MW00380772

Nelson's Trafalgar Captains and their Battles

Nelson's Trafalgar Captains and their Battles

A Biographical and Historical Dictionary

T. A. Heathcote

Pen & Sword

MARITIME

First published in Great Britain in 2005 by
Pen & Sword Maritime
an imprint of
Pen & Sword Books Ltd
47 Church Street
Barnsley
South Yorkshire
S70 2AS

Typeset in 10/12pt Palatino by
Mac Style Ltd, Scarborough, N. Yorkshire
Printed and bound in England by CPI UK.

For a complete list of Pen & Sword titles
please contact
PEN & SWORD BOOKS LIMITED
47 Church Street, Barnsley, South Yorkshire,
S70 2AS, England
E-mail: enquiries@pen-and-sword.co.uk
Website: www.pen-and-sword.co.uk

'After such a victory, it may appear unnecessary to enter into encomiums on the particular parts played by the several Commanders; the conclusion says more on the subject than I have words to express; the spirit which animated all was the same; when all exert themselves zealously in their country's service, all deserve that their high merits should stand recorded; and never was high merit more conspicuous than in the battle I have described.'

Dispatch to the Lords Commissioners of the Admiralty from Vice-Admiral Cuthbert Collingwood, C-in-C Mediterranean Fleet, in the frigate *Euryalus*, off Cape Trafalgar, 22 October 1805

In memory of Derek Stephen Baynham
1936–2000
Scholar, Soldier, Naval Administrator

CONTENTS

Preface

October 2005 is the 200th anniversary of the Battle of Trafalgar, a victory that confirmed British supremacy over the Combined Fleets of Napoleon and his allies and left the oceans of the world clear for British shipping and British trade. At the time, most British people saw it as they had the defeat of the Spanish Armada in 1588, or as they would the Battle of Britain in 1940 – a deliverance from the threat of invasion by a well-trained army with a record of recent victories. In fact, Napoleon had already despaired of gaining control of the Channel and abandoned his invasion plans eight weeks before Trafalgar. As the veteran Admiral St Vincent put it, it was not that the French could not come, but that they could not do so by sea. The significance of Trafalgar was not that it safeguarded British shores (the wooden wall of the Channel fleet and the choppy waters of the Channel tides did that), but rather that by the annihilation of the enemy's main fleet, it guaranteed British maritime ascendancy across the world. For the next century, British ships were free to carry British products to every part of the globe and return with raw materials for British mills and food for the British population. British traders and bankers had already created a society wealthy enough to defend itself and to subsidize its allies. Nelson's triumph ensured that the expanding British Empire and its financial heart, the City of London, would flourish under the unchallenged protection of the Royal Navy for another 100 years.

Most of the works, published or republished in connection with this occasion, are about Nelson himself, on the battle and its preceding campaign, or on the general history of the Navy in the Georgian period. This book is an account of the lives of all the men who commanded at Trafalgar under

Nelson. Often treated as extras in the biographies of their great commander, they are here collected together as a group in their own right. Some already have their own biographers. Others well deserve them, and many led lives that bear comparison, in terms of incident and adventure, with fictional counterparts such Aubrey, Bolitho, Hornblower or Ramage. The book is intended for anyone, whether academic or general reader, seafarer or landsman, who has an interest in the history of the Royal Navy and a liking for tales of ships and the sea. It is intended also as a tribute to all who fought at Trafalgar, including those of the French and Spanish Navies, whose modern successors, now British allies in NATO and the European Union, also commemorate the courage and chivalry shown by both sides.

Acknowledgements

I take this opportunity to acknowledge the assistance given in the preparation of this book by the staff of the Royal Military Academy Sandhurst Library, the National Maritime Museum, the City of Portsmouth Library, the Royal Naval Museum and the National Portrait Gallery, and by members of the 1805 Club and the Huguenot Society. I am especially grateful to Michael Orr and John Vignoles for their advice on historical sources; to Dr Debbie Goodwin and Neil Hearne for help with IT problems; to Surgeon Commander Sandy Cochrane, late RNR, and Surgeon Lieutenant Commander Dennis Freshwater, Royal Navy, for their naval medical opinions, and, as always, to my wife who acted as research assistant and who proofread the manuscript.

T. A. Heathcote
Camberley, February 2005

Note on the Classification of Sailing Warships

During most of the period covered by this book, the British fleet was made up of rated ships (corresponding to the modern term 'major surface combatants') and unrated vessels (the modern 'minor surface combatants'). The major combatants were divided into six rates, according to the official number of their guns, though in practice many carried additional pieces such as carronades (heavy ordnance for close combat) which were not shown in the rate. The official number was given after the ship's name, together with its rate. 1st-rates had 100 or more guns. 2nd-rates carried either ninety or ninety-eight. 1st and 2nd rates, the fleet's most powerful assets, were three-deckers, platforms for three tiers of guns that not merely outnumbered those of the smaller two-deckers that were the standard work-horses of contemporary navies, but were able to sweep the upper decks of such opponents. 3rd-rates carried between sixty-four and eighty-four guns. 4th-rates, with between fifty and sixty guns, were too weak to stand in the line of battle and were mostly used either as convoy escorts or on other detached duties. There were none in the fleet at Trafalgar. Frigates, technically ships that carried their main armament on a single deck, made up the 5th- and 6th-rates, with between thirty and forty-four or twenty and twenty-eight guns respectively. There were four frigates at Trafalgar, all of them 5th-rates. Rated ships were commanded by post captains, officers who were captains by rank as well as by title. The two unrated vessels at Trafalgar were a schooner and a cutter. Too small to merit the appointment of commander, which went with more important minor combatants such as sloops and brigs, each was under the command of a lieutenant.

Introduction

At five a.m. on 2 September 1805, Captain Henry Blackwood, travelling along the post road from Lymington to London, stopped at Merton, Surrey, to pay a hurried call on his old friend and recent C-in-C, Vice-Admiral Viscount Nelson. He was carrying dispatches reporting that Vice-Admiral Pierre Villeneuve's Franco-Spanish Combined Fleet, pursued to the West Indies and back by Nelson earlier that summer, was under blockade in Cadiz. Nelson greeted him with the words 'I am sure you bring me news of the enemy fleets' and, before they parted, told him 'Depend upon it, Blackwood, I shall yet give M. Villeneuve a drubbing'.

Before noon, Admiral Lord Barham, the octogenarian First Lord of the Admiralty, told Nelson to re-hoist his flag in the 1st-rate *Victory* and sail to take over command of the fleet off Cadiz. Handing him a copy of the Navy List, Barham invited Nelson to select his own officers. Nelson's reply was to hand the volume back and tell him to choose whom he would, saying, 'The same spirit actuates the whole profession. You cannot choose wrong.' When Barham insisted that he must choose, Nelson decided against making any changes in existing commands. In practice, this was little more than an exchange of courtesies and expressions of mutual confidence. Both Barham and Nelson were experienced admirals. Neither was likely to have perceived much merit in replacing large numbers of commanding officers in a fleet about to fight a decisive battle. Nelson was by no means as uncritical of other officers in his Service as the generous nature of his reply to Barham suggests, but his brilliance in leadership never waned. Only eight of the captains in the fleet gathering outside Cadiz had actually commanded ships under him, but he was known, at least by reputation, to all of them. All eagerly awaited his arrival to take over the command there. None, however, would have respected an admiral who turned captains out of their ships in favour of his own nominees before even meeting them.

Thus it was that Nelson appointed only two new captains, his old friend Sir Edward Berry to the 3rd-rate *Agamemnon*, and his distant cousin John Conn to the 1st-rate *Royal Sovereign*, both of which were being made ready for sea and had their commands vacant.

The aim of this book is to tell the stories of those whom Nelson judged typical of his profession in their day, and to show what it was that, in addition to the spirit which he specifically mentioned, they had in common. To avoid repetition, the battles in which two or more of them fought are summarized separately in the second part of the book. Between them, they served in almost every major naval engagement of their time. The individuals who commanded under Nelson at Trafalgar, (two flag officers; twenty-five captains of ships of the line and two lieutenants acting in command of ships of the line in the absence of their captains; four captains of frigates and two lieutenants in command of minor combatants) are treated alphabetically. For ease of cross-reference, where their names appear outside their own biographical sections, they are numbered from one to thirty-five within square brackets in bold print thus [1]. In the same way, where a battle, mentioned in the biographical sections, is treated in more detail in the second part of the book, its name is printed in **bold**. In both parts, Trafalgar is given more attention than any other battle, because it was the greatest battle in which any of the captains who were there ever fought.

An analysis of the background and careers of the Trafalgar captains shows that they were as much like their contemporaries in the Navy List as Nelson implied. All had first gone to sea as boys in their early teens (some indeed, as young as eight or ten). On average they had become midshipmen by the age of fourteen, though Rotheram [31], who began in the Merchant service, and Prowse [29], who was promoted from the lower deck, did not reach this rank until their mid-twenties. In theory, no one could become a midshipman without two years of reckonable sea service over the age of thirteen (or eleven in the case of sons of sea officers) but, in practice, this rule was commonly disregarded. Promotion from midshipman to lieutenant was notionally dependant upon completing at least six years' efficient seagoing service (including at least two as a midshipman or master's mate), reaching a minimum age of twenty, passing a viva voce examination by a board of captains and, above all, selection to a vacant post in this rank. An otherwise qualified midshipman who could not find a nomination might remain unpromoted for years, or indeed for his entire career. Even a promising candidate could experience difficulty in advancement during periods of peace, when the number of ships in commission was kept to a minimum and the demand for officers was limited.

The age qualification for promotion to lieutenant was as commonly evaded as that for appointment to midshipman. In both cases, in a period before the compulsory registration of births, it was a simple matter to obtain a false copy of a baptismal certificate. Clergymen might be induced to produce such an item to oblige an influential friend or patron or, if all else failed, the Navy Board's own underlings would, for a modest gratuity, produce a certificate of any age that a candidate specified. The average age of the thirty-five Trafalgar captains on becoming lieutenants was just under twenty-three, ranging from Duff [12] and Morris [26], both of whom made this step aged about sixteen, to Prowse [29], Rutherford [32] and Stockham [33], who did not become lieutenants until they were over thirty.

Promotion to substantive or 'post' captain (i.e. those who were captains by naval rank rather than by the title conventionally given to the master of any kind of ship) was by selection from officers holding the rank of lieutenant. Increasingly, those so selected had also reached the rank of commander, bestowed on those appointed to the command of a minor combatant such as a sloop, but many officers were 'made post' without passing through this intermediate stage, among them the two first lieutenants who were in acting command of their ships at Trafalgar. Advancement from lieutenant to post captain depended solely upon an individual being nominated by the Admiralty, or by a local C-in-C, subject to Admiralty confirmation. Much depended upon being noticed by a patron on whose judgement (or political support) the Admiralty felt able to rely. Generally, this produced competent captains, if only because, with so many eligible individuals to choose from, patrons rarely needed to risk having their own judgement called into question by recommending someone demonstrably unfit to command. Ships, especially the major combatants or 'rated' ships to which post captains were appointed, were too valuable to be entrusted to known incompetents. In most cases, individuals who proved themselves incapable after being appointed were not employed at sea again. Efficiency had no effect on their subsequent promotion to flag rank, which was by seniority to vacancies on the establishment as they occurred, so that after becoming a post captain an officer had only to outlive his contemporaries to become admiral of the fleet. It could, however, affect their income, since those not in employment were placed on half pay and also lost any chance of the valuable prize money which was the great attraction of naval service. There were, however, always more good captains than ships and more good flag officers than squadrons for them to command, so that (as in every walk of life) lack of advancement is not evidence of lack of ability.

An officer's age on promotion to post captain therefore reflected both the influence of his patron and the date on which he was born, because promotion in the Armed Services comes more slowly in peace than in war. Bayntun [1], for example, born in 1766, became a lieutenant at the age of seventeen in 1783, just after the end of the American War of Independence, but had to wait until he was twenty-eight to become a post captain, a year after the outbreak of the French Revolutionary War in 1793 . Berry [2], two years younger, began his career at much the same time, but because of the decade of peace, did not become a lieutenant until 1794, when he was twenty-six, though he then rose to post captain in only three years. Of the Trafalgar captains, the youngest to have been 'made post' were Richard King [21], son of Admiral Sir Richard King, promoted at the age of twenty in 1794, and the Honourable Thomas Capel [5], son of the Earl of Essex, promoted at the age of twenty-three in 1798. At Trafalgar, the two subordinate flag officers (Vice-Admiral Collingwood [8] and Rear-Admiral the Earl of Northesk [6]) were aged fifty-five and forty-nine respectively. The average age of captains of ships of the line (excluding the two first lieutenants who commanded in the absence of their post captains) was just over forty-two, with Grindall [16] the oldest, aged fifty-five and King the youngest, aged thirty-one. The four frigate captains, Capel [5], Blackwood [3], Dundas [13] and Prowse [29] were aged twenty-nine, thirty-five, forty-five and fifty-three respectively, all men of mature experience. Of the two lieutenants commanding minor combatants, Lapenotiere [23] of *Pickle* was thirty-five and Young [35] of *Entreprenante* was thirty-two. Though capable sea officers, neither had patrons to gain them more important commands, then or later.

Of the twenty-seven British ships of the line at Trafalgar, only six were under officers who had previously commanded such ships in battle. There had indeed, as in any war, been few enough battles in which they might have done so, and two of them were only commanding in the absence of their post captains. Nevertheless, this still meant that almost one in four had commanded a ship of the line in battle, while all of the remainder had been present in actions of some sort earlier in their careers. Ten of them had fought under Howe at **The Glorious First of June** in 1794, six under Rodney at the **Battle of the Saintes** in 1782, another six at **Bridport's Action** off Lorient in 1795, five (as well as Nelson himself) under Jervis at **Cape St Vincent** in 1797 and five in **Calder's Action** off Finisterre only three months previously.

Two of the captains, Cooke [10] and Duff [12], fell at Trafalgar. Along with their C-in-C Collingwood, who succeeded to the command on Nelson's death and was kept in post until 1810, when he died at sea on his way home, Conn [9] also died at sea in 1810. All the others survived the war except for Mansfield [24] and Stockham [33], who died ashore of natural causes. Of these survivors, all but seven eventually reached flag rank. Apart from Young, who never became a post captain and was thus ineligible, those who failed to obtain their flags did so simply because they died before the captains above them in the seniority list.

In social origins, the Trafalgar captains conformed to the general pattern of sea officers of their day. Twelve were the sons of sea officers (three admirals among them), reflecting the common tendency of sons to follow their fathers' profession. Eleven were related to noblemen or members of the landed gentry, whose wealth and influence brought the patronage necessary for promotion and appointment. Several came from Scots, Irish or Huguenot families with a tradition of military service. Two were the sons of medical men and one of an eminent churchman (who was himself a peer's son). The remainder were drawn from a broad range of social classes.

Almost all were younger sons, for although the Navy had become a profession suitable for gentlemen, it was rarely a first choice. Its great advantage, for those with several sons to provide for, was that it cost virtually nothing to join, compared with the Church, the Law or Medicine, all of which required expensive tuition at a university or similar institute. Cavalry and infantry officers normally purchased their commissions, involving an outlay that was not refunded until the individual left his regiment, while artillery and engineer cadets had to attend the Royal Military Academy, which charged substantial fees. The disadvantage of a naval career was that, in addition to the ordinary hazards of eighteenth century existence, seamen of every kind were liable to the additional dangers associated with life aboard ship, including tropical and other diseases, accidents and the violence of sea. The risk of death in battle, wounds or captivity (Berry [2], Hardy [17] and Hargood [18] were all prisoners of war at various times) is always present in a fighting service, but during the twenty years of the Revolutionary and Napoleonic Wars, the Navy lost nine times as many ships and men by foundering, wreck, fire or explosion it did to enemy action.

Bayntun [1], Capel [5], Collingwood [8], Morris [26], Tyler [34] and Young [35] were shipwrecked, Bullen [4] and Fremantle [15] were in ships that foundered at sea and Durham [14] was one of the few survivors of the famous loss of Kempenfeldt's flagship *Royal George* at Spithead. Berry [2] was captain of a ship lost by fire and Pellew [27] of one that blew up at her moorings.

Although the Trafalgar captains were only a small cross-section of the Navy's officers then, between them they had experience of virtually every major sea battle and sea duty of their time. Their lives demonstrate that Nelson was right when, before going to command them, he told Barham that 'the same spirit actuates the whole profession', just as was his successor Collingwood [8] when, after Trafalgar, he reported to Barham that 'the spirit that animated them all was the same'.

The Biographies of the Trafalgar Captains

BAYNTUN, Admiral Sir HENRY WILLIAM, GCB (1766–1840) **[1]**
Henry Bayntun, born in 1766, was the son of the British
Consul General at Algiers, one of the states of the North
African 'Barbary Coast' which were nominally part of the
Ottoman Empire, but in practice independent entities. Algiers
was a valuable source of provisions for the Mediterranean
fleet and consular officials played an important part in
encouraging this. Bayntun entered the Navy at an early age
and, after serving during the American War of Independence,
was promoted to lieutenant on 15 April 1783, a few months
after the end of the war. This was followed by ten years of
peace, so that Bayntun did not see active service until after
the outbreak of the French Revolutionary War in 1793. He was
then deployed to the West Indies, where he served ashore in
the capture of **Martinique (February–March 1794)**.

After this operation, the local C-in-C, Vice-Admiral Sir John
Jervis, appointed Bayntun commander of the 16-gun sloop
Avenger, whose previous commanding officer had been killed
in the fighting at Fort Royal Bay, Martinique, on 17 March.
After serving in the capture of **Guadeloupe (April–May
1794)** Bayntun was promoted to post captain on 4 May 1794
and appointed by Jervis to the frigate *Undaunted* (32),
formerly the French *Bienvenue* captured in the action at Fort
Royal Bay. He subsequently commanded another former
French frigate, *Réunion* (36), which was lost by shipwreck on
7 December 1796, though Bayntun and his crew were all

saved. He soon returned to sea and was present at the capture of Trinidad in February 1797.

As soon as hostilities ended in March 1802, Napoleon Bonaparte, as First Consul of France, sent a large army and fleet to recover French Santo Domingo (now Haiti). Counter-insurgency operations were still in progress in May 1803, when the war with France was renewed. On 30 June 1803 Bayntun, in the 3rd-rate *Cumberland* (74) as commodore of a squadron cruising off Spanish Santo Domingo (now the Dominican Republic), intercepted and captured the French frigate *Créole* and four consorts. He subsequently returned home, where he was appointed to the 3rd-rate *Leviathan* (74) and deployed to the Mediterranean. Under Nelson, he took part in the blockade of Toulon and the pursuit of the French Vice-Admiral Pierre Villeneuve from there to the West Indies and back during the summer of 1805. After returning to European waters, *Leviathan* went to Gibraltar, from where, on 8 October 1805, she joined Nelson's fleet blockading Villeneuve's Franco-Spanish Combined Fleet in Cadiz.

At **Trafalgar (21 October 1805)**, *Leviathan* went into action fifth in line in the British weather column, led by Nelson in the 1st-rate *Victory*. After breaking through the French line, *Victory* and her next astern, the 2nd-rate *Téméraire* (98), became entangled with the French *Redoutable* and *Fougueux*, and drifted slowly downwind. *Leviathan*, following the 2nd-rate *Neptune* (98), sailed through the gap behind *Bucentaure* (74), Villeneuve's command ship, firing into her stern as they passed, and then turning to engage her starboard side with their own port side batteries. Leaving *Bucentaure*, they engaged her next ahead, the four-decker Spanish flagship *Santisima Trinidad* (130). *Leviathan* then overtook *Neptune* to pursue the Spanish *San Agustin* (74). In the ensuing combat *San Agustin* was supported by the French *Intrépide* (74), part of the enemy van squadron under Rear-Admiral Dumanoir that had turned back, too late, to support Villeneuve's centre. *Conqueror*, the next in line, then engaged *Intrépide*, leaving *Leviathan* with a single opponent. Lying alongside *San Agustin*, Bayntun continued to fire on *Intrépide* and shouted to Captain Edward Codrington [7] of the approaching

3rd-rate *Orion* (74), 'I hope you will make a better fist of it'. With his ship badly damaged and 160 casualties among his crew, *San Augustin*'s captain, Commodore Don Felippe de Cajigal, surrendered his sword to Bayntun while *Leviathan*'s crew tore down the Spanish colours and shouted 'Huzza, *Conqueror*, she's ours!'

In the battle, *Leviathan* lost four men killed and just over twenty wounded, of whom the senior was a midshipman. Afterwards, when Vice-Admiral Collingwood [8], to whom command of the fleet passed on Nelson's death, decided that the prizes were to be destroyed in case they were recovered by the enemy, Bayntun took charge of the ships nearest to him and coordinated the evacuation of their crews. Later, when Captain Hope [20] of *Defence* arrived on the scene, Bayntun sent a report across to him as his senior in the Navy List, saying they had done their best to comply with Collingwood's orders but that, from the sea-state, '... much less has been done than I most ardently wished and many boats have been lost'. Bayntun and *Leviathan* remained off Trafalgar with Collingwood until 10 November 1805, when they were released to sail for Gibraltar. Four days earlier, when *Victory* and her two consorts had passed on their way home to England, Bayntun transferred into them *Leviathan*'s French prisoners of war and some of the British crews from recaptured prizes who, after surviving the storm, had been chivalrously returned by their Spanish captors. The many Spanish prisoners of war and remaining British prize crews crowded aboard *Leviathan* until she reached Gibraltar. Bayntun then went home and carried the guidon in the water procession that brought Nelson's body from Greenwich to Whitehall in January 1806.

During 1807 he was with the squadron supporting the British attack on the rich Spanish colonies of the River Plate. The expedition, initially successful, ended in ignominious failure, with the British Army suffering heavy street-fighting casualties in Buenos Aires and having to be evacuated by the fleet. Bayntun returned home to command first the new 3rd-rate *Milford* (78) in 1809 and then the royal yacht *Royal Sovereign* from 1811 until his promotion to rear-admiral on 12

May 1812. With Napoleon defeated and exiled to Elba, Bayntun was awarded the KCB in January 1815. Sir Henry Bayntun was promoted to vice-admiral on 19 July 1821 and to admiral on 10 January 1837. He became a GCB on 25 October 1839 and died in Bath on 17 January 1840.

BERRY, Rear-Admiral Sir EDWARD, Baronet, KCB (1768–1831) [2]

Born in 1768, Edward Berry was the son of a London merchant whose death at a relatively early age left his large family with limited means. Through the patronage of the influential Lord Mulgrave, who had been a pupil of Edward's uncle, the Reverend Titus Berry, and was at the time a lord commissioner of the Board of Admiralty, Berry was in 1779 appointed as a volunteer in the 3rd-rate *Burford* (70), under orders for the East Indies during the American War of Independence. *Burford* (with Berry soon appointed midshipman) formed part of Vice-Admiral Sir Edward Hughes's squadron at the capture of the Dutch port of Trincomalee, Ceylon [Sri Lanka] (17 January 1782) and in the subsequent fleet actions against the French under de Suffren off Sadras (17 February 1782), Providien (12 April 1782), Nagapatam (6–7 July 1782), Trincomalee (3 September 1782) and Cuddalore (20 July 1783), in which *Burford* lost a total of twenty-seven killed and 128 wounded. With the end of the war, Berry returned home in 1783 and was not again employed at sea until after the outbreak of war with Revolutionary France in February 1793. He was promoted to lieutenant on 20 January 1794, after distinguishing himself in boarding a French man-of-war, and was subsequently commended for similar conduct in **The Glorious First of June (1 June 1794)**.

During 1795 Berry served in the Mediterranean as Captain Horatio Nelson's first lieutenant in the 3rd-rate *Agamemnon* (64) and followed him to become first lieutenant of the 3rd-rate *Captain* (74) on 11 June 1796. When Nelson went ashore to land British troops at Porto Ferrajo, Elba, in July 1796, Berry was left in command of the ship and was subsequently mentioned in Nelson's report. Nelson's own appointment as commodore on 11 August 1796 allowed Berry to be given formal command of *Captain*, though he was superseded by the arrival of a more senior officer on 24 September. His promotion to the rank of commander was confirmed on 12 November 1796, but while waiting for an appointment he remained in *Captain* as a volunteer and served in her at **Cape St Vincent (14 February 1797).** There, during the boarding of the Spanish *San Nicolas*, as Nelson later reported, 'The first man who jumped into the enemy's mizen chains was Captain Berry, late my first lieutenant; he was supported from our spritsail-yard, which hooked into the mizen-rigging.' Nelson himself climbed into *San Nicolas* through her stern galleries and reached the quarterdeck to find Berry in possession of the poop and hauling down the enemy colours. Berry then joined the party that boarded the Spanish three-decker *San Josef* from *San Nicolas*, which became known as 'Nelson's patent bridge for boarding first rates' and was there to help his one-armed commodore get across.

Berry was promoted to post captain on 6 March 1797 and returned home with Nelson. At court, when George III remarked sympathetically on Nelson's loss of his right arm, Nelson immediately presented Berry as his right hand. Nelson also promised that, if he were ever given command as an admiral, Berry should be his flag captain. Accordingly, he wrote to Berry on 8 December 1797, 'If you mean to marry, I would recommend your doing it speedily, or the to-be Mrs Berry will have very little of your company ... you may expect to be called every hour'. Four days later Berry married his cousin Louisa, daughter of the Reverend Dr Forster of Norwich, and seven days after that became captain of the newly-refitted 3rd-rate *Vanguard* (74) at Spithead, where Rear-Admiral Sir Horatio Nelson joined him on 14 March 1798.

They left England on 10 April 1798 and joined St Vincent's fleet blockading Cadiz. On 8 May they sailed from Gibraltar as part of a small squadron under Nelson's command to re-establish a British naval presence in the Mediterranean and look for a French fleet believed to be taking troops to support a rebellion in Ireland. In fact, the expedition, under General Napoleon Bonaparte, sailed from Toulon on 19 May not for

Ireland but for Egypt. Nelson missed its departure as, on 20 May, *Vanguard*, still some distance away, was struck by a sudden gale, in which her under-strength and newly-commissioned complement lost the entire foremast assembly, together with the main and mizen topmasts, and was only saved by the efforts of her consort, the 3rd-rate *Alexander* (74). Nelson's three ships of the line were reinforced by the arrival of another ten on 6 June 1798, but Nelson kept his flag in the jury-masted *Vanguard*, and eventually found the French fleet moored under the protection of shore batteries and shoals in Aboukir (Abu Qir) Bay, near Alexandria, on 1 August 1798. On seeing the signal 'enemy in sight' Berry commented, 'If we succeed, what will the world say?' Nelson's reply was, 'There is no 'if' in the case. That we shall succeed is certain: who will live to tell the story is a very different question.'

Berry's own account of the consequent action, the battle of **The Nile (1–2 August 1798)** noted that Nelson viewed the French position with the eye of a seaman determined on attack. Although the British had no precise chart of the shoals, '... it instantly struck his eager and penetrating mind that where there was room for an enemy's ship to swing, there was room for one of his to anchor'. In the battle, when Nelson was temporarily blinded, Berry caught him and prevented him from falling. After the battle, in which *Vanguard* lost thirty-one men killed, Nelson sent him home with the dispatches, a customary reward for good service, in the 4th-rate *Leander* (50). On 18 October 1798 *Leander* encountered *Généraux* (74), one of the two French ships of the line that had escaped from the battle. After a five hours' long fight, in which *Leander* lost thirty-five killed and fifty-seven wounded out of 282, against 100 killed and 180 wounded out of 936 in *Généraux*, the British frigate was dismasted and obliged to surrender. Berry and *Leander*'s captain were among the wounded but none could be treated on board as the French looted the surgeon's implements. After being released on parole, he reached England early in December 1798. Duplicate dispatches had arrived ahead of him, and he was greeted as a hero, knighted and awarded the freedom of the City of London. On 13 October 1799, having been regularly exchanged for a French officer of equal rank, he assumed command of the new 2nd-rate *Foudroyant* (80), Nelson's flagship at Palermo, in succession to Captain Thomas Hardy [17] who had previously succeeded Berry in command of *Vanguard*.

On 29 October 1799 *Foudroyant* joined the blockade of French-occupied Malta and later returned several times to Palermo to collect British and Neapolitan troop reinforcements for the Malta operations. On 18 February 1800, sailing once more as Nelson's flagship, with two other 3rd-rates and a frigate, she encountered Berry's old opponent *Généraux*, with four smaller warships, escorting French transports en route to Malta. In the ensuing combat *Généraux* and one French frigate were captured, and Berry was once again mentioned in dispatches. Off **Malta (30 March 1800)** he played a major part in the capture of *Guillaume Tell* (80), as she tried to escape the British blockade.

Berry then took *Foudroyant* back to Palermo from where, as Nelson's flagship, she conveyed King Ferdinand IV of the Two Sicilies, his forceful Queen Maria Carolina and the British ambassador, Sir William Hamilton, to Leghorn (Livorno). There, as part of a new coalition against the French, they landed with an army in the rear of French operations against the Papal States. They reached Rome in triumph, but the French speedily recovered from their surprise and by the end of December 1799 Ferdinand IV had been driven out of all his mainland territories and forced to move from Naples to his Sicilian capital, Palermo. Nelson hauled down his flag at the end of June 1800 and travelled home overland with Sir William and Lady Hamilton. *Foudroyant* became the flagship of Admiral Keith on 15 August 1800 and remained as such until July 1802. Berry himself left the ship on 2 November 1800 and, after returning home in a frigate, was still ashore when peace with France and her allies was signed in March 1802.

Hostilities were renewed with France in May 1803 and with Spain in December 1804. Berry did not return to sea until 17 September 1805, when on Nelson's nomination he was appointed to the vacant command of the newly-refitted

3rd-rate *Agamemnon* (64), once the fastest ship of the line in the Navy, but by this time over twenty years old. En route to join Nelson in the blockade of Vice-Admiral Pierre Villeneuve's Franco-Spanish Combined Fleet at Cadiz, *Agamemnon* was sighted by a French squadron from Rochefort and Berry was obliged to jettison thirty casks of water in order to outpace a French 80-gun ship pursuing him. When he reached Cadiz on 13 October 1805, Nelson, alluding to Berry's reputation for having been in more fleet actions than any other captain in the Navy, said, 'Here comes that damned fool Berry! *Now* we shall have a battle.'

On 20 October 1805 Berry intercepted a merchant brig and took her in tow. After a signal from Captain Blackwood [3] of the frigate *Euryalus* that the Combined Fleet had put to sea and *Agamemnon* was heading towards it, the tow was cast off and Berry changed course to rejoin Nelson's main force. Even then, she proceeded without haste and, after a sudden squall carried away her main topmast and split the mainsail, stopped to repair the damage. At **Trafalgar (21 October 1805),** *Agamemnon* was stationed towards the rear of the weather column and did not come into action until about two hours after the first shot had been fired. She joined *Neptune* (98) and *Conqueror* (74) in their capture of the Spanish flagship *Santisima Trinidad* (130) and, under fire at various times from four enemy ships, received several hits along the waterline. With her pumps continuously manned, she briefly took the damaged 3rd-rate *Colossus* in tow, before turning northwards with a group of ships under the Earl of Northesk [6] in the 1st-rate *Britannia* to meet the enemy van division that had belatedly turned back to support Villeneuve's centre. After the battle, with only two men killed and eight wounded, but with her rigging badly damaged and three feet of water in her hold, *Agamemnon* towed *Colossus* to Gibraltar before returning to the blockade of Cadiz.

Agamemnon, with Berry still in command, was one of the eight British ships of the line under Sir John Duckworth that took part in the last major fleet action of the Napoleonic wars, off Santo Domingo (6 February 1806). *Agamemnon*, stationed fourth in line, was late into battle, but then supported

Duckworth's flagship, the 3rd-rate *Superb* (74), in her successive engagements with the French ships *Alexandre* (80), *Impérial* (120) and *Diomede* (84). *Diomede* ran aground but continued in action until her captain took off his hat as a gesture of surrender, when Berry ordered *Agamemnon* to cease firing. With one man killed and three officers, two marines and sixteen seamen wounded, and the ship badly damaged, *Agamemnon* was repaired in Barbados and then remained on patrol in the West Indies. She captured the French privateers *Dame Ernouf* (19) and *Lutine National* (16) on 18 and 24 March 1806 respectively, before escorting a convoy home to England during October–November 1806.

Berry was made a baronet on his return from the West Indies and remained ashore until 1811, when he was appointed to the 3rd-rate *Sceptre* (74) on the home station. In September 1812 Sir Edward Berry exchanged into the 2nd-rate *Barfleur* (98), in which he served in the Mediterranean, and then commanded successively the royal yachts *Royal Sovereign* and *Royal George* during 1813–15. He was awarded the KCB in January 1815 after Napoleon had been defeated and exiled to Elba. Berry became a rear-admiral on 19 July 1821, but never had the opportunity to hoist his flag. His three gold medals for service as a captain at The Nile, Trafalgar and Santo Domingo made him the only officer apart from Lord Collingwood [8] to be so decorated, and he had been present in at least eight major actions, as well as numerous smaller engagements. His health deteriorated in his later years and he died at Bath on 13 February 1831. There were no children of his marriage and his baronetcy became extinct.

BLACKWOOD, Vice-Admiral the Honourable Sir HENRY, Baronet, KCB, GCH (1770–1832) **[3]**
Henry Blackwood, born on 28 December 1770, was the fourth son of Sir John Blackwood, baronet, of Ballyleidy, County Down, and his wife Dorcas, who was later created Baroness Dufferin and Clanboye in her own right. In April 1781, during the American War of Independence, he joined the Navy as a volunteer in the 5th-rate frigate *Artois* (40), deployed on trade protection duties in the North Sea. He served in this ship at

the hard-fought battle of the Dogger Bank (5 August 1781), against the Dutch, and after the end of hostilities in 1783 continued at sea, with four years in the Mediterranean in the 4th-rate *Trusty* (50). In May 1790, when a fleet was mobilized to meet the threat of war with Spain over the possession of Nootka Sound (Vancouver, British Columbia), he was appointed signal midshipman in the 1st-rate *Queen Charlotte* (100), flagship of Admiral Earl Howe as C-in-C in the Channel, at a time when Howe was introducing his new code of flag signals. On 30 November 1790, when the fleet dispersed after the dispute was settled by diplomacy, Howe promoted Blackwood to lieutenant in one of the 'haul-down' promotions at the disposal of senior flag officers on ending their period in command.

During 1791 Blackwood served for a time in the 6th-rate frigate *Proserpine* (28) and was then given permission to go to France to improve his knowledge of the French language. He spent much of 1792 in Paris, at a time of increasing domestic and international tension, with the Revolutionary government declaring war on Austria in April 1792, and Prussia entering the war on Austria's side in the following July. The British government declared its neutrality, but Blackwood was suspected of espionage and narrowly escaped with his life. After France declared war on the United Kingdom in February 1793, Blackwood was appointed to the 5th-rate frigate *Active* (32), from which he transferred after a few months to the 3rd-rate *Invincible* (74). He served as first lieutenant of this ship in Howe's encounters with the French fleet on 28–29 May 1794 and in **The Glorious First of June (1 June 1794)**, after which he returned home in command of the French prize *St Juste* (80), and was promoted to commander on 6 July 1794.

Blackwood was then given command of the fireship *Megaera* (14) in the Channel, and was promoted to post captain on 2 June 1795. Still in *Megaera*, he took part in **Bridport's Action (23 June 1795)** when three French ships of the line were captured off the Île de Groix, Lorient. He subsequently was appointed to the guard-ship at Hull and a few months later was given command of the 6th-rate frigate

Brilliant (28) in the North Sea squadron under Admiral Duncan. Blackwood spent the next two years there and took part in capturing the French *Nonsuch* (64) in 1796. *Brilliant* was one of the ships affected by the naval mutiny at the Nore during late May and early June 1797, but when the mutiny collapsed Blackwood was able to resume command. On 26 July 1798, with Spain having joined the war on the French side, *Brilliant* stood into Tenerife, Santa Cruz (Canary Islands) to investigate a ship she had pursued the previous day. There she found the French 38-gun frigates *Vertue* and *Régéneree*, which immediately slipped their cables and gave chase. By the early evening they were close behind *Brilliant*, but Blackwood then crossed *Régéneree*'s bows and fired a series of broadsides that damaged her masts and rigging and forced her to stop for repairs. *Vertue* then came up and exchanged an ineffectual fire with *Brilliant* but a freshening breeze then enabled Blackwood to make his escape.

In 1799 Blackwood was given command of a larger frigate, the 5th-rate *Penelope* (36), in which he was deployed with the Mediterranean fleet under Nelson. Off French-occupied **Malta (30 March 1800)** he played a major part in the capture of *Guillaume Tell* (80) as she tried to escape through the British blockade. Nelson, from his base at Palermo, Sicily, sent Blackwood a personal letter of congratulation, expressing '… a sympathy which ties men together in the bonds of friendship without having a personal knowledge of each other'.

Following the end of hostilities in March 1802 Blackwood returned home and *Penelope* was paid off. In April 1803, a few weeks before the war with France was renewed, he was appointed to the frigate *Euryalus* (36) in which, during the next two years, he served successively off the coast of Ireland and in the Channel. In July 1805, with Spain having once more joined the war on the French side, *Euryalus* was dispatched to observe the Franco-Spanish Combined Fleet under Vice-Admiral Pierre Villeneuve as it made its way along the coast of Spain. Brushing aside the small blockading squadron under Vice-Admiral Collingwood **[8]**, Villeneuve entered Cadiz on 21 August. The next day Collingwood resumed his blockade and sent *Euryalus* home to inform the Admiralty.

En route to London, Blackwood stopped briefly to give his news to Nelson, who had gone ashore after pursuing Villeneuve to the West Indies and back, and was enjoying his leave with Lady Hamilton. Later in the day, Nelson was summoned to London and re-appointed to his command of the Mediterranean Fleet. Blackwood and *Euryalus* sailed in company with him and his flagship *Victory* from Spithead on 14 September 1805 and reached Cadiz two weeks later. Blackwood had been offered command of a ship of the line, but declined, on the basis that the Combined Fleet would never put to sea once it became known that Nelson was waiting there, and that there would be more chance of action by remaining in *Euryalus*. Nelson therefore gave him command of the fleet's four frigates, tasked with observing and reporting activity within Cadiz harbour. Withdrawing his main fleet fifty miles out into the Atlantic in the hope of tempting Villeneuve out, Nelson repeatedly stressed to Blackwood the vital importance of '… not letting the rogues escape without a fair fight'. When conditions looked favourable for the enemy to sail, he charged him '… watch all points and all winds and weather, for I shall depend on you'.

At dawn on 19 October 1805, *Sirius*, the nearest frigate to Cadiz, hoisted the signal flags for 'Enemy have their topsail yards hoisted', evidence that Villeneuve, contrary to Blackwood's earlier appreciation, was preparing for sea. As the Combined Fleet started to come out, the British frigates, covered by the two fast ships of the line that had linked them with Nelson's main force, kept it in sight. The next day Blackwood was able to warn Captain Berry [2] in *Agamemnon*, who had been busy with the capture of a merchant brig, that he was heading directly towards the enemy fleet. *Euryalus* then covered nearly thirty miles to windward in less than three hours, to signal Nelson with details of the enemy's numbers and path of intended movement. During the night of 20–21 October, Blackwood continued to shadow Villeneuve's ships, reporting their movements to *Victory* using gunfire and light signals, before going below at midnight to snatch a few hours' sleep. When he returned to the deck at first light and saw that a battle would take place, he finished a letter to his wife, his 'dearest dear Harriet', enjoining her to take care of their son and 'make him a better man than his father'.

As the two fleets made contact at **Trafalgar (21 October 1805)** Blackwood saw that the flagship had hoisted a signal ordering the frigate captains on board. His first thought was that Nelson might be about to appoint him to a ship of the line, as there were two in the fleet under the acting command of their first lieutenants. In fact Nelson had summoned all four frigate captains to give them their final pre-battle orders. They were to remain to windward of his column, repeating his signals to rearward ships, to shadow any enemy vessels that attempted to escape, to capture any damaged ones that had evaded ships of the line, and to take in tow any British or captured enemy ships that had been dismasted. He then asked them to witness the codicil to his will, leaving Lady Hamilton and his illegitimate daughter Horatia, as a legacy to his king and country. Discussing the likely outcome of the battle Nelson invited Blackwood to say what he would judge as a victory. Blackwood replied that, given the proximity of the land, the capture of fourteen enemy ships would be a glorious achievement. Nelson admitted that the enemy coast was near, but said that twenty would be a better figure.

Blackwood, like the other officers on board, was concerned for his admiral's safety. He tried to persuade him to shift the flag to *Euryalus*, from where he would be better able to observe the conduct of the battle, but Nelson would not hear of it. He did agree, however, to Blackwood's subsequent proposal to allow *Téméraire*, the next ship astern, to take *Victory*'s place at the head of the line, so as to draw enemy fire away from the flagship. *Téméraire* drew closer to *Victory*, but when Blackwood pointed out to Hardy [17], the flag captain, that unless the flagship shortened sail, *Téméraire* could not pass, Hardy said he was sure that Nelson would not agree. Nelson resolved the question by hailing Captain Harvey [19] of *Téméraire* and ordering him back to his proper station.

As the two fleets crept closer together, Nelson said to Blackwood 'I will now amuse the fleet with a signal. Do you not think there is one yet wanting?' Blackwood thought that all knew what to do, but Nelson persisted and, after some discussion with Pascoe, his flag lieutenant, eventually made the famous signal 'England expects that every man will do his duty'. Shortly afterwards he ordered the frigate captains back to their commands, instructing Blackwood to tell all the captains of ships of the line that he relied on them to do their best and, if the operational plan did not allow them to come into action at once, they were to do so at their own discretion. Blackwood, taking his leave, said he would return to *Victory* as soon as possible and hoped to find Nelson the master of twenty prizes. Nelson answered 'God bless you, Blackwood, I shall never speak to you again'.

In the concluding phase of the battle, Collingwood, leading the fleet's lee column in his flagship the 1st-rate *Royal Sovereign*, ordered *Euryalus* to close and act as a repeater, before taking dismasted *Royal Sovereign* in tow. Blackwood was therefore with Collingwood when a boat, sent by Hardy from *Victory*, arrived with the news that Nelson had been wounded. Both of them understood the gravity of the message and Blackwood hoped he would be allowed back to *Victory* to see his friend, but Collingwood ordered him instead to the Spanish ship *Santa Ana*, to take the surrender of Admiral Alava. Blackwood boarded her to be told that the admiral was mortally wounded. He courteously left him there (in fact, Alava was only unconscious) and made a prisoner only of her captain, who had already sent his sword to *Royal Sovereign*. Subsequently, an enemy shot cut the towing cable between *Euryalus* and *Royal Sovereign* and Blackwood took the chance to wear ship (changing tack by turning away from the wind rather than going though it) and go to *Victory*. On boarding her, he was told that Nelson still lived but, on reaching the cockpit, learned that he had died of his wounds.

Collingwood, who had succeeded Nelson in command, shifted his flag to *Euryalus* where a few days later he was joined by the defeated Villeneuve, who had previously been held as a prisoner of war first in *Mars* and then in *Neptune*.

Blackwood, one of the few who appreciated Collingwood's problems in handling the fleet during the vicious storm that followed the battle, was equally sympathetic towards Villeneuve and treated him with as much courtesy and personal generosity as he could. When the weather improved, Collingwood dispatched Blackwood into Cadiz under a flag of truce to negotiate sending the wounded prisoners of war ashore. Blackwood, in his smartest uniform, was received graciously by the Spaniards, who chivalrously reciprocated Collingwood's gesture by offering to care for any of the British wounded that he chose to send them, and to return the captured British prize-crews of ships retaken or driven ashore during the storm.

Blackwood was then sent home with Villeneuve and his senior officers, and was therefore in England for Nelson's state funeral on 8 January 1806, where he was train-bearer to the Admiral of the Fleet, Sir Peter Parker. He was later appointed to the 3rd-rate *Ajax* (80) in which he rejoined Collingwood, still blockading Cadiz, on the first anniversary of Trafalgar. From there, at the beginning of 1807, he formed part of a squadron sent to the Turkish Straits under Sir John Duckworth.

On the night of 14 February 1807, while the squadron lay becalmed off the entrance to the Straits, Blackwood was roused from his cabin by the officer of the watch reporting fire in the after cockpit. Within ten minutes the smoke was so dense that, in spite of bright moonlight, officers and men on the upper decks could not see each other. Many escaped by jumping from the bowsprit into the sea, where boats from other ships in the squadron came to their rescue. Blackwood, who saved himself by jumping from the spritsail yard and clinging to an oar, was picked up after an hour in the sea, badly affected by exposure. *Ajax* burned throughout the night and drifted ashore on the island of Tenedos, where the next morning she blew up when the fire reached her magazine. Of her company of 633, only 381 survived. Blackwood and his surviving officers were honourably acquitted by the court martial customarily convened after the loss of any ship, and the cause of the fire was attributed to carelessness or drunkenness on the part of the purser's steward or else to spontaneous combustion in the coal carried on board. Without a ship, Blackwood joined Duckworth's flagship, the 1st-rate *Royal George*, as a volunteer and remained there, gaining a mention in dispatches, during the subsequent operations in the **Turkish Straits (19 February – 3 March 1807)**.

After returning home in May 1807, he was offered the appointment of pay commissioner at the Navy Board, but declined. Instead, he accepted command of the new 3rd-rate *Warspite* (76), in which he served from 1807 to 1813, first in the North Sea and then in the Mediterranean, mostly in the blockade of Toulon. On 20 July 1810, commanding the inshore squadron of six ships of the line, he turned back a sortie by a larger French force and received the thanks of the C-in-C, Sir Charles Cotton. He returned to home waters at the end of 1812 and during the following year captured three privateers. In May 1814, when the allied sovereigns visited the United Kingdom as part of the celebrations following Napoleon's first abdication, Blackwood was captain of the fleet in the escort squadron, commanded by Admiral of the Fleet the Duke of Clarence (later William IV), and was created a baronet.

Sir Henry Blackwood was promoted to rear-admiral on 4 June 1814. In 1819 he was awarded the KCB and served as C-in-C in the East Indies from then until late in 1822, with promotion to vice-admiral on 19 July 1821. He became groom of the bedchamber to William IV in 1824 and was C-in-C at the Nore from 1827 to 1830. He died from fever on 17 December 1832, at Ballyleidy, the family seat then held by his eldest brother, the 2nd Baron Dufferin and Clanboye.

In December 1795 Blackwood had married Jane Crosbie, daughter of a country squire. She died without issue in December 1798 and six moths later he married again, to Eliza, daughter of Captain Martin Waghorn. Eliza Blackwood died in October 1802, leaving Blackwood with a son, Henry, who in due course succeeded to his baronetcy. Blackwood married a third time, to Harriet Gore, daughter of the Governor of Grenada. With her he had a family of three sons, of whom the youngest became a captain in the Navy, and a daughter, Harriette. Lady Blackwood survived her husband and lived until 1851.

BULLEN, Admiral Sir CHARLES, GCB, KCH (1769–1853) **[4]**
Charles Bullen was born at Newcastle-upon-Tyne on 10 September 1769, the son of John Bullen of Weymouth, who from 1779 to 1781, during the American War of Independence, was naval Surgeon General on the North America station. John Bullen's wife, Ruth, née Liddell, was a cousin of the influential lawyer and politician, Lord Eldon. Charles Bullen entered the Navy in 1779 as a 1st Class volunteer in the 3rd-rate *Europe* (64) and was a midshipman in the 4th-rate *Renown* when she was dismasted in a heavy gale while escorting a merchant convoy from New York to Quebec. In the sloop *Loyalist* he served at the capture of Charleston, South Carolina, in May 1780, the most severe defeat suffered by American forces until Pearl Harbor in December 1941. He returning home to pay off in the sloop *Halifax* (14), in July 1781 and remained ashore until after the war ended in 1783.

In 1786 Bullen was appointed midshipman in the 3rd-rate *Culloden* (74) deployed in the Channel under Captain Sir Thomas Rich. In October 1789 he transferred to the 4th-rate *Leander* (50), flagship of Rear-Admiral Joseph Peyton in the Mediterranean, and on 9 January 1791 became acting lieutenant in the 6th-rate frigate *Mercury* (28). In the same year he married a distant cousin, Miss Wood, with whom he subsequently raised a family. Bullen's promotion was confirmed on his appointment, still in the Mediterranean, to the 6th-rate frigate *Euridyce* (24) on 9 August 1791. When she paid off in December 1792, Bullen remained ashore until he was again appointed to *Culloden*, once more under Sir Thomas Rich. Following the outbreak of war with Revolutionary France in February 1793, *Culloden* was deployed to the West Indies and served at **Martinique (14 – 21 April 1793)**. Bullen subsequently returned home with his ship and in March 1794 transferred to the 3rd-rate *Ramillies* (74), in which he fought at **The Glorious First of June (1 June 1794).** In August 1796 he re-joined Admiral Peyton, then flying his flag in the 3rd-rate *Oberyssel* (64) and in January 1797 became first lieutenant of the 3rd-rate *Monmouth* (64), under Captain the Earl of Northesk [6]. *Monmouth* was involved in the mutiny at the Nore during late May and early June 1797. Northesk seems to have been respected by his crew and was nominated by the mutineers to put their case to the Admiralty, but Bullen, who as first lieutenant was responsible for enforcing discipline in the ship, was roughly handled.

The North Sea fleet under Admiral Adam Duncan, based at the Nore, was responsible for countering the navy of the Batavian Republic (the Netherlands), a French ally since May 1794. The two fleets met at Camperdown (11 October 1797) where, after a hard-fought battle, Bullen took possession of *Delft*, one of two Dutch 50-gun ships that had surrendered. Three days later, badly damaged in the battle and caught in a gale on the way to England, she began sinking under him. Bullen told her Dutch first lieutenant, Lieutenant Heilberg that there was no hope of saving the ship and invited him into the longboat. Heilberg said he could not leave his wounded. Much moved, Bullen shook him by the hand and, after ordering the prize crew into the boat, remained with Heilberg and his men, saving as many of the wounded as they could until *Delft* suddenly foundered. Bullen and a few survivors were rescued from the sea by boats from neighbouring British ships, but the gallant Heilberg and many others went down with their ship. In recognition of his bravery in the battle and his humanity aboard *Delft*, Bullen was promoted to commander on 2 January 1798.

As commonly happened, Bullen's promotion to a higher rank brought a transfer to the half pay list until he could obtain an appointment at the appropriate level. It was not until June 1801 that he was given a command, the sloop *Wasp* (18), deployed to the coast of West Africa, where he protected British trading stations in Sierra Leone against neighbouring African rulers. This brought him promotion to post captain on 29 April 1802, just after peace was signed with France and her allies and he returned home in August 1802 after serving in the West Indies. The war with France was renewed in April

1803 and Bullen served in temporary command of the frigate *Minerve* off Cherbourg from 8 May to 3 June 1803, where he captured twenty-three French coastal vessels and fishing boats and forced the French to deploy a large frigate in the area. He was then given command of the Plymouth division of the Sea Fencibles, troops maintained by the Admiralty for the protection of dockyards and shore installations. In November 1803 he was appointed to a flotilla being fitted out in the Thames for the defence of creeks and tidal estuaries against the threat of a French invasion. Bullen returned to sea in May 1804, when he was invited by his former captain in *Monmouth*, Rear-Admiral the Earl of Northesk, to be his flag captain in the 1st-rate *Britannia* (100), in the blockade of Brest.

From there they became part of the squadron under Vice-Admiral Sir Robert Calder that, on 30 August 1805, arrived at Cadiz to join the blockade of Vice-Admiral Pierre Villeneuve's Franco-Spanish Combined Fleet. In the approach to **Trafalgar (21 October 1805)** Nelson signalled *Britannia*, *Prince*, and *Dreadnought*, all powerful 2nd-rates, but the three slowest ships in the fleet, to 'take station as convenient without regard to established order of sailing' so as to allow faster ships to come into action without delay. With no special role allotted to Northesk in Nelson's battle plan, *Britannia* came into action fifth behind *Victory* and joined the attack on Villeneuve's command ship *Bucentaure*. Subsequently she turned with other undamaged ships to counter the belated attempt of the enemy van division to come to Villeneuve's support. In the fighting she lost a lieutenant and nine men killed, and her master, a midshipman and forty men wounded. After the battle Bullen returned home with three of the four surviving prizes and paid off *Britannia* in June 1806. He subsequently served in the western Mediterranean, where between September 1807 and December 1810 he commanded the 5th-rate frigate *Volontaire* (38), in the blockade of Toulon and operations on the coast of Spain.

In May 1808, when the Spanish rose against French occupation and the rule of King Joseph Bonaparte, the British declared that, though Spain had joined the war on the French side in December 1804, they would support any nation that opposed French tyranny. British money and arms were sent from Gibraltar to aid the insurrection. Bullen was ordered to Fez, Morocco, from where he proceeded overland to Tangiers and negotiated the purchase of provisions to be sent to the Spanish patriots. During 1809, he led a series of attacks on the French coast near Marseilles, taking the island of Pomegues and destroying a shore battery of fourteen guns at Fort Rioux, Cape Croisette. Off Rosas at the eastern edge of the Pyrenees, where British seamen were fighting alongside the city's Spanish defenders, he supported a boat action that captured a convoy of seven merchant vessels and their three armed escorts. Bullen remained on the coast of Catalonia, cooperating with the Spanish patriots, and in January 1811 took command of the 5th-rate frigate *Cambrian* (40). In April 1811 he destroyed the French shore batteries at St Philon and Palamos and took their guns on board. Returning to Rosas, he captured a total of nineteen enemy merchantmen off Cadaques, and then sailed south to support the Spanish in **Tarragona (June 1811)**, where he was wounded while serving with a battery ashore at La Selvas.

Bullen left *Cambrian* in December 1811 and did not return to sea until November 1814, after Napoleon had been defeated and exiled to Elba. He was then appointed to the 4th-rate *Akbar* (54), as flag captain first of Rear-Admiral Sir Thomas Martin off the Scheldt, supervising the disposal of former enemy naval assets at Antwerp. He was awarded the CB in June 1815. From the Scheldt he took *Akbar* to Halifax, Nova Scotia, where he remained as flag captain of the C-in-C, North America, until going ashore in January 1817. Bullen became commodore on the West Coast of Africa on 12 Dec 1823, with his broad pendant in the frigate *Maidstone* (42). During the 1st Ashanti War he supported operations along the Gold Coast (Ghana) and landed seamen to defend the British depot at Cape Coast, where his men had to cast extra bullets from the lead on the roofs in anticipation of an Ashanti attack. Subsequently, in anti-slave trade operations, he freed nearly 10,000 slaves before his return home in 1827.

In July 1830 Bullen was appointed Superintendent of Pembroke Dockyard and captain of the royal yacht *Royal Sovereign* and retained both appointments until promoted to rear-admiral on 10 January 1837. During this time he served as Dockyard Commissioner at Chatham in 1831 – 32 and was made a knight of the Guelphic Order of Hanover in January 1835. Sir Charles Bullen was awarded the KCB in April 1839 and became a vice-admiral on 9 January 1846. He became a GCB in April 1852 and, promoted to admiral on 30 July 1852, died at Shirley, Southampton, on 2 July 1853.

CAPEL, Admiral the Honourable Sir THOMAS BLADEN, GCB (1776–1853) **[5]**
The Honourable Thomas Capel was born on 25 August 1775, the second son of William Capel, 4th Earl of Essex, and his second wife, Harriet, daughter of another influential figure, Colonel Thomas Bladen. He entered the Navy on 22 March 1782 as captain's servant in the frigate *Phaeton*, on whose books he remained until first going to sea in the 3rd-rate *Assistance* (50), deployed to the Newfoundland station in 1783 at the end of the American War of Independence. On 1 March 1793, with the French Revolutionary War just beginning, he was appointed midshipman in the frigate *Syren* (32) under Captain John Manley, whom he subsequently followed into the frigate *Apollo* (24). He then served under the command of Lord Hugh Seymour, first in the 3rd-rate *Leviathan* (74) and then in the 3rd-rate *Sans Pareil* (80). Capel was present in *Sans Pareil* at **Bridport's Action (23 June 1795), Île de Groix, Lorient** and remained with her on blockade duty in the Channel until April 1797, with promotion to acting lieutenant on 16 May 1796. He became a lieutenant on 5 April 1797, on appointment to the new 5th-rate frigate *Cambrian* (40) in the Channel under Captain the Honourable Arthur Legge.

In April 1798, for the first time not under the command of a fellow-nobleman, Capel joined the flagship of Rear-Admiral Sir Horatio Nelson, the newly-refitted 3rd-rate *Vanguard* (74) under Captain Edward Berry **[2]**. From the blockade of Cadiz, they were deployed to the Mediterranean to look for a French fleet that had sailed from Toulon with General Napoleon

Bonaparte and his army. After weeks of hunting, Nelson brought the French to battle at **The Nile (1–2 August 1798)**, in which Capel served as Nelson's signal lieutenant and was commended in dispatches as 'a most excellent officer'.

He was made acting commander of the brig *Mutine* (16) and, as a mark of honour, sent home with the dispatches, and the sword of the senior surviving French admiral. These dispatches were sent in duplicate, but the capture of Captain Berry, carrying the first set, meant that Capel was first home with the news. His promotion to commander was confirmed, with appointment to the sloop-rigged fireship *Alecto* (12) on the home station, followed by promotion to post captain on 27 December 1798.

Capel commanded the 6th-rate frigate *Arab* (22) on the West India station from January 1799 and then the 5th-rate frigate *Meleager* (32) from 19 July 1800 until 9 June 1801, when she was wrecked on the Triangle Rocks in the Gulf of Mexico. In May 1802, shortly after the conclusion of peace with France, he was appointed to the 5th-rate frigate *Revolutionnaire* (38) at Spithead, from where he went to the Mediterranean as captain of the 5th-rate frigate *Phoebe* (36). War with France was renewed in April 1803 and with Spain in December 1804. Capel remained in *Phoebe*, observing French naval movements in the Mediterranean and in April 1805 was the first to inform Nelson that Vice-Admiral Pierre Villeneuve's squadron had sailed from Toulon. While Nelson pursued Villeneuve to the West Indies and back during the summer of 1805, Capel was left in the Mediterranean with a force of five frigates and two bomb vessels in case the French moved against Sardinia or Sicily. After Villeneuve's Franco-Spanish Combined Fleet entered Cadiz on 20 August 1805, *Phoebe* joined the British blockading fleet there and became one of the four frigates on whom Nelson relied to keep the enemy under surveillance.

When Villeneuve again put to sea, *Phoebe* was one of the chain of ships whose signals reported to Nelson, forty-eight miles away with the main fleet, that enemy ships were coming out of harbour. After the two fleets made contact at **Trafalgar (21 October 1805)** Capel and the other three frigate captains were summoned aboard Nelson's flagship to receive their final orders. They were to remain to the windward of the column led by Nelson and to repeat his signals to the ships in the rear. Any enemy ships attempting to escape were to be followed, and damaged ones forced to strike their colours. Dismasted British or captured enemy ships were to be taken in tow. The four captains were then asked to go below and witness the codicil to Nelson's will in which he left his mistress, Lady Hamilton, and their daughter Horatia, as legacies to the State, a provision which the Cabinet would later decline to accept. During the action Capel kept his ship clear of the battle line as ordered and subsequently helped save the French *Swiftsure* and the Spanish *Bahama*, two of only four prizes that survived the great storm after the battle. The disabled French *Fougueux* (74) was taken in tow by *Phoebe* after surrendering but drifted away when the line parted. Capel made repeated efforts to retrieve her, but on 22 October she was blown ashore and broke up with *Phoebe*'s boats rescuing only a few survivors. After returning to England, Capel sat as a member of the court martial that Vice-Admiral Sir Robert Calder had demanded in response to criticism of his encounter with Villeneuve's fleet in **Calder's Action, Finisterre (22 July 1805)**.

In December 1805 Capel was appointed to the 4th-rate *Endymion* (40). Early in 1807, at a time of increasing tension between the British and Ottoman governments, *Endymion* carried Sir Charles Arbuthnot, the new British Ambassador, to Constantinople. While a British fleet under Sir John Duckworth waited at the entrance to the Turkish Straits, Capel learned of a plan to kidnap Arbuthnot and the leading British merchants in the city. He countered it by inviting them to dine with him in *Endymion* and then escaped with them to the fleet. He returned to Constantinople in Duckworth's operations in the **Turkish Straits (19 February–3 March 1807)**. As the fleet fought its way back to the Aegean, *Endymion* was hit by two immense stone shot, each weighing nearly 800 lbs and measuring two feet across, and lost three men killed with ten wounded.

Capel, mentioned in dispatches for his part in this action, was appointed to the 3rd-rate *La Hogue* (74) in December

1811 and served on the North America station during the War of 1812. There he commanded a small squadron in the blockade of New London, Connecticut, at the mouth of Long Island Sound, and along the eastern seaboard of the United States. He returned home after the end of hostilities in 1814 and was awarded the CB in June 1815. In May 1816 he married Harriet Catherine Smyth, the only daughter of a country gentleman. Between 15 December 1821 and 27 May 1827, when he was promoted to rear-admiral, Capel commanded successively the royal yachts *Royal George* and *Apollo*. In February 1832 he was awarded the KCB. Sir Thomas Capel was C-in-C in the East Indies from May 1834 to July 1837, with his flag in the 4th-rate frigate *Winchester* (50), and was promoted to vice-admiral on 10 January 1837. Between 1848 and 1852 he was C-in-C Portsmouth. He was awarded the GCB in April 1852 and died at Rutland Gate, London, on 4 March 1853.

CARNEGIE, Admiral the Right Honourable WILLIAM, 7th Earl of Northesk, GCB (1758 – 1831) **[6]**
The Honourable William Carnegie was born on 10 April 1756, the second son of Admiral the 6th Earl of Northesk and his wife, Anne, eldest daughter of the 5th Earl of Leven. He entered the Navy in 1771 on the books of the 3rd-rate *Albion* (74) and later served successively in the 5th-rate frigate *Southampton* (32) and the 6th-rate frigate *Squirrel* (20). On 7 December 1777, during the American War of Independence, he was promoted lieutenant and appointed to the 5th-rate frigate *Apollo* (32). He subsequently moved to the 1st-rate *Royal George* (100) in Sir George Rodney's fleet, escorting a large convoy to the relief of Gibraltar. On the way they captured a Spanish South American convoy and its escort off Finisterre (8 January 1780) before a further success in **The Moonlight Battle, Cape St Vincent (16 January 1780)**. With Gibraltar relieved, Rodney sailed for the West Indies. Carnegie joined his flagship, the 2nd-rate *Sandwich* (98) and served in the fleet action off **Martinique (17 April 1780)**, after which he was promoted to commander (confirmed on 10 September 1780) and appointed to the fireship *Blast*.

When news reached the West Indies that the Netherlands had entered the war, Rodney immediately attacked the rich Dutch island of St Eustatius (known as 'the Golden Rock') and captured it on 3 February 1781. Carnegie took part in this action commanding a hired vessel, formerly the Dutch frigate *Eustachia* (20), and was promoted to post captain on 7 April 1782, appointed to the 6th-rate frigate *Enterprise* (28). With the war ended by the Treaty of Versailles in January 1783, he returned home to pay off and then went ashore. On the death, without offspring, of his elder brother on 19 February 1788, he succeeded to the courtesy title of Lord Rosehill and soon afterwards married Mary Ricketts, the only daughter of a Hampshire country gentleman and a niece of Rear-Admiral Sir John Jervis (later Admiral of the Fleet Earl St Vincent).

Rosehill returned to sea in 1790, when a fleet was mobilized to meet the threat of war with Spain over the possession of Nootka Sound (Vancouver Island, British Columbia). He commanded the 5th-rate frigate *Heroine* (32) in the Channel for a few months, after which Spain, with her former ally France in the throes of revolution, acceded to British pressure. In 1792 he succeeded his father to become the 7th Earl of Northesk. During 1793, after the outbreak of war with Revolutionary France, Northesk successively commanded the 5th-rate frigates *Beaulieu* (40) and *Andromeda* (32). He then went ashore until 1796, when he was appointed to the new 3rd-rate *Monmouth* (64), in which he was serving with the North Sea fleet at the time of the mutiny at the Nore in May–June 1797.

Northesk (unlike his first lieutenant, Charles Bullen [4]) was respected by his crew but was detained in his cabin before being nominated by the mutineers' committee of delegates to put their case to the Admiralty. Northesk travelled to London, where Lord Spencer, First Lord of the Admiralty, agreed that a Royal Pardon should be granted to the Nore mutineers, as it already had been to those at Spithead. Northesk did not return to the Nore and, after the mutiny collapsed, resigned his command of *Monmouth*. In 1800 he was appointed to the 2nd-rate *Prince* (90) in the

Channel fleet and remained in command until the conclusion of peace in March 1802.

When war with France was renewed in May 1803, Northesk was given command of the 1st-rate *Britannia* (100) in the Channel fleet, and served in the blockade of Brest, where he remained with *Britannia* as his flagship on his promotion to rear-admiral on 23 April 1804. Spain entered the war on the French side in December 1804 and *Britannia* was sent to Cadiz in August 1805 as part of a squadron under Vice-Admiral Sir Robert Calder. There, they reinforced Vice-Admiral Cuthbert Collingwood [8] in the blockade of Vice-Admiral Pierre Villeneuve's Franco-Spanish Combined Fleet. After Nelson assumed command on 25 September 1805, Collingwood became his second-in-command and Calder returned to England. Nelson's subsequent detachment of Rear-Admiral Thomas Louis's squadron to escort a troop convoy into the Mediterranean left Northesk, as the only other flag officer present, third in command of the fleet.

Northesk had no experience of commanding a major warship in battle, still less a squadron, and neither Nelson nor Collingwood had served with him before. At **Trafalgar (21 October 1805)** he was allotted no special responsibility in Nelson's battle plan, and *Britannia*, old and slow, but still one of the fleet's most powerful assets, was placed in the weather column led by Nelson himself. In the approach to battle, together with the other slow sailers, the 2nd-rates *Prince* and *Dreadnought*, she was ordered to 'take station as convenient', so as to allow faster ships to come into action without waiting for them. Despite this, Collingwood's flag captain, Edward Rotheram [31] thought that the rear-admiral (and for that matter, Captain Grindall [16] of *Prince*) had behaved 'notoriously ill' in the action, and Northesk's own flag captain, Captain Bullen (his former first lieutenant in *Monmouth*) is said to have objected when Northesk ordered him to shorten sail, thereby reducing speed, in the approach to battle. After joining the fight around Villeneuve's command ship, *Bucentaure*, Northesk and others drove off the returning French van division under Rear-Admiral Dumanoir as it attempted to enter the battle. *Britannia* was only slightly damaged in the action but her crew suffered heavy casualties, with one officer and nine men killed and her master, one midshipman and forty men wounded.

On Nelson's death, command devolved upon Collingwood and Northesk served as his second-in-command until returning home in *Britannia* early in 1806. He was awarded the KB, the thanks of Parliament, the freedom of the City of London and the other honours and financial awards bestowed on the senior officers of the battle and was promoted to vice-admiral on 28 April 1808 and admiral on 4 June 1815, as the war came to an end. He was made Rear-Admiral of Great Britain in 1821 and was C-in-C Plymouth from 1827 to 1830. In Parliament, he sat in the House of Lords for several sessions as one of the representatives elected by the Scottish peers. Northesk's eldest son, the sixteen year old Midshipman Lord Rosehill, was lost in the Indian Ocean with Sir Thomas Troubridge and the 3rd-rate *Blenheim* in 1807. With his countess, who died in 1836, he had five daughters and three other sons, of whom the eldest succeeded in due course as 8th Earl and the youngest became an admiral. Lord Northesk died on 28 May 1831 and was buried near Nelson and Collingwood in the crypt of St Paul's Cathedral, London.

CODRINGTON, Admiral Sir EDWARD, GCB, GCMG (1770–1851) [7]

Edward 'Ned' Codrington was born on 27 April 1770, the grandson of a baronet with family estates at Dodington, Gloucestershire. He joined the Navy in July 1783, carried on the books of the yacht *Augusta*, and during the next ten years served as a midshipman on the North American, Mediterranean and home stations, successively in the sloop *Brisk*, the 4th-rates *Assistance* (44) and *Leander* (50), the 5th-rate frigate *Ambuscade* (32), the 2nd-rate *Formidable*, the 1st-rate *Queen Charlotte* (flagship of Lord Howe as C-in-C of the Channel Fleet), and the frigate *Santa Margarita* (36). Following the outbreak of war with Revolutionary France in February 1793, Codrington was promoted to lieutenant on 28 May 1793 and appointed by Howe to the frigate *Phoebe* (28), employed in repeating the flagship's signals to the rest of the fleet. He was then recalled to *Queen Charlotte* for signalling duties and performed this role during the operations of May 1794 leading to the **Glorious First of June (1 June 1794)**. During this action he commanded the flagship's forward lower deck batteries and personally fired her guns into the stern of the French *Montagne* as *Queen Charlotte* broke through the enemy line. As a mark of honour, he was sent to the Admiralty with the duplicate dispatches announcing Howe's victory.

Codrington was promoted to be commander of the fireship *Comet* on 7 October 1794 and to post captain on 6 April 1795, appointed to the frigate *Babet* (22) in which he served in **Bridport's Action, Île de Groix, Lorient, (23 June 1795)**. In July 1796 he transferred to the frigate *Druid* (32), on the Lisbon station, and took part with two other frigates in the capture of the French troopship *Ville de L'Orient* (7 January 1798), part of a French expedition intended for the invasion of Ireland. After returning home with *Druid* he remained ashore for some years. Peace with France and her allies was signed in March 1802 and Codrington married Jane, daughter of Jasper Hall of Kingston, Jamaica, in the following December. Hostilities were renewed against France in May 1803 and Spain in December 1804. Codrington's brother, the Member of Parliament for Tewkesbury, a wealthy landowner and a regular supporter of the Tory ministry, attempted to use his influence to obtain another command for him. When this did not materialize, the MP stayed away from the division lobbies, so that in May 1805, the Prime Minister, Pitt the Younger, learning of the reason for his absence, told Lord Barham, First Lord of the Admiralty, to find Codrington a ship. On 24 May 1805, accordingly, Codrington was appointed to the 3rd-rate *Orion* (74) which, in August 1805, joined Vice-Admiral Collingwood **[8]** in the blockade of Vice-Admiral Pierre Villeneuve's Franco-Spanish Combined Fleet at Cadiz.

Collingwood's policy of discouraging captains from paying social visits to each other's ships left Codrington with little to distract him from the sadness of parting from his good-looking wife and their small family, and he complained in a letter home that his C-in-C was a 'stay-on-board

Admiral'. He felt more warmly towards the fleet's second-in-command, Vice-Admiral Sir Robert Calder, who was of a more convivial disposition and generally popular with captains who served under him. Calder was at this time the subject of criticism at home for his inconclusive encounter with Villeneuve's fleet in **Calder's Action, Finisterre (22 July 1805)**. Codrington was one of those who felt that it was ungenerous of Collingwood not to allow his captains to leave their ships to dine with Calder and give him moral support. As the blockade continued, he wrote home that morale among officers and ratings alike suffered under Collingwood's stern leadership and that all were looking forward to Nelson's imminent assumption of the command.

At **Trafalgar (21 October 1805)** *Orion* was eighth in the column led by Nelson in *Victory*. In this position, Codrington joined the action when it was well under way, passing the *Victory* and Collingwood's *Royal Sovereign* in the mêlée, and being frustrated in his attempts to close with the enemy by other British ships forestalling him. He encountered the damaged French *Swiftsure* and dismasted her with a single broadside before reaching the northern edge of the battle area, where he found the French *Intrépide*. Her commander, Captain Infernet, had broken away from the returning enemy van division with the intention of supporting Villeneuve's command ship *Bucentaure* and was already exchanging shots with two other British ships. Codrington then engaged *Intrépide* in a fifteen-minute duel that cost *Orion* one man killed and two midshipmen and nineteen ratings wounded, together with several spars and her maintopsail yard. Finally, with her masts gone and rudder smashed, *Intrépide* was forced to surrender and her valiant commander, with his young son, was taken on board *Orion*.

In the storm that followed the battle, *Orion* was among the British ships that took on board the crews of the prizes that Collingwood ordered to be scuttled or burnt. As well as her own 500-strong complement, she then had an additional 100 members of prize crews from other ships and 580 prisoners of war, all in conditions of overcrowding, stench and dirt. Captain Infernet, after a few weeks, was sent to England to await an exchange. Codrington, who had discovered that Infernet's wife and family were at Toulon with no income but his naval pay, chivalrously wrote to his own wife to spend up to £100 on Infernet's needs while in captivity. *Orion* and Codrington remained at sea until December 1806, when they returned home to pay off.

In December 1808 Codrington was given command of the 3rd-rate *Blake* (74). During the summer of 1809 he served in the North Sea and was flag captain to Admiral Lord Gardner, C-in-C of the Channel Fleet, prior to the British expedition to Walcheren (August – September 1809). There, he was mentioned in dispatches for his conduct on 14 August 1809 when *Blake*, with no pilot on board, went aground under fire from shore batteries during the bombardment of Flushing (Vlissingen) and fought an engagement lasting two and three-quarter hours, losing two men killed and nine wounded and being twice set on fire before getting off.

With the rising of Spanish patriots against French occupation in 1808, Spain became a British ally. Cadiz came under siege by the French in March 1810, but held out with a garrison of Spanish, British and Portuguese troops and supplies brought in by sea under the protection of British warships. Codrington was deployed to the coast of Spain and in August 1810, when it seemed as if the French might enter Cadiz, was tasked with taking four ill-found Spanish warships, under-manned and crowded with refugees, from there to Port Mahon, Minorca, which he reached after a stressful voyage lasting thirty-eight days.

During 1811 Codrington commanded a squadron on the east coast of Spain and was mentioned in dispatches for supporting the Spanish defenders of **Tarragona (June 1811)** and for helping refugees escape by sea before the city was stormed by the French on 28 July 1811. He continued to support the patriots along the Catalonian coast and was once more mentioned in dispatches for his part in a raid on Tarragona on 28 April 1812, in which he swept the harbour mole with naval gunfire and destroyed the enemy vessels sheltering there. He returned home early in 1813, commended for his services by the Spanish government and by Sir Edward Pellew, C-in-C Mediterranean.

Codrington returned to sea at the beginning of 1814, deployed to the North America station in the War of 1812 as commodore, with his broad pendant in the new 4th-rate *Forth* (50). He was promoted to rear-admiral on 4 June 1814 and served as captain of the fleet to the local C-in-C, Sir Alexander Cochrane, in the 3rd-rate *Tonnant* (80). In this campaign he organized naval transport supplying the British army that captured and burnt Washington DC, and planned the successful British attack on Baltimore, Maryland, a base for American privateers, for which he was mentioned in dispatches a fourth time. Late in 1814 Collingwood was given command of a squadron with his flag in the 5th-rate frigate *Havannah* (36), deployed at the mouth of the Mississippi where he supported the British Army's landing before the battle of New Orleans (8 January 1815) and its re-embarkation following the British defeat there. Awarded the KCB on 2 January 1815, Sir Edward Collingwood took part in the more successful British operations leading to the capture of Fort Bowyer, Mobile Bay, Alabama, early in February 1815 and, when news came that the American war was over, was sent home with the dispatches. The Napoleonic Wars ended in the same year, followed by Collingwood's promotion to vice-admiral on 10 July 1821.

In February 1826 Codrington returned to sea as C-in-C, Mediterranean Fleet, with his base at Malta and his flag in the 2nd-rate *Asia* (84). The Greek War of Independence from Turkish rule was at this time in progress, with many acts of genocide on both sides and a multinational British, Russian and French fleet was assembled under Codrington's command to enforce an uneasy truce. Rising tension between this force and the Turks led to the Battle of Navarino (20 October 1827), the last fleet action between wooden sailing ships in naval history, in which sixty Turkish and Egyptian ships were destroyed, with 4,000 casualties among their crews. The multi-national fleet lost 167 men killed and over 600 wounded, among whom was Codrington's youngest son, serving in the flagship as a signal midshipman. Codrington himself had four bullets through his hat and clothing and a fifth through his watch, and was nearly killed by *Asia*'s falling mizen mast. Although public opinion in the United Kingdom (Codrington among them) strongly supported the Greeks, the destruction of a fleet belonging to a friendly state, together with the disproportionate number of casualties, led to an outcry and the British government described the battle as 'an untoward event'. Despite this, the Lord High Admiral, the Duke of Clarence (later William IV), a professional sea officer who was an old friend of Codrington, sent him personal congratulations and distributed honours to the fleet on an unprecedented scale. As well as a GCB from his own sovereign, Codrington later received awards from the Emperor of Russia and the kings of France and Greece, but in June 1828 was recalled by the British Cabinet.

Between June and October 1831, during the Belgian War of Independence, Codrington commanded a squadron of observation in the Channel, with his flag in the 1st-rate *Caledonia* (120). From 1832 to 1840 he was Member of Parliament for Devonport. He was promoted to admiral on 10 January 1837 and was C-in-C, Portsmouth, from November 1837 to December 1842. Sir Edward Codrington died on 28 April 1851 and was buried in St Peter's Church, Eaton Square, Belgravia. With his wife Jane, who died in 1837, he had a family of three sons and two daughters. Their eldest son, Edward, midshipman in the frigate *Cambrian*, was drowned when the ship's cutter overturned off the island of Hydra. Their youngest became an admiral of the fleet and their elder daughter married a naval officer.

COLLINGWOOD,   Vice-Admiral   **CUTHBERT**,   Baron
Collingwood of Caldburne and Hethpool (1748 – 1810) [8]
Cuthbert 'Cuddy' Collingwood was born in Newcastle-on-Tyne on 26 September 1748, the eighth child and eldest son in a middle-class Northumberland family of ten children. Their father died in 1775, leaving his widow and three surviving daughters ill-provided for, so that Collingwood

was always aware of the family's limited means. After attending the local grammar school, he joined the Navy in 1761, during the Seven Years War, as a volunteer in the 6th-rate frigate *Shannon* (28), commanded by his maternal cousin, Captain (later Admiral Sir George) Braithwaite. He served under Braithwaite first in this ship and then in the 6th-rate *Gibraltar* on trade protection duties in the North Atlantic, North Sea, Baltic and eastern Mediterranean until the war ended in 1763. Collingwood remained at sea and was appointed a midshipman in 1766. He became a master's mate (a rank given to midshipmen who had passed the examination for promotion to lieutenant but were still under the requisite age) in 1767, in the 6th-rate frigate *Liverpool*, employed on survey and other duties in the eastern Mediterranean.

In March 1772 Collingwood was appointed to the 3rd-rate *Lenox* (74), guard-ship at Portsmouth, and during 1773 was briefly deployed to Jamaica in the 4th-rate *Portland* (50). Early in 1774 he joined the 4th-rate *Preston*, flagship of Vice-Admiral Samuel Graves as C-in-C, North America, and was with him at Boston, Massachusetts, at the outbreak of the American War of Independence. In the initial hostilities, Collingwood served ashore with a party of seamen from Graves's squadron, carrying supplies to the embattled redcoats in the Battle of Bunker Hill (17 June 1775). He was promoted to lieutenant by Graves and returned home in the 3rd-rate *Somerset* (74) where his commission was confirmed with effect from the date of the battle.

Collingwood returned to sea in March 1776 in the new sloop *Hornet* (14) on the West Indies station. He found himself out of sympathy with his new captain, Commander Robert Haswell, whom he regarded as over-insistent on his own prerogatives while leaving all the work of commanding the ship to Collingwood. In 1777 Collingwood was charged by Haswell with neglect of duty. A court martial acquitted him, but commented on the lack of cheerfulness with which he had performed his duties and recommended him to conduct himself in the future 'with the alacrity essential in the King's service'. In the summer of 1778 he moved to the newly-arrived 5th-rate frigate *Lowestoffe* (32), in place of Lieutenant Horatio Nelson, who had been transferred to the 4th-rate *Bristol*, flagship of the local C-in-C, Sir Peter Parker. Collingwood flourished in his new appointment and on 20 June 1779 was promoted to commander and succeeded Nelson in the brig *Badger* (12) in which he pursued a number of small vessels, though all escaped, taking the prospect of prize money with them. Collingwood was promoted to post captain on 22 March 1780 and was appointed to the 6th-rate frigate *Hinchinbroke* (28), once more succeeding Nelson, on 2 May 1780.

The entry of Spain into the war in June 1779 opened her colonies to British attack and early in 1780 the British tried to cross Central America and reach the Pacific by way of the San Juan river and Lake Nicaragua. The expedition was defeated by the geography and fever, and Collingwood, who took over *Hinchinbroke* from Nelson at the mouth of the river, recorded that many of the transports no longer had troops to carry nor crews to keep them afloat. In the first four months of his command, despite all the measures recommended by the ship's surgeon, 180 out of his 200 men died of tropical illnesses. In August 1780 *Hinchinbroke* returned to Port Royal, Jamaica, where on 19 December 1780 Collingwood transferred to the 6th-rate frigate *Pelican* (24). During the night of 2 August 1781, when a hurricane drove over 100 vessels ashore at Port Royal, *Pelican* was wrecked on the Morant Keys, a group of small islands thirty-five miles from Jamaica, but the next day Collingwood managed to get his crew ashore on rafts made from broken yards. They eked out their food and water for ten days until getting a boat away to Port Royal, from where the frigate *Diamond* came to their rescue.

Collingwood returned to England and in January 1783 was appointed to the new 3rd-rate *Sampson* (64). When the war ended in January 1783, *Sampson* was paid off, but Collingwood obtained command of the new 5th-rate frigate *Mediator* (44) in which he returned to the West Indies. There, together with his friend Nelson as the senior officer, and his own younger brother Wilfred as commander of the sloop

Rattler (16), Collingwood displeased the local community in Antigua by enforcing the Navigation Acts, which excluded foreign merchantmen from British ports. Most planters and businessmen in the West Indies, like those in the former North American colonies, had looked forward to resuming their pre-war trade with each other and regarded American independence as a mere technicality. The London government supported the sea officers, though both Nelson and Collingwood continued to be threatened with writs from the indignant Antiguans. Collingwood went home with *Mediator* in 1786 and rejoined his sisters in Northumberland. There they received the news from Nelson that their brother Wilfred had died at sea.

In the spring of 1790, when a British fleet was mobilized during the dispute with Spain over the possession of Nootka Sound (Vancouver), Collingwood was offered the choice of commanding a 64-gun ship of the line or a frigate. He declined the 64-gun ship on the grounds that, smaller than most 3rd-rates, they were usually deployed as convoy escorts or on detachment away from the main fleet and were, moreover, the most likely to be sent to Indian waters. A frigate, although rated lower than a ship of the line, with a corresponding lower rate of pay for her captain, involved fewer expenses and, if deployed to the West Indies, held out prospects of ample prize money. In June 1790 therefore, he was appointed to the 5th-rate frigate *Mermaid* (32) in which he sailed to the West Indies, but Spain, with her old ally France distracted by revolution, accepted British terms and the crisis was resolved by diplomacy.

Collingwood once more returned home and in June 1791 married Sarah Blackett, daughter of a wealthy Newcastle merchant, and granddaughter of Admiral Roddam, who had been Collingwood's captain in *Lenox*. They set up house in Morpeth, Northumberland, and together had two daughters, born in 1792 and 1793 respectively. Collingwood was destined to see little of them, but he was a loving and careful father, and in later years wrote home urging that they should not be allowed to develop a provincial accent, nor to read romantic novels (which, he said, developed imagination at the expense of judgement). After seeing the fate of refugees unable to cross a river as the French Revolutionary armies swept into Italy, he sent to say that his daughters should be taught to swim, an unusual accomplishment among young ladies of the time. Equally unconventionally, when they were young teenagers, he wrote home to say they should be taught to handle a musket, like the Spanish patriot women then fighting against French occupation.

Following the outbreak of the French Revolutionary War in February 1793, Collingwood was given command of the 2nd-rate *Prince* (90), flagship of his old friend, Rear-Admiral George Bowyer, in the Channel fleet under Lord Howe. This ship, launched barely five years earlier, proved to be one of the slowest in the fleet and in January 1794 Bowyer, with Collingwood remaining as his flag captain, moved to the older but faster 2nd-rate *Barfleur*. Collingwood's first fleet action was **The Glorious First of June (1 June 1794)** where Bowyer lost a leg to cannon-shot and Collingwood, after catching him as he fell, took his place when he was carried below. Collingwood therefore felt the more aggrieved when, along with a number of other captains, he was not mentioned in Howe's dispatches and accordingly not awarded the gold medal that the King decided to give to all those so mentioned. Howe himself had declared that those whose names were omitted because he had not personally noticed them, should not, simply on that account, be considered less deserving.

With Bowyer invalided ashore, *Barfleur* was given to a new admiral who selected his own flag captain. Collingwood took the chance to visit his small family in Northumberland before returning to Portsmouth to take over the 3rd-rate *Hector* (74). When it proved impossible to find a crew for this ship, he was given the 3rd-rate *Excellent* (74) in December 1794 and joined her at Plymouth after another few days in the north. He then sailed for the Mediterranean where he joined his old friend Nelson off Leghorn (Livorno). After a year on blockade duty *Excellent* was nearly run down by the 2nd-rate *Princess Royal* (90) in a squall on 27 February 1796. Collingwood, on deck at the time, saw her coming and altered course to reduce the impact, but *Excellent* lost her foremast and bowsprit and returned to the British base at Ajaccio, Corsica, under jury rig in gale force winds. Like Nelson, Collingwood welcomed the arrival of Admiral Sir John Jervis to command the Mediterranean fleet (other captains, aware of Jervis's reputation as a disciplinarian, were less enthusiastic). By the end of 1786, however, allied defeats on land had driven the Navy from its Central Mediterranean bases and forced the fleet to move to Gibraltar.

From there, Collingwood took part in Jervis's victory over the Spanish fleet at the battle of **Cape St Vincent (14 February 1797)** in which *Excellent* played a prominent role. She first engaged *Salvador del Mundo* (112) which struck her colours only to hoist them again after *Excellent* had passed, so that afterwards, to Collingwood's chagrin, she was taken by another British ship. She next encountered *San Yidro*, which surrendered after a ten-minute duel, and was left to be boarded by the frigate *Lively*. She then passed between the British and Spanish lines to support Nelson's 3rd-rate *Captain* (74), heavily engaged with *San Nicolas* (80) and *San Josef* (112). Collingwood came up to within ten feet of *San Nicolas* and poured in a fire that passed through her into *San Josef*. The two Spanish ships collided with each other and with *Captain* and, as the pressure on Nelson eased, Collingwood left them and joined other British ships in attacking the Spanish flagship, the four-decker *Santisima Trinidad*. Collingwood's conduct was commented on with approval by Jervis himself, by Rear-Admiral William Waldegrave and his flag captain in *Barfleur*, and by Nelson who wrote to him that 'a friend in need is a friend indeed'.

All the captains of ships of the line that took part in the battle were awarded a gold medal issued to mark this victory. Collingwood, informed by Jervis of the award, at first declined to accept it, on the grounds that by doing so he would seem to be admitting that he had been treated fairly when not given the medal for **The Glorious First of June**. Jervis supported his stand and Lord Spencer, First Lord of the Admiralty, sent him the two together, with a congratulatory letter stating that the delay in sending the medal for the former action (which indeed had only become available for issue three months previously) was due to the lack of a suitable means of delivery.

The surviving Spanish ships escaped to their base at Cadiz, where they were blockaded by Jervis (newly created Earl of St Vincent) and his fleet. Collingwood remained there for almost two years until he returned home with *Excellent* to pay off. He was offered immediate re-appointment as captain of the 2nd-rate *Atlas* (90) but, after an absence of almost four years, determined to re-join his family in Northumberland. On 14 February 1799, with a large increase in the establishment of flag officers, he was promoted to rear-admiral. On offering his services, he was appointed to a command in the Channel fleet and on 27 May 1799 hoisted his flag in the 3rd-rate *Triumph* (74). A few weeks earlier the French Admiral Bruix had escaped from Brest and entered the Mediterranean. St Vincent, seeing Bruix pass Gibraltar, ordered Vice-Admiral Lord Keith to abandon the blockade of Cadiz and concentrate his ships off the eastern coast of Spain. Collingwood and other reinforcements joined Keith on 25 May but, by then, Bruix had first reached Toulon and then sailed back to Cartagena, where he joined the Spanish fleet that had escaped from Cadiz. With Keith in close pursuit, the combined French and Spanish fleet put into Brest early in August.

Collingwood found himself on blockade duty there once again, though as a flag officer he now had a share of the prize money from the fleet's ever-questing frigates. In January 1800 he shifted his flag to the more spacious *Barfleur*, in which he had previously been flag captain and remained in her for the next two years, apart from a brief spell during 1800 in the new 2nd-rate *Neptune* (98). For part of this time Sarah Collingwood and their elder daughter came south and lived variously in Plymouth and Paignton. St Vincent, now in command of the Channel Fleet, rigorously enforced standing orders forbidding captains to go ashore without permission and Collingwood's family saw little of him. When they joined him on board *Barfleur*, they were caught in a gale and so badly affected by motion sickness that they were glad to get ashore again.   During the last winter of the war, with hostilities suspended while the diplomats negotiated, Collingwood was deployed to Bantry Bay, where the fleet could lie safely in port and its officers could enjoy what social life this remote Irish region had to offer. He then returned to Torbay where, with the coming of peace and the demobilization of the Channel fleet, he struck his flag and went ashore on 7 May 1802.

War with France was renewed on 16 May 1803 and three days later a British squadron under Vice-Admiral the Honourable Sir William 'Billy Blue' Cornwallis resumed the blockade of Brest. Collingwood, leaving his home at Morpeth for the last time, hoisted his flag in the 5th-rate frigate *Diamond* (38) on 3 June 1803 and sailed from Spithead to join Cornwallis. 'Here comes my old friend Coll', remarked Cornwallis 'the last that left and the first to join me.' Early in August Collingwood's intended flagship, the 3rd-rate *Venerable* (74), arrived on station and he shifted his flag accordingly, only to transfer it briefly to the 3rd-rate *Minotaur* (74) while *Venerable* returned to port for replenishment. He spent a few weeks ashore at Plymouth over Christmas 1803 while his new flagship, the 3rd-rate *Culloden* (74), was being made ready in place of the unseaworthy *Venerable*. During June 1804 he flew his flag briefly in the larger but slower 2nd-rate *Prince* (90) and then returned to *Culloden* until she was given to Sir Edward Pellew in August 1804. Collingwood was irritated at not being given warning of this, but his new flagship, the 2nd-rate *Dreadnought* (98), proved a good substitute and more appropriate to the rank of vice-admiral, to which he had been promoted on 23 April 1804. He spent the winter of 1804 off Brest, during which time Spain joined the war on the French side.

At the beginning of March 1805 Collingwood was ordered to prepare a small 'flying squadron' for deployment in an emergency without the need to weaken the main Channel fleet. A month later Vice-Admiral Pierre Villeneuve escaped from Toulon with eleven French ships of the line and, after collecting six Spanish ships of the line at Cadiz, disappeared from British view. Collingwood was reinforced and sent south to join in the hunt for him. After learning that Villeneuve had gone to the

West Indies with Nelson in pursuit, he took station off Cadiz to prevent a junction between the Spanish ships there and in Cartagena. The Cartagena squadron put to sea, but returned to port on hearing of Collingwood's arrival. Collingwood sent two ships to join Nelson and divided the remainder between Cadiz and Cartagena. He was at Cadiz with *Dreadnought*, the 3rd-rates *Colossus* and *Achille*, the old 5th- rate frigate *Niger* (33) and the bomb-vessel *Thunder* (8) when Villeneuve and his Franco-Spanish Combined Fleet of thirty-six ships arrived there on 20 August 1805.

Collingwood retired south towards Gibraltar, pursued by sixteen enemy ships of the line. *Thunder*, a slow sailer, was nearly captured but took advantage of her shallow draft to run into shoal water where she could not be followed. When the pursuers broke off the chase and went back to Cadiz, Collingwood resumed his station and over the next few days was joined by another five ships of the line, the 3rd-rate *Mars* (74) from Gibraltar and the rest from Cartagena. At the end of August another eighteen arrived, under Vice-Admiral Sir Robert Calder. Confident of victory if Villeneuve were to come out, but determined not to relax his guard, he ordered all captains to remain in their ships and forbade the practice of inter-ship visiting for social engagements. On 28 September 1805, with Nelson's long-awaited arrival from England, Collingwood became his second-in-command and, reluctantly but in accordance with Admiralty orders, shifted his flag into the 1st-rate *Royal Sovereign* on her arrival a week later. *Royal Sovereign* had previously been noted for her poor sailing and was known in the fleet as the 'West-Country Wagon' but her bottom had recently been re-coppered, and her speed improved in consequence.

Collingwood and Nelson, with the former older than his C-in-C by some ten years, and the latter as warm and extrovert as Collingwood was reserved and austere, formed an ideal combination of commander and second-in-command. While they waited for Villeneuve to sail, Nelson made his plans clear. They would attack the enemy line in two lines. 'No man has more confidence in another than I have in you', he told Collingwood and, in his Tactical

Memorandum, laid down that, ' The entire management of the Lee line after the intentions of the Commander-in-Chief are signified is intended to be left to the Admiral commanding that Line'.

At **Trafalgar (21 October 1805)** Collingwood led the lee column as planned. As the fleet neared the enemy line, Nelson signalled *Mars* to take station ahead of *Royal Sovereign*, not wishing to see his old friend in the most dangerous position. Collingwood ordered *Royal Sovereign* to make more sail, so preventing this just as Nelson later prevented *Téméraire* from overtaking *Victory*. Meeting his flag lieutenant on deck, he recommended him to change his boots for silk stockings, as he himself had done, because 'if one should get a shot in the leg, they would be so much more manageable for the surgeon'. He then toured the ship, encouraging the officers and ratings and giving orders for the men to lie down and keep quiet while the fleet slowly approached the enemy. Seeing more flags hauled aloft in *Victory*, he said 'I wish Nelson would stop signalling, we all know what to do', but afterwards expressed his approval of 'England expects ...' and passed on the message to his men.

As *Royal Sovereign* approached the enemy line, Collingwood ordered a gun to be fired so as to make smoke and give the ship some cover. When hostile fire cut down one of her studding-sails so that it trailed over the side, a midshipman in one of the following ships supposed that the loss of good canvas would grieve Collingwood, who was noted for his careful husbandry of naval stores. In fact, the admiral called on his flag lieutenant to help him haul it in and, under fire, they stowed it away in a boat for future use. Nelson, watching *Royal Sovereign* become the first to come under fire, declared 'See how that noble fellow Collingwood takes his ship into action. How I envy him.' At about the same time Collingwood remarked to his flag captain, Captain Edward Rotheram [31], whom he had brought with him from *Dreadnought*, 'What would Nelson give to be here'.

Collingwood, calmly munching an apple, remained on the poop deck for most of the action. At one point, with *Royal Sovereign* under fire from four enemy ships, he ordered the

Marines down to the quarterdeck and eventually joined them there, telling the gunners to be sure to aim carefully and looking along the barrels to ensure they were properly laid. Although the ship's master was mortally wounded while standing alongside him, Collingwood himself escaped serious injury, and suffered only cuts and bruises from flying splinters and other wreckage. Of all those on the poop and quarterdeck, only Collingwood, his Secretary and Rotheram were not killed or wounded. News that Nelson had been seriously wounded arrived at about the same time that the Spanish flagship *Santa Ana* (112) surrendered to *Royal Sovereign*, but the British ship had suffered so much damage to her masts and rigging that she could no longer function as a command platform. Collingwood, unaware of the precise nature of his old friend's wound, but fearing the worst, shifted his flag to the frigate *Euryalus* and ordered her to take *Royal Sovereign* in tow.

As the battle ended, Captain Thomas Hardy [17] of *Victory* was pulled across in her sole remaining boat to report Nelson's death and to repeat his last emphatic order, to anchor. Collingwood, on whom command of the fleet now devolved, found himself with three ships of the line totally dismasted and another eleven with badly damaged masts or rigging. He had also seventeen ships of the line as prizes, all badly damaged, with six totally dismasted and several others kept afloat only by constant pumping. Although Nelson, before the battle, had signalled 'Prepare to anchor at close of day', Collingwood now told Hardy 'Anchor the fleet, why, that is the last thing I should have thought of '. With the late October dusk approaching, he decided to abandon any pursuit of the remaining enemy ships and signalled the fleet to follow him westwards, away from the shoals of Cape Trafalgar. Later, when the wind had changed and strengthened and they had made less than ten miles from a lee shore, Collingwood ordered 'Prepare to anchor' but as several ships reported that they had lost their anchors or cables, he decided not to make the 'Execute' signal. Some anchored on their own discretion, but the remainder followed him seawards.

The wind steadily strengthened to gale force and, on the morning of 23 October, Collingwood ordered the prizes to be evacuated and destroyed. As many of their crews as possible were taken off, but many, especially the wounded, were lost when their ships were scuttled or driven ashore by the storm. When the weather improved on 27 October, Collingwood sent a boat into Cadiz under a flag of truce with Captain Blackwood [3] of *Euryalus* to negotiate the landing of wounded prisoners of war and the return of British prize crews who had been wrecked with their ships. The Spanish Captain-General of the province, the Marquis de la Solana, sent a cask of wine to Collingwood who, not to be outdone in courtesy, responded by sending him an English cheese and a cask of porter. Collingwood then resumed the blockade with his serviceable ships and sent the worst damaged, with the four remaining prizes, to Gibraltar for repair. On 29 October Rear-Admiral Louis rejoined the fleet from Gibraltar with his squadron of four ships, including the 2nd-rate *Queen* (98) into which Collingwood shifted his flag.

Several of his captains, regretting the loss of their prize money and disappointed in their hopes of a triumphal return home, were critical of his decision not to anchor immediately after the battle. Collingwood, in his puritanical way, noted that such 'might have made us proud and pretentious, and we ought to be content with that good fortune which Providence has thought sufficient'. As for the destruction of the prizes, rather than risk British ships in trying to retain them, 'my object was their ruin and not what might be made of them'. He was also concerned to maintain the blockade in case those ships that had escaped came out, as indeed some did, attempting to recover the prizes. In the distribution of honours after the battle, Collingwood was raised to the peerage as a baron of the United Kingdom with the thanks of Parliament and a pension for himself, his wife and daughters. He was confirmed as C-in-C, Mediterranean, with all the diplomatic and other authority that had previously been exercised by Nelson.

In April 1806 Lord Collingwood shifted his flag to the new 2nd-rate *Ocean* in which he remained at sea for the rest of that year and into the next. His reluctance to delegate and his refusal to appoint a captain of the fleet added much to the burden of his command, though he was convinced that it was his duty to bear it as long as the Admiralty so wished and, despite worsening health and a longing to see his family, stayed faithfully at his post. During August 1807 he negotiated a settlement with the Ottoman government, following the failure of Sir John Duckworth in the **Turkish Straits (February–March 1807)**, and then returned to the western Mediterranean and the blockade of Toulon. In the spring of 1808 he prepared to meet a threat to British-protected Sicily from the combination of the Toulon ships with a squadron that had escaped from Rochefort and entered the Mediterranean. With insufficient frigates to track them, and distracted by the arrival off the Balearics of a Spanish squadron from Cartagena, he failed to make contact and the French escaped back into Toulon.

In May 1808 Spanish patriots rose against French occupation. The British, with whom Spain was still technically at war, sent arms and money to the patriots and ended the blockade of Spanish ports. At the beginning of August Collingwood landed at Cadiz where, still held in regard for his chivalry after Trafalgar, he was lavishly entertained. Hoping that the tide of the war had at last changed, he wrote to the Admiralty asking to be allowed to go home for the sake of his health. The Cabinet, reluctant to lose the services of so experienced an officer at this critical time, told him he could not be spared. He was told he might fly his flag ashore if he so wished, but he spent the stormy winter of 1808 at sea between Toulon and Spain. In April 1809 he shifted his flag to the 1st-rate *Ville de Paris* (110). With no exercise except walking in his great cabin, where he spent all his working hours, he increasingly complained of weaknesses in his legs and bad eyesight. In August he was saddened by the loss overboard of his old dog, Bounce, a faithful seagoing companion that for the last four years had been his only link with home. At the end of October 1809, from a distance, he witnessed his last action, the destruction of a French convoy and its escorts in Rosas Bay. On 22 February 1810, after another winter at sea, he wrote to the Admiralty from Minorca, insisting that he was no longer physically able to exercise command. At last the ministers agreed to let him go and he sailed for home in *Ville de Paris* on 6 March.

Collingwood died at sea on the evening of 7 March 1810, from what is now believed to have been cancer of the stomach. He was buried near Nelson in St Paul's Cathedral, London. His request that his peerage might be granted with a remainder in the female line, as he had no sons, was never granted and his barony became extinct. One of his habits had been to carry a pocketful of acorns and to plant them as he travelled about his native land, so that the Navy would never be short of oak for its ships. They, or their descendants, survive as his living memorial.

CONN, Captain JOHN (1764–1810) [9]

John Conn, scion of an ancient Irish family of Mount Ida, County Waterford, was born in 1764 and joined the Navy in 1778 during the American War of Independence. He was promoted to lieutenant on 1 June 1793, five months after the outbreak of the French Revolutionary War, and served in the 1st-rate *Royal Sovereign* (100) at **The Glorious First of June (1 June 1794)**. On 11 August 1800 he became a commander, appointed to the bomb vessel *Discovery* (10) in which he took part in the battle of **Copenhagen (2 April 1801)**, engaging Danish shore batteries and ships at anchor. With his experience of this type of combat, he subsequently commanded a division of mortar vessels in a raid on French invasion barges at **Boulogne (15 August 1801)**.The attack was led by Vice-Admiral Viscount Nelson, to whom Conn was related by marriage (his wife was the daughter of the Reverend Isaac Nelson, incumbent of the Northumbrian parishes of Meldon and Milford) but proved one of his rare failures. With both the French and British governments anxious for peace, hostilities effectively ceased in October 1801. A formal treaty was concluded in March 1802 but the war was renewed in May 1803.

Conn was promoted to post captain on 29 August 1802, and appointed to the 3rd-rate *Canopus* (80) as the flag captain of Rear-Admiral George Campbell, deployed under Nelson in the blockade of Toulon. On 24 August 1804, Vice-Admiral Latouché-Tréville (promoted following his repulse of Nelson's raid on Boulogne) put to sea with eight ships of the line and drove away the inshore British frigates. Just over the horizon, he encountered Nelson's five ships of the line, including *Canopus*. Realizing he had fallen into a trap, he returned to harbour and reported that the British Navy had been forced to flee. This was published in the Paris newspapers, leading a furious Nelson to declare that if he captured Latouché-Tréville he would make him eat his report, but a few weeks later Latouché-Tréville died of a heart attack, caused, it was said, by continually climbing up to his signal station at Sepet to watch for the British fleet. 'I always said it would be his death' was Nelson's comment.

Spain entered the war on the French side in December 1804. Latouché-Tréville's successor, Vice-Admiral Pierre Villeneuve, sailed from Toulon late in March 1805 with orders to collect his Spanish allies, join other French ships in the West Indies and return to the Channel, where he was to free the French squadrons under blockade there and cover Napoleon's invasion of England. Villeneuve, with Nelson and his captains, including Conn, in pursuit, reached the West Indies but Napoleon's admirals were unable to carry out their emperor's design and by the end of August the Franco-Spanish Combined Fleet was back in Cadiz. Late in September 1805, when Lord Barham, First Lord of the Admiralty, told Nelson to select his own officers for the fleet blockading Cadiz, Conn was appointed to the newly-refitted 1st -rate *Royal Sovereign* (100), with orders to follow Nelson as he sailed to take over command from Vice-Admiral Collingwood **[8]**. On her arrival early in October, Collingwood shifted his flag into *Royal Sovereign* from the 2nd-rate *Dreadnought* (98) which was due to return home for a refit. In fact, *Dreadnought* remained at Cadiz, as Nelson allowed Vice-Admiral Sir Robert Calder to go home in his own flagship, the 2nd-rate *Prince of Wales*, for the court martial he had demanded in response to his conduct of **Calder's Action, Finisterre (22 July 1805)**. On 11 October 1805 Conn took over *Dreadnought* from Collingwood's flag captain,

Edward Rotheram **[31]**, who moved with his admiral to *Royal Sovereign*.

At **Trafalgar (21 October 1805)** *Dreadnought*, along with the other slow sailers, was ordered to take station as convenient, and joined the battle fourth from last in Collingwood's column. As his former flagship, she had a reputation for the best gunnery in the fleet and, though entering the action at a late stage, was determined to justify it. Conn hailed the 3rd-rate *Polyphemus* (64) to ask for room to pass so as to attack the three-decker *Principe de Asturias* (112), flagship of the Spanish Vice-Admiral Don Frederico de Gravina. After scoring hits on this ship, *Dreadnought* then attacked *San Juan de Nepomuceno* (74), the rearmost ship of the enemy line, already damaged by British gunfire but being supported by *Principe de Asturias* and the French *Indomptable* (80). After an engagement lasting fifteen minutes and with her captain dead, *San Juan de Nepomuceno* surrendered to Conn who then tried to re-engage *Principe de Asturias*. *Dreadnought* proved too slow to come up with the Spanish flagship, which was by this stage fleeing for Cadiz in company with *Indomptable* and others, so Conn broke off the pursuit, having lost seven men killed and one lieutenant, two midshipmen and twenty-three men wounded. In the years after Trafalgar Conn commanded in succession, as a flag captain, the 1st-rates *San Josef* (112) and *Hibernia* (110). In 1810, he was drowned off Bermuda while in command of another Trafalgar veteran, the 3rd-rate *Swiftsure* (74).

COOKE, Captain JOHN (1763–1805) [10]

John Cooke, the son of an Admiralty cashier, was born in 1763 and joined the Navy in 1776 at the beginning of the American War of Independence. In December 1776, as a midshipman in the 3rd-rate *Eagle* (64), he took part in the British capture of Rhode Island, and thereafter remained on the North American station with promotion to lieutenant on 21 January 1779. He served in the 2nd-rate *Duke* (90) at Rodney's victory at the **Battle of the Saintes (12 April 1782)** and went ashore after the war ended in January 1783. With the outbreak of the French Revolutionary War in February 1793, Cooke returned to sea with promotion to commander on 21 February 1794 and commanded the fireship *Incendiary* (16) at **The Glorious First of June (1 June 1794)**. He was promoted to post captain on 23 June 1794 and appointed to the 5th-rate frigate *Nymphe* (38). With others, they captured the French frigate *Résistance* (40) and corvette *Constance* (22) off Brest (9 March 1797). Cooke was still in command of *Nymphe* when the mutiny of the fleet at the Nore broke out on 12 May 1797. He was arrested and put ashore by his men but returned to his ship after the mutiny collapsed four weeks later. As captain of the 3rd-rate frigate *Amethyst* (38), Cooke carried the Duke of York, C-in-C of the British Army, to the Helder as part of the combined Anglo-Russian invasion of the Batavian Republic (the French-dominated Netherlands) in September 1799. After some initial successes the logistic weaknesses of the expedition became apparent and, with the weather beginning to break, the troops were evacuated in October 1799.

With Spain having been a lukewarm ally of France for the previous three years, the British Cabinet believed that a descent upon the Spanish naval arsenal at Ferrol would achieve great results. In fact, when a British army was landed upon the coast of Galicia in July 1800, it found Ferrol's defences to be impregnable and, after a few skirmishes, re-embarked at the end of August much to the indignation of the Navy, which had looked forward to lavish prize money. As part of these operations, *Amethyst*'s boats took part in cutting out the French vessels *Cerbere* (29 July 1800) and *Guêpe* (29 August 1800). At sea, Cooke captured the French corvette *Vaillante* later in 1800 and the French frigate *Dédaignneuse* and Spanish *General Brune* in 1801.

Peace was signed in March 1802 but war was renewed with France in May 1803 and with Spain in December 1804. Cooke returned to sea with command of the 3rd-rate *Bellerophon* (74) and in May 1805 formed part of the flying squadron with which Vice-Admiral Collingwood **[8]** was deployed in the hunt for Vice-Admiral Villeneuve and his Franco-Spanish Combined Fleet. The squadron reached Cadiz on 9 June, from where Collingwood detached two of his nine ships of the line to reinforce Nelson as he pursued Villeneuve in the West

Indies, and sent Rear-Admiral Sir Richard Bickerton with *Bellerophon* and three other ships into the Mediterranean to blockade Cartagena. When Villeneuve reached Cadiz on 20 August 1805, Collingwood recalled Bickerton, who rejoined him two days later. Further reinforcements were sent and Nelson arrived to take over from Collingwood on 28 September.

During the morning of 19 October 1805, Nelson invited Cooke and several other captains to dine with him in his flagship, the 1st-rate *Victory*. Before they could comply, *Bellerophon*'s first lieutenant, William Cumby, who prided himself on his good eyesight, saw the 3rd-rate *Mars*, far away on the horizon, repeating a message from the chain of frigates watching Cadiz. He read the signal flags as the figures 370 'Enemy ships are coming out of port or getting under sail' but because the colours of the flags were too faint for anyone else to read, Cooke declined to repeat the message to *Victory* unless a second pair of eyes confirmed it. *Mars* (as Cumby had said she would) then hoisted the distant signal for the same figures, using a system of flags, pendants and balls at different mastheads. To Cumby's chagrin, *Victory* acknowledged *Mars* before *Bellerophon* could repeat the signal. At dusk, as the fleet steered towards the enemy, Nelson ordered his six fastest ships to proceed ahead and show a light for the remainder to follow. Cooke and Cumby began to stand watch and watch about until contact was made, so that one of them would always be on the quarterdeck.

At **Trafalgar (21 October 1805)** Cumby was wakened by the sailing master, Mr Overton, with the news that the Combined Fleets was in sight and, after a brief prayer for his wife and children, joined Cooke on the quarterdeck. At breakfast, Cooke asked Cumby to read Nelson's tactical memorandum, so that he would know what to do if Cooke fell. Cumby responded that the same shot that disposed of the captain might also make his first lieutenant a casualty, so the memorandum was also shown to the sailing master, as the only other officer whose station would be on the quarterdeck in battle. When Nelson made his famous signal 'England expects ...' Cooke went below and told the gunners (who could see nothing of what was happening above them) of their admiral's message. Cooke, with *Bellerophon* fifth in line in the lee column led by Collingwood, originally intended not to open fire until Collingwood reached the enemy line, but did so when heavy enemy fire began to damage *Bellerophon*'s masts and rigging and cause casualties among her crew.

Bellerophon cut the enemy line astern of the Spanish *Monarca* (74), pouring in a heavy fire as she passed, but then, in the smoke, collided with the French *Aigle* (74). Cumby had earlier urged Cooke to take off his epaulettes as they made him too conspicuous a mark for the musketeers stationed in the enemy's tops. Cooke replied 'It is too late to take them off. I see my situation, but I will die like a man'. With the two ships locked together, he sent Cumby below with orders to the lieutenants commanding the gun divisions. *Aigle*'s boarders made several attempts to cross and each time Cooke fired his pistols at them. While reloading, he was hit in the chest by two musket balls. The quartermaster asked if he should be taken below, but Cooke answered 'No, let me lie quietly one minute' before giving his last order 'Tell Lieutenant Cumby never to strike' and dying shortly afterwards. Cumby returned to the quarterdeck to find the captain dead and the master mortally wounded, in one of the fiercest combats of the entire battle. With *Bellerophon*'s main and mizen topmasts gone, her running rigging unserviceable, and the quarterdeck, poop and forecastle almost cleared by enemy musketry, Cumby mustered a party to repel *Aigle*'s boarders, and told his gunners that all depended on them. Eventually *Aigle* closed her gun-ports and moved away to leeward, where ten minutes later, with her own captain killed, she surrendered to the 3rd-rate *Defiance* (74). *Bellerophon* lost two officers and twenty-four men killed and seven officers (the captain of Marines, the master's mate, four midshipmen and the boatswain) and 119 men wounded out of a total complement of 540.

Cooke was buried at sea with his fallen shipmates. Ashore, he was commemorated by a plaque in St Paul's Cathedral, near to the memorials to Nelson and Collingwood, and by a tablet in his family's parish church at Dunhead, Wiltshire. Cumby commanded *Bellerophon* until 6 November, when Captain Edward Rotheram [31], previously Collingwood's flag-captain in *Royal Sovereign*, took command. Cumby was promoted to post captain and served in operations at Santo Domingo in 1808–09. He survived the war and died in harness as Superintendent of Pembroke Dockyard in September 1837. *Bellerophon*, 'Billy Ruffian' to the lower deck, was the ship that carried Napoleon to exile in St Helena after his final defeat at Waterloo.

DIGBY, Admiral Sir HENRY, GCB (1770–1842) [11]
Henry Digby, grandson of the 1st Earl of Digby and son of the Very Reverend Dr the Honourable William Digby, Dean of Durham and chaplain to George III, was born in Bath in 1770 into a long-established naval family. He entered the Navy in 1783, after the end of the American War of Independence, and became a lieutenant on 20 October 1790. Following the outbreak of the French Revolutionary War in February 1793, Digby was appointed to the 5th-rate frigate *Pallas* (32), in which he was serving on 1 May 1795 when the 2nd-rate *Boyne* (98) caught fire while anchored at Spithead, drifted ashore and eventually blew up. With boats from *Pallas* and neighbouring ships, he joined in rescuing the crew of the burning vessel, a task which became the more dangerous when *Boyne*'s loaded guns started to go off as the flames reached them. He was promoted to commander on 11 August 1795 and appointed to the sloop-rigged fireship *Incendiary* (16), followed by promotion to post captain on 16 December 1796 and appointment to the 6th-rate frigate *Aurora* (28). In these two ships during 1796 he captured a Spanish frigate (Spain, at first a partner in the coalition against the Revolution, had become a French ally in October 1796), a French corvette, a privateer, seven other armed vessels and forty-eight merchantmen.

It became his practice, rather than waiting for his prizes officially to be judged as such by an Admiralty court, to sell them on his own authority and immediately distribute the proceeds among his crew in the usual proportions. Had the courts eventually decided that they were not lawful prizes, he would have been obliged to compensate the owners out of his own pocket, but in each case his decision was upheld and he was never short of volunteers to sail under him nor senior officers (who received their own share of *Aurora's* prize money) ready to send him to sea. During 1798 he commanded the 3rd-rate *Leviathan* (74), pendant-ship of Commodore John Duckworth in the British capture of Minorca (7–15 November 1798).

In 1799 Digby was appointed to the 5th-rate frigate *Alcmene* (32) in which he patrolled the sea-lanes between the coast of Portugal and the Azores and captured the French privateer *Courageux* (28) and several other vessels, bringing the total of his prize money accrued thus far in his career to some £20,000. While at sea, Digby, by his own account, was woken three times by a dream, in which he heard someone calling his name and urging him to change course. He eventually did so and at dawn on 16 October 1799 met with the British 5th-rate frigates *Naiad* and *Ethalion* pursuing the Spanish 34-gun frigates *Santa Brigida* and *Thetis*. While *Naiad* and *Ethalion* followed and eventually captured *Thetis*, Digby, joined by another new arrival, the 5th-rate frigate *Triton* (32), pursued *Santa Brigida* during the rest of that day and the following night and finally, with *Naiad* in company, ran her down some forty miles north of Vigo. The two captured frigates were found to be carrying an immense amount of treasure, which was then taken home to Plymouth and thence, in a triumphal convoy of sixty-three wagons, to London. *Alcmene* lost one seaman killed and eight more, with a petty officer, wounded. Her share of the prize money for *Santa Brigida's* cargo (after a long struggle in the courts) brought Digby £40,731 and even her ordinary seamen and marines were awarded £182 each.

In 1801 Digby was appointed to the new 5th-rate frigate *Résistance* (36) and added the French ship *Elizabeth* to his list of prizes before an armistice with France and Spain effectively ended hostilities at the end of the year. The war with France was renewed in May 1803 and that with Spain in December

1804. Digby returned to sea in the 3rd-rate *Africa* (64) and in August 1805 was with the squadron under Vice-Admiral Sir Robert Calder that reinforced the blockade of Vice-Admiral Pierre Villeneuve's Franco-Spanish Combined Fleet in Cadiz.

When Villeneuve began putting to sea on 19 October 1805, *Africa*, along with the rest of the British fleet under Nelson's command, sailed south-eastwards throughout that day and the following night, expecting to meet the enemy near the Strait of Gibraltar. With no enemy in sight during the next day, Nelson turned back towards Cadiz and, after nightfall, ordered his ships to change course, so taking them in the same direction as Villeneuve but fifteen miles ahead of him. In the darkness *Africa* missed this signal and continued northwards so that on the dawn of **Trafalgar (21 October 1805)** she was alone, six miles away from Nelson's flagship *Victory* at the head of the British line, but much nearer, and in full view of, the leading enemy ships. As the morning wore on, Nelson twice signalled Digby to 'make all sail possible with safety to the masts', intending *Africa* to rejoin the main body of the fleet at her best speed, so as to avoid being intercepted by the enemy. Digby chose to comply by steering a course parallel to the enemy van, but in the opposite direction, passing port to port and exchanging broadsides as he passed until reaching the Spanish flagship *Santisima Trinidad* (130) which, by that time, was already under attack from the 3rd-rate *Conqueror* (74).

When the totally dismasted *Santisima Trinidad* ceased firing, Digby assumed she had surrendered and, with his zeal for taking prizes, sent his first lieutenant across ahead of any other British ship. This officer made his way to the quarterdeck to find that all the senior officers had been wounded, but that the ship had not struck her flag and was merely bringing up fresh ammunition for the guns. The Spanish, accepting that he had arrived by mistake, chivalrously escorted him and his men back to their boat and allowed them to return to *Africa*.

Digby then continued back along the enemy line and attacked the French *Intrépide* (74) which, after a forty-minute close engagement, finally surrendered to Captain Edward

Codrington [7] of *Orion*. She was the last French ship to yield in this part of the battle and the bravery of her commanding officer, Captain Infernet, was much admired by his British captors. *Africa* lost eighteen men killed and seven officers and thirty-seven men wounded. Her masts, bowsprit, rigging and sails were badly damaged and her hull sustained numerous hits, including several on the waterline. After the battle she was towed to Gibraltar by the 3rd-rate *Conqueror*.

In 1815, the year in which Napoleon was finally defeated, Digby was awarded the CB. He was promoted to rear-admiral on 12 August 1819 and vice-admiral on 22 July 1830 and became a KCB in March 1831 on the accession of William IV. Between 1840 and 1841, Sir Henry Digby was C-in-C, Sheerness, with promotion to admiral on 23 November 1841 and the award of the GCB in 1842. He died at Minterne, Dorset, on 13 August 1842.

DUFF, Captain GEORGE (1764 – 1805) [12]

George Duff was born in 1764, the son of George Duff of Banff and grandson of Alexander Duff of Banff and his wife Anne, eldest daughter of the 1st Earl of Fife. Alexander Duff's brother Robert became a vice-admiral and, through his influence, the young George Duff entered the Navy in 1777 in the early part of the American War of Independence. He was promoted to lieutenant on 15 September 1779 and appointed to the 4th-rate *Panther* (60) in which he took part in Sir George Rodney's victory at **The Moonlight Battle, Cape St Vincent (16 January 1780)**. Following the relief of Gibraltar, Duff sailed with Rodney to the West Indies, where he served in the 3rd-rate *Montagu* (74) in various actions against the French during April and May 1780, including the battle of **Martinique (17 April 1780)**. He also took part in Rear-Admiral Sir Samuel Hood's operations at **St Kitts (25 January–13 February 1782)**, where Hood outmanoeuvred the French fleet only to find that the British garrison was too far inshore to be relieved. Duff also served at the **Battle of the Saintes (12 April 1782)**, the last major naval engagement of the war.

Duff was promoted to commander on 21 September 1790, when a fleet was mobilized to meet the threat of war with

Spain over the disputed possession of Nootka Sound (Vancouver, British Columbia). He was promoted to post captain on 9 February 1793, eight days after the outbreak of the French Revolutionary War, and returned to the West Indies with the 2nd-rate *Duke* (90), where he served at **Martinique (14–21 April 1793)**. During 1797 he commanded the 3rd-rate *Vengeance*, deployed to Bantry Bay to prevent a French landing in support of Irish republicans.

Late in 1799 Duff, in command of 5th-rate frigate *Glenmore* (36) and in company with the frigate *Aimable* (32), was deployed on escort duty with a convoy outward bound to the West Indies. On 17 December off the island of Porto Santo, north-east of Madeira, they encountered the French frigate *Sirène* (36) and corvette *Bergère* (18), carrying troops from Rochefort to Cayenne, and the East Indiaman *Calcutta*, captured by the French earlier that day. Large East Indiamen, well-armed and frigate-built, were sometimes mistaken for men-of-war, as happened on this occasion. After an hour's chase *Calcutta*'s prize crew hoisted British colours and Duff sent a boat to recapture her. *Aimable*, with Duff's permission, pursued the two French warships over the horizon, while *Glenmore* remained with the convoy. Making a recapture was not so lucrative as taking a prize, but *Calcutta*'s owners proved suitably grateful and Duff was rewarded accordingly. Nevertheless, his frigate commands did not bring him the financial benefits that he hoped for and the war ended in March 1802 without his having made the fortune that luckier captains gained.

War was renewed with France in May 1803 and with Spain in December 1804. Duff was appointed to the 3rd-rate *Mars* (74), manned mostly by fellow Scots and deployed to the blockade of Brest. From there, expecting imminent action, he wrote home to his wife in March 1805, about how she might be left if he fell. 'I hope that our friends [i.e. relatives] will take care of you and our dear little ones. I have done all, my dearest Sophia, to make you and them comfortable, that our small funds would allow; but I am sorry to say, they are very small indeed. I regret much you would never allow me to speak of making a settlement, nor would look at the one I made.'

In May 1805, while Nelson hunted in the West Indies for Vice-Admiral Pierre Villeneuve and his Franco-Spanish Combined Fleet, Duff and *Mars* formed part of a flying squadron under Vice-Admiral Collingwood [8]. Collingwood, after sending two ships to reinforce Nelson, blockaded Cadiz with three ships of the line, and sent the remaining five, including *Mars*, into the Mediterranean to blockade Cartagena. When the Combined Fleet arrived at Cadiz on 20 August 1805, Collingwood sent a frigate to recall the Cartagena detachment and located *Mars* revictualling in Tangiers. Well supplied with enough fresh meat for the whole squadron, Duff joined Collingwood the next day and remained there as part of the steadily reinforced blockade. He wrote home to his wife in Edinburgh that he was pleased to be with his old friend Captain John Cooke [10] who had returned from Cartagena with *Bellerophon* and that he hoped they might take rich prizes together. Cooke was known to be lucky in making prizes, though his luck would run out at Trafalgar.

Duff thought that Collingwood was 'a fine steady good officer' and Collingwood, who normally discouraged captains from visiting other ships, invited Duff aboard his flagship *Dreadnought* on 27 August 1805, where they dined on a fresh turtle Duff had shot. Nevertheless, like the other captains, Duff was glad when Nelson arrived on 28 September to take over command from the austere Collingwood. Writing home to his Sophie, he commented 'He is certainly the pleasantest admiral I ever served under ... we all wish to do what he likes, without any kind of orders.' In the morning of 19 October, when Villeneuve began to put to sea, *Mars*, as one of the fastest sailers in the fleet, was at the end of the chain linking the inshore frigates to Nelson's main force fifty miles away and thus was the first to repeat their messages to Nelson in *Victory*. Nelson took his fleet southwards and, at nightfall, ordered *Mars* and five others to go ahead and steer for the Gibraltar Strait. During 20 October, after the fleet failed to contact Villeneuve and turned back to look for him, *Mars* led an advanced squadron of eight ships, with the rest of the fleet following in two columns led respectively by Nelson and Collingwood. Nelson's original battle plan had been to engage the enemy in these three formations, but at the end of the day he redeployed the advanced ships to form part of the two main columns.

In the morning of **Trafalgar, 21 October 1805**, Nelson signalled *Mars*, in the lee column, to take station astern of Collingwood's flagship *Royal Sovereign*. He subsequently twice signalled *Mars* to take the lead of this column, probably with the intention of reducing the danger to which his old friend Collingwood would be exposed at the head of the line. Collingwood, however, would not allow *Royal Sovereign*, a quarter of a mile ahead of *Mars* on the port bow, to be overtaken, so that *Mars* was actually the third ship of his column to reach the enemy line. Encountering the French *Pluton* (74) Duff fought a duel with her for twenty minutes before he changed direction to avoid colliding with the Spanish flagship *Santa Ana* (dismasted by *Royal Sovereign*). This allowed the Spanish *Monarca* (74) and French *Algesiras* (74) to fire into *Mars*'s stern, causing heavy casualties. *Pluton* renewed her engagement and at about the same time the French *Fougueux* (74), disabled by *Mars*'s next ahead, the 3rd-rate *Belleisle* (74), but still in action, appeared through the smoke. Captain Norman of the Royal Marines, spotting her from the poop, went down to the quarterdeck to warn Duff, who asked him if *Mars*'s guns would bear on *Fougueux*. Norman said he could not see for smoke, but thought they would not. Duff went to the side to see for himself and then sent a midshipman below to order the guns to be trained against *Fougueux*. Before this could be done, *Fougueux* fired her broadside into *Mars*, adding to the existing casualties and causing more damage. Duff was hit in the head by a cannon ball and died instantly.

Mars, with her steering gear damaged and no rigging left to support her masts, so that no sail could be set, drifted away under the command of her first lieutenant, Lieutenant Hannah. In addition to her captain, she lost a master's mate and two midshipmen killed, and two lieutenants, her master, the captain of Royal Marines and two midshipmen wounded. Among the lower deck, the casualties amounted to twenty-six killed and sixty-three wounded. Duff's headless body, covered by an ensign, lay where it fell until the end of the battle. Villeneuve, having been taken prisoner when his command ship *Bucentaure* surrendered to the 3rd-rate *Conqueror* (74), was brought aboard by Captain James Atcherly of her Royal Marines, whose boat had been unable to find its way back to *Conqueror* through the battle smoke. With no more senior British officer present, Villeneuve gave up his sword to Hannah.

Duff had earlier that day written his last letter to his wife, to say that action was at hand, and that he hoped everyone would behave as they should and he hoped soon to take her and their children in his arms again. He told her he had ordered their twelve year old son Norwich, who was with him as a volunteer, off the quarterdeck, a prudent decision in view of the subsequent casualties among the other young gentlemen. Norwich Duff survived the battle to send the letter home, with his own, starting 'My Dear Mamma, you cannot possibly imagine how unwilling I am to begin this melancholy letter'. In due course he rose to become a vice-admiral. Captain George Duff was granted a posthumous augmentation of his arms for his service at Trafalgar, and a memorial to him was placed near those to Nelson, Collingwood and Cooke in St Paul's Cathedral, London.

DUNDAS, Vice-Admiral Sir Thomas, KCB (c.1765–1842) **[13]**
Thomas Dundas entered the Navy in 1778, during the American War of Independence. He became a lieutenant on 15 July 1793, a few months after the outbreak of the French Revolutionary War and was promoted to commander on 2 September 1795. He became a post captain on 9 July 1798 and was appointed to the 6th-rate frigate *Prompte* (20) in which, during 1799 (with Spain having joined the French side three years earlier), he captured a valuable Spanish whaling ship. After the brief peace with France between March 1802 and May 1803, Dundas returned to sea in 1804 as captain of the 5th-rate frigate *Naiad* (36). He was deployed off the western coasts of Spain (which entered the war on the French side in December 1804) and in the Channel, where he made a

number of valuable prizes and fought an engagement in the Bay of Gibraltar with a flotilla of Spanish gunboats. In mid-August 1805, patrolling off the north Spanish coast, *Naiad* encountered a large fleet which challenged her, using the correct British code. It was, in fact, the Franco-Spanish Combined Fleet under Vice-Admiral Pierre Villeneuve on its way from Ferrol. *Naiad* made a narrow escape, with shots from French frigates passing over her as she ran and, a few days later on 20 August, reached Vice-Admiral Sir Robert Calder's squadron as it sailed to resume its blockade of Ferrol, while the Combined Fleet was actually entering Cadiz.

Calder's squadron was then sent to reinforce the British fleet gathering outside Cadiz and *Naiad* played a useful part in harrying the coastal shipping on which that port relied for its supplies. After Nelson arrived on 28 September 1805 to take over command from Vice-Admiral Cuthbert Collingwood [8] and withdrew his fleet beyond the horizon, *Naiad* was deployed in the chain of ships linking the fleet with Cadiz. On 19 October 1805, when Villeneuve began to put to sea, she was third in the chain, between the frigate *Phoebe* and the 3rd-rate *Defence*. During the following day and night, together with Nelson's other three frigates, she shadowed the Combined Fleet and reported its movements.

In the morning of **Trafalgar (21 October 1805)**, with the enemy fleet in sight, Dundas and the other frigate captains were ordered on board Nelson's flagship *Victory* to receive their final orders. They were to remain to windward of his column (and thus of the entire fleet), repeat his signals to rearward ships, shadow any enemy vessels that attempted to escape, capture any damaged ones evading British ships of the line and to take in tow any British or captured enemy ships that had been dismasted. Nelson then asked them to witness the codicil to his will, leaving his mistress Lady Hamilton and their daughter Horatia, as a legacy to his king and country. During the battle, Dundas kept *Naiad* at her appointed station and, at about five o'clock, as the firing died away, took in tow the dismasted 3rd-rate *Belleisle* (74). The next day, as the weather worsened, the frigates handed over their tows to undamaged ships of the line and resumed their place as the eyes of the fleet. Dundas remained in command of *Naiad* and their subsequent service included the blockade of Rochefort in 1808. He then went ashore and, surviving the war, became a rear-admiral on 27 May 1827 and a KCB in September 1835. Sir Thomas Dundas was promoted to vice-admiral on 28 June 1837 and died on 29 March 1841.

DURHAM, Admiral Sir PHILIP CHARLES CALDERWOD HENDERSON, GCB (1763–1845) **[14]**
Philip Durham, the second son of James Durham of Largo, Fife, was born in 1763 and entered the Navy in July 1777, as captain's servant in the 3rd-rate *Trident* (64). He served in this ship in the American War of Independence where he was at the British evacuation of Philadelphia, Pennsylvania, in June 1778. Durham remained in Admiral Lord Howe's fleet protecting New York and Rhode Island until the end of August 1778. He returned home with Howe and was appointed to the new 3rd-rate *Edgar* (74) in which he took part in **The Moonlight Battle, Cape St Vincent (16 January 1780)**. After the relief of Gibraltar, he served there for several months with inshore gunboats.

In July 1781 Durham was appointed acting lieutenant in the 1st-rate *Victory*, flagship of Rear-Admiral Richard Kempenfelt in the Channel, in which he served in the battle of **Ushant (12 December 1781)**. In May 1782 he followed Kempenfelt into the 1st-rate *Royal George* (100) as his signal lieutenant and, as officer of the watch, was one of the few survivors when that ship foundered at Spithead on 29 August 1782. Durham was immediately appointed signal lieutenant in the 2nd-rate *Union* (90) in which he took part in Howe's final relief of Gibraltar during October 1782. Durham then sailed to the West Indies, with his promotion to lieutenant confirmed on 26 December 1782. After the war ended in January 1783 he stayed in the West Indies, appointed first to the 3rd-rate *Raisonnable* (64) in May 1783 and then to the 6th-rate frigate *Unicorn* (20) in October 1783. He then returned home and went ashore until March 1786, after which he joined the 4th-rate *Salisbury* (50), flagship at Halifax of the C-in-C, North America, Rear-Admiral John Elliott, his former captain in *Trident* and *Edgar*. He followed Elliott into the 2nd-rate *Barfleur* (98) and served as his flag lieutenant until 12 November 1790, when he was promoted to commander and appointed acting captain of the 6th-rate frigate *Daphne* (20), sent with dispatches to Jamaica. On arrival there, he was given command of the sloop *Cygnet* (14) and ordered home to report that Afro-Caribbean slaves in the French colony of Santo Domingo (Haiti), inspired by news of the French Revolution and the Declaration of the Rights of Man, had risen in revolt and massacred many of their European masters.

On 12 February 1793, eleven days after the outbreak of the French Revolutionary War, Durham was appointed to the fireship *Spitfire* (16) in the Channel, where on the following day he captured the French privateer *Afrique*, the first ever vessel to be taken flying the Revolutionary tricolour. He was promoted to post captain on 24 June 1792 and appointed to the 6th-rate frigate *Narcissus* (20). In January 1794, commanding the 6th-rate frigate *Hind* (28), he was pursued by a squadron of five French frigates and escaped after a running fight of several hours. Durham was next deployed to the Mediterranean, from where he safely escorted home a large merchant convoy before being appointed in October 1794 to the large frigate *Anson* (44), newly-converted from her original configuration as a 3rd-rate ship of the line. As part of the Channel fleet, *Anson* supported **Bridport's Action, Île de Groix, Lorient (23 June 1795)** and was with Sir John Warren's squadron in the unsuccessful French Royalist expedition to Quiberon Bay in the following month. During the next four years, Durham and *Anson* captured or destroyed eight privateers, over thirty merchant vessels and the major combatants *Etoile* (30), *Calliope* (36), *Daphne* (28) and *Flore* (36).

On 20 September 1798 *Anson* joined in shadowing a French squadron from Brest as it carried troops intended for the invasion of Ireland and maintained contact, culminating in 'Warren's Action' off Donegal (12 October 1798). *Anson* suffered considerable damage to her masts and yards in the violent gale preceding this engagement and arrived too late to take part in the main fight. She was, however, engaged by four French frigates in succession and sustained further damage with the loss of two men killed and thirteen wounded. During the night of 17 October 1798 Durham met the brig-sloop *Kangaroo* (16) and ordered her to keep in company with his disabled *Anson*. The next morning they encountered the equally disabled French frigate *Loire* (46), which had suffered severe damage in an earlier action. After an hour's gunnery duel *Loire* surrendered with forty-eight men killed and seventy wounded. *Anson* lost another two men killed, and one officer, two midshipmen and ten men wounded. Durham received the gold medal and thanks of Parliament given to all the captains engaged and was singled out for special recognition by Vice-Admiral the Duke of Clarence, later William IV, on being presented to George III at Weymouth.

During 1799 Durham, whose prizes had made him an eligible suitor, married Lady Charlotte Bruce, daughter of the Earl of Elgin. After serving with *Anson* in the Mediterranean, he was appointed on 27 February 1801 to the 4th-rate *Endymion* (50), in which he captured the privateer *Furie* (14) and escorted a convoy of East Indiamen safely home to England from St Helena. In April 1802, following the end of hostilities, he went ashore, but returned to sea in April 1803 on appointment to the 2nd-rate *Windsor Castle* (98) in the Channel. At the end of May 1803, with the renewal of war with France, he transferred to the 3rd-rate *Defiance* in which he remained in the Channel after Spain joined the war on the French side in December 1804. Durham took part in **Calder's Action, Finisterre (22 July 1805)**, against the Franco-Spanish Combined Fleet under Vice-Admiral Pierre Villeneuve. In this inconclusive action *Defiance* suffered damage to her yards, with eight men killed or wounded and subsequently went into Portsmouth dockyard, where she still was on 14 September 1805, when Vice-Admiral Viscount Nelson sailed to take command of the fleet blockading Villeneuve in Cadiz.

Rather than wait for *Defiance* and her consorts *Royal Sovereign* and *Agamemnon*, Nelson told their captains to follow him as soon as they were ready for sea. His orders from the Admiralty were that Calder was to go home for the court martial he had demanded in response to criticism of the way he had conducted the action off Finisterre and that captains who had been present in the action and who were willing to testify on his behalf could go with him. Captain Eliab Harvey **[19]** and Durham, who reached Cadiz shortly after Nelson, both chose to remain on station in anticipation of a battle. Durham moreover, unlike most officers in the fleet, had little sympathy for Calder, whom he considered had given insufficient credit to *Defiance* for being the first ship to sight the Combined Fleet and so bring on the Finisterre action.

At **Trafalgar (21 October 1805)**, *Defiance* was one of the last three ships in Collingwood's column as it approached the enemy line. In the mêlée she exchanged broadsides with the Spanish flagship *Principe de Asturias* (112) and later engaged the French *Aigle* (74). As *Aigle*'s fire slackened, Durham prepared to send a boarding party to take possession, but found all his boats damaged. Midshipman Spratt, ordered to take *Aigle*'s surrender regardless of difficulties, thereupon swam across and entered through a lower port. He fought his way to the quarterdeck, where he was rescued by boarders from *Defiance* after Durham had laid his ship alongside. They hoisted the British flag, but *Aigle*'s crew rallied and drove them back to *Defiance*. Durham then cut loose the lashings and stood away to open a heavy fire that, after twenty minutes, obliged *Aigle*'s surviving officers, with their captain dead and 270 other casualties, at last to surrender.

Spratt, badly wounded after a series of hand-to-hand encounters with French bayonet-men, defied the surgeon's wish to amputate his mangled leg. The surgeon appealed to Durham, who said he could not order him to agree but, though wounded himself, went to see Spratt and urged him to accept the surgeon's advice. Spratt refused and survived to become a commander. His useless leg brought him a pension for his wounds but did not prevent him from retaining his skill as a swimmer and, at the age of sixty, for a wager, he won a swimming race of fourteen miles. *Defiance*'s total casualties were a lieutenant, a midshipman, a boatswain and fourteen men killed, and Durham, Spratt and two other midshipmen, a master's mate and forty-eight men wounded.

Durham returned home and took part in Nelson's funeral procession, in which he carried Nelson's Order of the Bath banner. Early in 1806 he was appointed to the 3rd-rate *Renown* (74) in which he served in the Mediterranean, becoming commodore of a squadron in the blockade of Toulon and taking part in the chase and destruction of the French *Robuste* (80) and *Lion* (74) off Cette (Sette) at the mouth of the Rhône (26 October 1809). He was promoted to rear-admiral on 31 July 1810 and, with his flag in the 3rd-rate *Ardent* (64), served as C-in-C in the Baltic during the absence of Sir James Saumarez in 1811. Durham was then deployed to the mouth of the Texel, with his flag in the 3rd-rate *Hannibal* in command of five ships of the line blockading a Dutch squadron. After shifting his flag to the 3rd-rate *Venerable* (74) he led a squadron in pursuit of a French force that escaped from the blockade of Lorient He subsequently returned to blockade duty, commanding a squadron off Rochefort with his flag in the 3rd-rate *Bulwark* (74).

In December 1813, during the American War of 1812, Durham was appointed C-in-C in the Leeward Islands. En route to take up his new command, with his flag once more in *Venerable*, he captured the French 40-gun frigates *Iphigenie* (16 Jan 1814) and *Alcmene* (20 Jan 1814). Once there, his main task was the defence of British shipping against American privateers. During 1815 he supported troops landed in Martinique and Guadeloupe to restore Bourbon rule under Louis XVIII, so that the last French tricolour of the war was struck to him in *Venerable* just as the first had been to him in *Spitfire* twenty-three years earlier. He was awarded the KCB in January 1815.

Sir Philip Durham returned home in April 1816 and assumed the additional surname of Henderson in October 1817 when, his first wife having died, he married Miss Ann Henderson, the daughter of a Fifeshire baronet, and entered county society there. He was promoted to vice-admiral on 12 August 1819 and to admiral on 22 July 1830. Durham became a GCB on the accession of William IV in 1830 and in the same year became MP for Queenborough, Isle of Sheppey, a seat associated with the naval interest at nearby Sheerness. After the first Parliamentary Reform Act, he sat from 1835 to 1836 as MP for Devizes, Wiltshire. He was C-in-C, Portsmouth, between March 1836 and April 1839 and, with his flag in the 1st-rate *Britannia*, took a small squadron along the Sussex coast on Queen Victoria's visit to Brighton following her accession in 1837. Sir Philip Henderson Durham adopted a third surname in 1840, when he inherited the family estates from his elder brother, Lieutenant-General James Durham, and added the name Calderwood, that of their mother's family, to his own. He died at Naples on 2 April 1845.

FREMANTLE, Vice-Admiral Sir THOMAS FRANCIS, GCB (1765–1819) **[15]**

Thomas Fremantle was born on 20 November 1765, the third son of John Fremantle, a country gentleman, of Aston Abbotts, Buckinghamshire. He entered the Navy in 1778, during the American War of Independence, and served off the coast of Portugal in the 6th-rate frigate *Hussar* (28). In 1780 he moved to the 4th-rate *Jupiter* (50) and then to the 5th-rate frigate *Phoenix* (44) in which he was serving as a midshipman when she sank in a hurricane off Cuba in October the same year. Fremantle subsequently served in several other ships, with promotion to lieutenant on 13 March 1782, remaining on the Jamaica station after the war ended in 1783 and returning home in 1788. He went back to sea in 1790, when he joined Captain Hyde Parker (his former captain in the ill-fated *Phoenix*) in the new 3rd-rate *Brunswick* (74), in the fleet mobilized to meet the threat of war with Spain over the possession of Nootka Sound (Vancouver Island). He was promoted to commander on 3 November 1790 and commanded the fireship *Spitfire* (16) during 1791.

Following the outbreak of the French Revolutionary War in February 1793, Fremantle was given command of the fireship *Conflagration* (14), from which in May 1793 he was promoted to post captain and appointed to the 6th-rate frigate *Tartar* (28). She sailed to the Mediterranean as part of Lord Hood's fleet tasked with the blockade of Toulon and was the first ship to enter the harbour on 27 August 1793, when the citizens, terrified by reports of republican atrocities at

Marseilles, invited Hood to take possession of their city in the name of Louis XVII. Fremantle served in the subsequent operations at **Toulon (August–December 1793)** until the city was retaken by the Republican government in December 1793. Fifteen thousand refugees fled to the fleet while many of those left ashore were massacred by their vindictive countrymen. Deprived of Toulon, the British turned to Corsica, where in the spring of 1793 the population had renewed its long-standing rebellion against French rule and driven the Republican troops into their coastal fortresses.

In February 1794 the British troops that had been sent, too late, for the defence of Toulon, disembarked for a campaign in **Corsica (February–August 1794)**. Lack of siege artillery obliged the Army to rely on the Navy for heavy guns, and the pieces engaging the fortress of Bastia were provided mainly by Captain Horatio Nelson and his 3rd-rate *Agamemnon* (64). In April, Fremantle, whose ship formed part of the squadron under Nelson's command and who had struck up a friendship with him, was invited ashore to dine in his tent and afterwards to inspect a new battery. As they walked back they took a short cut and a shot from the defenders landed near enough for the wind of its passage to knock Nelson over and cover Fremantle with earth. 'Determine never to go the short way again' Fremantle noted in his journal. Bastia was starved into surrender on 15 May 1794 and *Agamemnon*'s guns then went to Calvi, which capitulated on 10 August. On 12 July Nelson, serving in the batteries, had been hit by flying debris that eventually cost him the sight of his right eye.

In January 1795 the fleet, now under Vice-Admiral William Hotham, moved its base from Corsica to Leghorn (Livorno),Tuscany. At the beginning of March the French fleet in Toulon put to sea and headed for northern Corsica. It was intercepted by Hotham off **Leghorn (13–14 March 1795)**, in an action for which Fremantle was mentioned in dispatches for his command of the 5th-rate frigate *Inconstant*. *Inconstant* was subsequently part of a squadron operating off the coast of Genoa with Nelson as commodore, comprising the 3rd-rate *Agamemnon* (64), four frigates and two minor combatants. There, in the summer of 1795, the Austrians and Piedmontese launched a successful offensive, capturing the anchorage of Vado and opening the flank of the French Army of Italy to British amphibious operations. On 26 August 1795 the squadron's boats cut out a number of small French warships and store vessels from the nearby bays of Allassio and Langueglia, without losing a man. In the spring of 1796, Bonaparte's victories drove the Austrians from Lombardy, forced the Piedmontese to sue for peace and left the rest of Italy at his mercy. British ships continued to patrol French-held coasts and Fremantle was one of the captains involved in the capture of the French frigate *Unité* (36) in April 1796. They were, however, at the mercy of events ashore and in June 1796 Bonaparte sent the dashing cavalry general Joachim Murat into neutral Tuscany to seize Leghorn, with its warehouses full of the property of British merchants and naval stores gathered for the British fleet.

On the news of Murat's advance, Fremantle, with *Inconstant* and several merchantmen, was ordered into Leghorn to evacuate the British and carry away anything of military or commercial value. Within a few days he had taken the British residents on board and got thirty-seven cargo vessels to sea, laden with most of the contents of the warehouses and a 240-strong herd of oxen that had been bought for the Mediterranean fleet. When the French entered the city on the morning of 27 June 1796, *Inconstant* made sail and escaped with the sole remaining freighter and its cargo of ship timber, under ineffectual fire from the hastily-manned shore batteries. Admiral Sir John Jervis, who had succeeded Hotham in November 1795, mentioned Fremantle in dispatches and paid tribute to his 'unparalleled exertions'.

Among the refugees who had hurried down to *Inconstant* was a wealthy and well-connected Englishman, Richard Wynne, with his French wife and their unmarried daughters, including the seventeen year old Elizabeth ('Betsey') and her sixteen year old sister Eugenia ('Jenny'). The elder Miss Wynne then became one of the many young ladies, before and since, to lose their hearts aboard a British warship, where the ambience seems to exert an irresistible influence over the female psyche. Two days after going on board, she confided to her diary 'How kind and amiable Captain Fremantle is. He pleases me more than any man I have yet seen. Not handsome, but there is something pleasing in his countenance and his fiery black eyes are quite captivating ... he seems to possess all the good and amiable qualities that are required to win everybodies heart the first moment one sees him ... he did the honor's so well that we all got a good Bed or Cot and he had *none*.'

Transferred, to her chagrin, from *Inconstant* into a merchantman before the French arrived, Betsey Wynne was carried off with her family to join the main fleet lying in San Fiorenzo Bay. There they were entertained in Sir John Jervis's flagship *Victory*, where the admiral demanded a kiss from the ladies as tribute, which they paid 'very willingly'. Her affection for Fremantle soon became known and she was allowed to accept a ring as a keepsake and to correspond with him. Her father objected to Fremantle's lack of a fortune, but Jervis told him that the captain was in a very good way to get one. Fremantle himself returned Miss Wynne's regard and noted in his diary for 13 July 1796, 'Serious thoughts about Betsey. If only I was not such a poor wretch.'

On 9 July 1796, with Leghorn under British blockade, Fremantle took part in Nelson's unopposed occupation of the nearby Tuscan island of Elba. In August he was sent on a mission to the Dey of Algiers, on whom, with most of Italy under French influence, Jervis's fleet would depend for fresh meat. He then escorted a Levant convoy to Smyrna (Izmir, Turkey) before returning to the fleet and taking part in the British descent on Piombono, on the mainland promontory between Leghorn and Elba (7 November 1796). This was little more than a gesture, as French successes ashore led the British Cabinet to abandon Corsica and withdraw from the Mediterranean. Spain had entered the war on the French side on 5 October 1796 and Jervis, with French troops already landing in Corsica, sailed for Gibraltar on 2 November.

Meanwhile, as Betsey Wynne refused to marry anyone except Fremantle, her parents allowed them to meet, and her mother let him know she would have £5,000 a year on marriage and stood to inherit £10,000. At the end of December 1796 Fremantle, who earlier in the year had been much attracted to another young lady while Betsey ruefully noted that *Inconstant* was living up to her name, noted, 'Am amazingly attached to Betsey but cannot make up my mind to marry'. Ten days later, having at last decided he could afford to take a wife, he made an offer and was accepted. The couple were married on 12 January 1797 at Naples, in the house of the British Ambassador Sir William Hamilton, with all the arrangements made by Lady Hamilton and the bride given away by George III's son, Prince Augustus (the future Duke of Sussex). Betsey and her sisters thought Lady Hamilton beautiful and charming, but Fremantle himself disliked her. Two more ceremonies had to be conducted by Roman Catholic priests for the sake of the bride's mother, who had brought up her children as devout Catholics. The new Mrs Fremantle set up home in her husband's frigate, while the British in Elba continued to defy Bonaparte until hostilities ended in 1802.

On 1 July 1797 Fremantle exchanged from *Inconstant*, which had been ordered home, into the 5th-rate frigate *Seahorse* (38), part of Nelson's inshore squadron blockading Cadiz. Two days later, in company with Nelson, he took part in a fiercely-contested boat action protecting the bomb vessel *Thunder* while she bombarded the Spanish ships anchored inside the harbour. Their next action together was in the night assault on **Santa Cruz, Tenerife (24–25 July 1797)**. Betsey Fremantle, like everyone else in the British squadron, anticipated an easy victory. After watching her husband and his men climb down into their boats, she retired to her berth in a cabin fitted up for her on the lower deck, near to that of the sail-maker's wife, who provided her with the female company that the conventions of the time required. The landing, based on faulty intelligence, proved to be one of Nelson's few defeats. With blood pouring from his shattered elbow, he was rowed out to *Seahorse*, the nearest ship to the fighting.

Despite being told that it was urgent for him to see a surgeon, Nelson refused to go aboard, saying that he would die, if he had to, 'rather than alarm Mrs Fremantle by her seeing me in this state, when I can give her no tidings whatever of her husband '. He was therefore taken on to his flagship, the 3rd-rate *Theseus* (74), where his own surgeon amputated Nelson's useless right arm. Fremantle was badly wounded by two musket balls in the arm as soon as he landed. Evacuated in one of the first boats to return to the frigates, he was eventually taken back to *Seahorse* where he was treated by her surgeon, Mr Fleming, a man whose clumsy treatment, his professional colleagues later said, was responsible for Fremantle's slow recovery. Betsey Fremantle, still only nineteen (though her husband thought she was twenty-one) and suffering from morning sickness with her first pregnancy, found herself nursing a wounded husband and his maimed commodore, as Nelson was sent home with Fremantle in *Seahorse*. 'I find it looks shocking to be without one arm' she noted and added that, with the constant groans of so many other sick and wounded on board, 'this ship is worse than a hospital'. *Seahorse* arrived at Spithead on 1 September 1797 and Betsey landed in England for the first time in her life.

Fremantle's wounded arm healed but severe pains in his hand (eventually diagnosed as gout) continued to depress him. He was awarded a wound pension of £200 annually and bought a house in Swanbourne, Buckinghamshire, where during the next few years he enjoyed the life of a country gentleman and began to raise a family with his Betsey. In August 1800 she was much distressed to find that Fremantle had been ordered back to sea, appointed to the 3rd-rate *Ganges* (74). In March 1801 he sailed from Great Yarmouth as part of the fleet sent to counter a threat by the Armed Neutrality of the North to close the Baltic against British shipping. Off the Danish coast, he wrote home to his wife that, what with the bitter weather, half the fleet coughing and virtually all Europe leagued against the British, only some superhuman figure could save the situation. Soon afterwards, he fought under his old friend Nelson in the battle of **Copenhagen (2 April 1801)**. After a brief peace between March 1802 and May 1803, Fremantle reluctantly returned to sea, once more in *Ganges*, in August 1803. He spent the winter in Bantry Bay before being deployed to the western coasts of Spain in the spring of 1804 and, after returning to Portsmouth to pay off in November 1804, was able to rejoin his family.

Spain entered the war on the French side in December 1804, but Fremantle remained ashore until May 1805 when, with the Franco-Spanish Combined Fleet under Vice-Admiral Pierre Villeneuve at sea and its path of intended movement unclear to the British, he was appointed to the 2nd-rate *Neptune* (98) at Plymouth. He spent the next two months as part of the squadron deployed off Ushant to close the Channel against Villeneuve as he returned from the West Indies, with Nelson in pursuit. *Neptune* went back into Plymouth in July and was still there at the time of **Calder's Action, Finisterre (22 July 1805)** when Vice-Admiral Sir Robert Calder encountered, but failed to destroy, Villeneuve's fleet. Fremantle sailed again on 3 August and, ten days later, was back off Ushant in Sir William Cornwallis's Channel fleet. From there, on 16 August 1805, *Neptune* was detached as one of the major assets in a squadron of eighteen ships of the line with which, on 30 August, Calder joined Vice-Admiral Cuthbert Collingwood **[8]** blockading Villeneuve in Cadiz.

Like many of his fellows, the extrovert Fremantle chafed under Collingwood's austere ways, especially his ban on captains inviting each other to dine in their respective ships and so escape briefly from the loneliness of command. Nelson's arrival on 28 September 1805 to take over from Collingwood lifted everyone's spirits. Fremantle was called to *Victory* to meet his old friend, who asked him whether he had wanted Betsey (whom he had left advanced in her fourth pregnancy) to give him a boy or a girl. He replied that he would like a girl. Nelson then told him to be content, as mother and daughter were doing well.

At **Trafalgar (21 October 1805)** *Neptune* was third in line, behind the 2nd-rate *Téméraire*, in the weather column led by Nelson in *Victory*. In the slow approach to the enemy line, Fremantle toured his ship's three gun decks in a final inspection and told his men of Nelson's 'England expects ...' signal. Under all sail, so as to close with the enemy as quickly as possible, *Téméraire* and *Neptune* both proved faster than the flagship in the light airs of the morning and had to make course corrections to starboard and port respectively, so as to keep their proper stations. Fremantle at one time seemed likely to pass *Victory* but, according to the recollections of one of his midshipmen, was hailed by Nelson in person, telling him to take in his studding-sails and drop astern, so allowing Captain Harvey [19] in the 2nd-rate *Téméraire* (98) to take station between *Neptune* and *Victory*. *Neptune* came into action at about 1.30 p.m., about fifteen minutes later than *Victory*, and broke the enemy line immediately ahead of Villeneuve's command ship *Bucentaure* (74), which she engaged before going onto the Spanish flagship, the four-decker *Santisima Trinidad* (130). After sustaining a heavy fire from *Neptune* into her vulnerable stern without being able to reply, this ship lost her main and mizen masts overboard, to be followed fifteen minutes later by her foremast as Fremantle shifted his attack to her starboard beam. She then surrendered to *Neptune*, which survived the battle with damage to her masts, rigging and hull, but lost only ten men killed and thirty-three wounded, of whom the senior was Fremantle's clerk.

After the surrender of *Bucentaure*, Villeneuve and his staff were first taken aboard *Mars* but as her commanding officer, Captain Duff [12], had been killed in the battle, and the ship was in any case so badly damaged as to be unable to make sail, they were subsequently transferred to *Neptune*. Fremantle wrote home to Betsey that Villeneuve himself was 'a very pleasant and Gentlemanlike man' and felt sorry for him, saying 'the poor man was very low'. The staff, who included General Contamine, the commander of the military contingent in Villeneuve's fleet, were more like his idea of Frenchmen, at whose *gasconnade* he felt able to laugh. In the days immediately after the battle, however, there was little to laugh about as gales tore at the battered ships. Fremantle had little confidence in the way Collingwood handled the fleet after the battle and told Betsey that 'the poor man does not know his own mind 5 minutes together'. On 27 October *Neptune* took the dismasted *Victory* in tow and was ordered by Collingwood to make for Gibraltar, which they reached, with their flags at half-mast, a day later. From there he wrote home that the next five ships returning to England for repair would go under Captain Eliab Harvey **[19]** of *Téméraire* of whom he said 'Never having been in action before he thinks every Ship was subdued by him, and he wears us all to Death, with his incessant Jargon'. On a more positive note, he said that he had taken a little pug-dog out of *Santisima Trinidad* and the animal had now become his companion, together with his cat and a pet monkey which the marine sentries refused to allow into his cabin.

Fremantle subsequently rejoined Collingwood in the continuing blockade of Cadiz, where he remained until returning home at the end of October 1806. He enjoyed the patronage of the powerful Nugent-Grenville-Temple family, whose members included the Marquis of Buckingham (at whose country seat, Stowe Park, Betsey was often a guest while her husband was at sea) and Lord Grenville, the then Prime Minister in the Whig Ministry of All the Talents. Through their influence he was elected MP for Sandwich on 3 November 1806 and appointed a lord commissioner of the Admiralty, a post that he took up at once, with Betsey and their young sons and daughters following him to an official residence there. After a few months enjoying London society, they were obliged to leave it at the end of March 1807, as the Ministry resigned when George III again refused to accept a bill for Catholic Emancipation. Fremantle left office with the other political appointees on the Board of Admiralty, but was consoled by being made captain of the newly-built royal yacht *William and Mary* (8), an appointment he retained until his promotion to rear-admiral on 31 July 1810. He went back to the Mediterranean in September 1810 and spent much of 1811 at Minorca with his flag in the 3rd-rate *Rodney* (74).

In April 1812 he was given command of a detached squadron in the Adriatic, with his flag in the 3rd-rate *Milford* (74). This sea, with its western shores ruled by Napoleon's Kingdom of Italy, and its north-eastern coasts (taken from Austria) annexed as provinces of France itself, was nevertheless one which the Royal Navy sailed at will, preying on enemy merchantmen and sending parties ashore to raid French-held harbours and batteries. As the tide of war on land turned against France, the Austrians marched into their lost Adriatic provinces and Fremantle cooperated in the capture of the great seaports of Fiume (Rijeka) on 3 July 1813 and Trieste on 8 March 1814.

When his ships were withdrawn after Napoleon's abdication in April 1814, Fremantle was able to say that every place on the coasts of Dalmatia, Croatia, Istria and Friuli had surrendered to ships under his command. They had taken over 1,000 guns and sunk or captured over 700 vessels. He returned home to take part in the victory celebrations and was awarded the KCB and a Austrian barony. Sir Thomas Fremantle was recalled to duty in March 1815 when Napoleon returned to France and the war was renewed. Offered the choices of being second-in-command in the Mediterranean, C-in-C at the Cape of Good Hope, or command of the Channel Islands, he chose the latter, and remained there until Napoleon's defeat at Waterloo. With his wife and daughters he then travelled on the Continent before taking up his final appointment, C-in-C of the Mediterranean fleet, with the award of the GCB in 1818. He hoisted his flag in the 2nd-rate *Rochefort* (80) and for a time lived on board with his wife and daughters, in defiance of Admiralty instructions, but to the pleasure of the ladies, with Lady Fremantle remembering her previous time at sea in a warship. He was promoted to vice-admiral on 12 August 1819 and awarded the GCMG in October 1819. Fremantle died suddenly on 19 December 1819, at Naples. With the approval of King Ferdinand IV of the Two Sicilies, whom British sea power had restored to his mainland capital, Sir Thomas Fremantle was buried there with full military honours. In appreciation of his services, his eldest son, also called Thomas Francis, was granted a baronetcy in 1821. Betsey Fremantle long survived her husband and died in November 1857, having lived to see her eldest son raised to the peerage as Lord Cottesloe and a younger one serve as an admiral in the Crimean War.

GRINDALL, Vice-Admiral Sir RICHARD, KCB (1750–1820) **[16]**
Richard Grindall, born in 1750, entered the Navy at about the age of twelve towards the end of the Seven Years War. He subsequently served in the American War of Independence and was promoted to lieutenant on 29 November 1776, commander on 21 December 1781 and post captain on 13 March 1783, soon after the war ended. After the outbreak of the French Revolutionary War in February 1793 he was appointed to the 5th-rate frigate *Thalia* (36), in which he captured the French *Requin* (12) off Dunkirk in 1795. Remaining in the Channel, Grindall transferred to the 3rd-rate *Irresistable* (74) in which he served in **Bridport's Action (23 June 1795)** off the Île de Groix. His ship was the first to engage the enemy and suffered severe damage to her mainmast and main topsail yard, with three seamen killed and two officers (Grindall himself and the ship's master) and nine seamen and marines wounded. His next command was the 3rd-rate *Ramillies* (74), in the blockade of Rochefort during 1799. In May 1800, in *Ramillies,* he was with a squadron detached from the blockade of Brest in order to land British troops on Belle Île in support of French Royalists in Brittany who, despite their defeat in 1795, had again risen against the Republic. By the time British aid arrived, however, their cause was lost. The defences of Belle Île were judged to be too strong for a successful assault and after five weeks the expedition was abandoned.

The war ended in March 1802 but hostilities were renewed with France in May 1803 and Spain in December 1804. Grindall was appointed to the 2nd-rate *Prince* (98) and deployed in the Channel. His ship had been built in 1788 and lengthened as part of a major refit in 1796, though this had not improved her sailing qualities and she was said to 'sail like a haystack'. On 30 August 1805, as part of a squadron under Vice-Admiral Sir Robert Calder, she joined the blockade of Vice-Admiral Pierre Villeneuve's Franco-Spanish Combined Fleet in Cadiz. When Vice-Admiral Viscount Nelson, with his flag in the 1st-rate *Victory,* took over command of the blockade on 28 September 1805, he withdrew his main force beyond the horizon, to tempt Villeneuve out.

After Villeneuve put to sea on 19 October 1805, Nelson sailed in pursuit and ordered *Prince*, together with his other two slowest ships, the 1st-rate *Britannia* and 2nd-rate *Dreadnought*, to 'take station as convenient', allowing them to catch up with the rest of the fleet when they could.

On the morning of **Trafalgar (21 October 1805)** *Prince* and *Dreadnought* were assigned to the lee column led by Collingwood, but in view of their known sluggishness were, with *Britannia*, once more ordered to take station as convenient without regard to the established order of sailing. At 8.40 a.m., an hour and twenty minutes after his previous order to her, Nelson signalled *Prince* to 'bear up and sail large on course steered by the Admiral'. Accordingly, Grindall turned his ship to port and, making the most of the light wind, went across towards the weather column led by Nelson.

Prince eventually regained her station at the rear of Collingwood's column and was the last ship into battle, at about 3 p.m., when the outcome had already been decided. Nevertheless, enemy ships were still fighting, among them the Spanish *Principe de Asturias* (112) with whom *Prince* briefly exchanged broadsides before encountering the French *Achille* (74). This ship had suffered heavy casualties earlier in the engagement and her musketeers, shooting from the mizen top, had set the sails on fire. As she dropped out of the line, her crew left the upper-deck guns and tried to cut down the burning mizen assembly while the lower-deck battery remained in action. *Prince* fired two broadsides, completely dismasting *Achille* and bringing down burning wreckage that smashed the fire pump and spread flames throughout the ship. Although *Achille*'s flag still flew, Grindall ordered *Prince* to cease firing and, after placing some distance between the two vessels so as to escape from the inevitable explosion, launched her boats to rescue survivors who had jumped into the sea. They were joined in this dangerous task by the boats of the 3rd-rate *Belleisle*, the frigate *Euryalus*, the schooner *Pickle* and the cutter *Entreprenante*, and saved about 200 men from the water before *Achille* finally blew up. Meanwhile, *Prince* had captured the dismasted Spanish flagship *Santisima*

Trinidad (130) and sent a prize crew aboard. Her own damage in the battle was a shot in her bowsprit and three each in her fore and mizen masts and she was the only ship of the line to record no casualties among her crew (though one diarist on board later claimed six wounded and four shots in the hull).

When Collingwood regrouped his fleet, Grindall was ordered to take *Santisima Trinidad* in tow but two days later, in response to the worsening wind and sea state, she was cast off along with the other prizes. In gale conditions, boats from *Prince* and *Neptune* took off the prize crew and as many Spaniards as they could, including between 300 and 400 wounded, before this giant warship, the largest then afloat, was left to sink. With her damaged masts and rigging, *Prince* was glad to stand clear of the lee shore and head for Gibraltar. Grindall left the ship soon afterwards, following his promotion to rear-admiral on 9 November 1805. He became a vice-admiral on 31 July 1810 and was awarded the KCB in January 1815. Sir Richard Grindall died in 1820.

HARDY, Vice-Admiral Sir **THOMAS MASTERMAN**, Baronet, GCB (1769–1839) **[17]**
Thomas Hardy, the second son of Joseph Hardy of Portisham, Dorset, was born on 5 April 1769. After attending Crewkerne School, he entered the Navy in 1781 during the American War of Independence, but was at school in Milton Abbas from 1782 to 1785, while carried successively on the books of the 6th-rate frigate *Seaford* (22) and the 3rd-rate *Carnatic* (74). Hardy first went to sea in the Merchant Service but in February 1790 was appointed a midshipman in the 5th-rate frigate *Hebe* (38), from which he moved to the 6th-rate frigate *Tisiphone* (20). Three months after the outbreak of the French Revolutionary War in February 1793 he joined the 6th-rate frigate *Amphitrite* (24), deployed in the Mediterranean fleet under Lord Hood. Hardy served off Marseilles and **Toulon (August–December 1793)** and was promoted to lieutenant on 10 November 1793, appointed to the 5th-rate frigate *Meleager* (32). During 1794 he served in this ship as part of a squadron under Captain Horatio Nelson, operating between Corsica

and Leghorn (Livorno). In June 1794, command of *Meleager* passed to Captain (later Admiral of the Fleet Sir) George Cockburn who, in August 1796, moved to the 5th-rate frigate *Minerve* (38) and took Hardy with him, subsequently to became his first lieutenant. Spain had joined the war on the French side in October 1795, but *Minerve* remained off the north-western coasts of Italy, cooperating with the Austrians until Bonaparte's victories on land drove the British fleet away from its Italian bases. Between 15 December 1796 and 14 February 1797 *Minerve* wore the pendant of Commodore Horatio Nelson, whose own ship, the 3rd-rate *Captain* (74), was too slow for the task of evacuating naval stores from the threatened island of Elba.

On 20 December 1796, en route from Gibraltar to Elba, *Minerve* and her consort, the 5th-rate frigate *Blanche* (32), encountered two Spanish frigates, *Ceres* and *Santa Sabina*. After a night action, the latter, with 164 casualties among her crew of 268, including all the officers except her captain, surrendered to *Minerve*. Hardy was sent on board with another lieutenant and a prize crew of twenty-four men. The arrival at dawn of another Spanish frigate obliged Cockburn to cast off his prize in order to commence a new engagement, but the combat was broken off and a further three Spanish ships came into sight. *Santa Sabrina*, flying British over Spanish colours to indicate her captured status, drew the largest of these, a ship of the line, away from the two British frigates, but with her mizen mast already lost, was overhauled and brought to action. Manned only by a prize crew, she lost her remaining masts and was recaptured by the Spanish. *Minerve*, having suffered nearly fifty casualties in the two actions as well as the twenty-six captured in *Santa Sabrina*, eventually escaped after a lengthy chase, repairing her battle damage as she ran. Hardy and his fellow lieutenant were soon exchanged for Don Jacobo Stewart, the captain of *Santa Sabrina*, and rejoined their ship when she returned to Gibraltar on 9 February 1797.

Minerve sailed on 12 February 1797 to join the main fleet under Sir John Jervis off the south-eastern coast of Spain. With two enemy warships following him, Cockburn ordered the topgallant masts to be swayed up. In the strong breeze, one of her seamen fell overboard and the ship hove to while a boat, with Hardy in it, was lowered to search for him. The man was nowhere to be found but the enemy moved closer and Cockburn got *Minerve* under way. Despite the danger, Nelson overruled him, shouting 'By God, I'll not lose Hardy. Back that mizen topsail'. This checked the frigate's way and enabled the boat's crew, pulling desperately, to come up to her. The Spaniards, mistaking the backed topsail for a signal to a fleet over the horizon, checked their own way, so allowing *Minerve* to escape and Hardy to avoid a second spell as a prisoner of war. She joined the fleet on the following day, when Nelson returned to *Captain* just in time to take part in the battle of **Cape St Vincent (14 February 1797)**, while *Minerve*, like the other frigates, stood apart from the main action.

Hardy remained in *Minerve* until May 1797 when, together with the 5th-rate frigate *Lively* (32), they located the French brig-sloop *Mutine* (16) in the harbour of Santa Cruz, Tenerife, Canary Islands. On 29 May 1797, he commanded the boats of these two ships in a successful cutting-out action. He was wounded, but gained promotion to be master and commander of the captured *Mutine*. Almost a year later, Rear-Admiral Sir Horatio Nelson sailed from Gibraltar to investigate reports of a large French expedition being assembled at Toulon under General Napoleon Bonaparte. On 19 May 1798 a violent storm scattered his squadron and damaged his flagship, the 3rd-rate *Vanguard* (74), so badly that she had to be taken in tow. They made repairs in Sardinia and reached their rendezvous off Toulon on 31 May 1798, but the squadron's frigates were nowhere in sight. On 5 June Hardy arrived in *Mutine* to report that the missing frigates had made their way back to Gibraltar and that seven days earlier he had left another squadron, under Captain Thomas Troubridge, on their way to reinforce Nelson. The two forces made contact on 7 June and eventually located Bonaparte in Egypt, where they destroyed the French fleet at **The Nile (1–2 August 1798)**. In the approach to the battle the 3rd-rate *Culloden* grounded on a shoal and *Minerve* helped her get clear. Afterwards, Nelson's flag captain, Edward Berry [2], was sent home with the dispatches as a mark of honour and Hardy was promoted to captain of the badly-damaged *Vanguard* in his place on 5 August 1798.

Hardy remained Nelson's flag captain in subsequent operations in the central Mediterranean, including the blockade of Malta, which had been captured and garrisoned by Bonaparte on his way to Egypt. At the end of December 1798, *Vanguard* carried King Ferdinand IV of the Two Sicilies and his court (including the British ambassador, Sir William Hamilton and his wife Emma) to Sicily, just before an invading French army reached his mainland capital at Naples. Nelson shifted his flag to the newly-arrived 2nd-rate *Foudroyant* (80), taking Hardy with him as flag captain, on 8 June 1799. The Parthenopian Republic, a puppet state set up in Naples by the French, lasted only a few months before it was faced with a patriotic uprising that drove the French occupiers out. In June 1799 the main fleet, led by *Foudroyant*, returned to Naples and landed marines to cooperate with the patriots and restore Bourbon rule. On 19 September *Foudroyant* carried the exiled Piedmontese royal family from their island of Sardinia to Leghorn (Livorno) in the still neutral Duchy of Tuscany.

Like others who served with Nelson at this time, Hardy disapproved of the extent to which the admiral had fallen under the spell of Lady Hamilton, though he was careful to keep his views to himself except when she attempted to interfere with the running of his ship. When she interceded with him on behalf of a boat's crew that had sought her influence, he gave her a non-committal reply, but then had the men flogged twice, once for the original offence and once for applying to the lady. Hardy handed over command of *Foudroyant* to Sir Edward Berry on 13 October 1799 and transferred to the 5th-rate frigate *Princess Charlotte* (38) before returning home.

After a year ashore, Hardy was appointed to the newly-refitted 1st-rate *San Josef* (114) at Plymouth on 28 December 1800. He was once more flag captain to Nelson (by this time a vice-admiral) and in early February 1801 transferred to the

2nd-rate *St George* (90) at Spithead. Nelson was appointed second-in-command of the fleet sent to the Baltic to force the Danes to withdraw from the recently-formed Armed Neutrality of the North. On the night of 1 April 1801, while the fleet lay off Copenhagen, Hardy went in by boat with a long pole to measure the depth of the channel around the anchored Danish ships. It was already known that *St George* drew too much water to enter the channel, so Nelson had transferred his flag to the 3rd-rate *Elephant* (74), with the consequence that Hardy's ship was not closely involved in the subsequent battle of **Copenhagen (2 April 1801)**. Nevertheless, his soundings proved of great value and the only two ships to go aground, *Agamemnon* and *Bellona*, were ones that had relied on local pilots rather than Hardy's recommended course. The main body of the fleet returned home in June 1801 and Nelson was succeeded in *St George* by Vice-Admiral (later Admiral of the Fleet Sir) Charles Pole. Hardy remained as flag captain until 18 August 1801 and subsequently transferred to the 4th-rate *Isis* (50).

Hostilities with France, briefly ended by the Treaty of Amiens in March 1802, were renewed on 18 May 1803. In the autumn of 1802 Hardy had been appointed to the 5th-rate frigate *Amphion* (32) in which, during October–November 1802, he took a new British ambassador to Lisbon before returning to Portsmouth. Nelson, appointed C-in-C, Mediterranean Fleet, at the outbreak of war, reached Portsmouth on 20 May 1803 to hoist his flag in the 1st-rate *Victory*. Finding her not only unready for him, but also provisionally promised to Sir William Cornwallis as his flagship in the blockade of Brest, he transferred his flag to *Amphion* and sailed for the Mediterranean the next day. While the question of *Victory*'s future deployment was being resolved, her commanding officer, Captain Samuel Sutton, took her to join Cornwallis off Ushant, and then joined the Mediterranean fleet off Toulon. *Amphion*, delayed by visits to Malta and Naples, arrived later and Nelson hoisted his flag in *Victory* on 31 July 1803, with Hardy exchanging with Sutton. Hardy served not only as Nelson's flag captain but as his captain of the fleet, though not formally appointed as such.

Spain, long under French influence, declared war on the United Kingdom in December 1804. Nelson's fleet continued the blockade of Toulon until the beginning of April 1805, when the French, under Vice-Admiral Pierre Villeneuve, escaped and sailed to join forces with their Spanish allies. Hardy remained with Nelson in their subsequent pursuit of Villeneuve's Franco-Spanish Combined Fleet to the West Indies and back. They returned to Spithead on 20 August 1805, when Nelson went ashore and Hardy began to prepare *Victory* for returning to sea.

Nelson's flag was again hoisted in *Victory* on 14 September 1805 and the ship sailed the next day for Cadiz, where Villeneuve had taken refuge. After arriving there on 29 September 1805 Nelson assumed command of the blockading British fleet from his old friend Vice-Admiral Cuthbert Collingwood [8] and Hardy undertook the duties of captain of the fleet, no additional officer having been provided for this post. Indeed, as Nelson had absolute confidence in Hardy, there was scarcely a need for one.

On the morning of **Trafalgar (21 October 1805)** Hardy, together with the four frigate captains summoned aboard *Victory*, witnessed the codicil to Nelson's will. As *Victory* slowly approached the enemy line, Hardy urged Nelson to shift his flag to one of the frigates, to avoid exposing himself to needless risks in the inevitable mêlée. Nelson refused, believing that a C-in-C not closely involved in a battle would lose control of it. Hardy then asked Nelson not to wear the decorations that would make him a target for enemy sharpshooters, but Nelson said it was too late to change into something less conspicuous and that, as he had won them in battle, he would wear them in battle. Finally, prompted by Captain Blackwood [3] of the frigate *Euryalus*, Hardy asked him to allow the 2nd-rate *Téméraire* to go past and take the lead, so drawing attention away from *Victory*. Nelson at first agreed, but when *Téméraire* drew level, called across for her to resume her proper station astern of the flagship.

In the battle, *Victory*, leading the weather column, came under heavy and effective fire from several enemy ships as she approached their line. Nelson's secretary was killed by a round shot, as were seven or eight marines on the poop deck. The mizen topmast and fore topgallant mast were brought down and all the studding-sails and their booms were shot away, so reducing the ship's speed. Another cannon ball smashed the steering wheel, leaving her out of control until the ship's master hastily rigged an emergency system, with the tiller operated by forty men hauling on ropes and controlled by orders shouted from above. As Nelson and Hardy paced the quarterdeck together, a flying splinter passed between them and tore the buckle from Hardy's left shoe. They stopped for a moment and Nelson remarked 'This is too warm work, Hardy, to last for long'. He had previously ordered Hardy to alter course so as to cut the enemy line astern of Villeneuve's command ship *Bucentaure* (74). To protect *Bucentaure*, her next ahead, the Spanish four-decker *Santisima Trinidad*, slowed down, while her next astern, *Redoutable* (74) closed up, so that Hardy warned Nelson that *Victory* would collide with one of them. Nelson told him it did not matter which, but at this point *Redoutable* left a gap through which Hardy took *Victory* so close to *Bucentaure* that they almost touched. After firing a broadside through *Bucentaure*'s vulnerable stern, thus devastating the length of her gun decks, *Victory* ran into *Redoutable*, pushing her out of the line and creating a gap through which *Téméraire*, followed by three other British ships, then passed, all firing into the stricken *Bucentaure* as they did so.

With *Victory* and *Redoutable* entangled alongside each other, the two ships exchanged fire at point-blank range. *Redoutable* closed her lower gun-ports and continued the fight with her upper tier of guns and a hail of grenades and small-arms fire from aloft, aimed mostly at the quarterdeck. There, at about 1.15 p.m., Nelson was struck by a French musket ball and was carried below, mortally wounded, while Hardy continued to engage *Redoutable* on his port side and *Bucentaure* and *Santisima Trinidad* on his starboard. When *Redoutable*'s guns ceased to fire, Hardy thought she was about to surrender and ordered his own starboard guns to stop. Captain Jean-Jacques Lucas of *Redoutable*, however, had no intention of giving up and thought that *Victory*'s silence meant that Hardy was about to surrender, especially as the French musketeers had driven almost everyone from her upper deck. He decided to board the British flagship and, as his men could not climb up *Victory*'s side, ordered the slings of *Redoutable*'s main yard to be cut so that it crashed down and formed a bridge. His boarders began to swarm across, but *Victory*'s seamen and marines came up to meet them while the two ships drifted downwind through the smoke to collide with *Téméraire*, on *Redoutable*'s starboard side.

Redoutable, a two-decker, had little chance against the three-decker *Téméraire*, whose upper tier of guns wiped out most of Lucas's boarding party as it assembled ready to cross into *Victory*. Some 200 men were killed or wounded by a single broadside, with the heroic Lucas among the latter. *Victory*, having cleared the boarders from her own deck, had a prize crew ready to take the now silent *Redoutable*, but no way of reaching her. Some seamen offered to swim across and climb into her bows, but Hardy would not hear of it. Breaking free of the entangled group of four ships (the original three having drifted alongside the French *Fougueux*) he sent two midshipmen and a party of marines in a small boat to take possession of *Redoutable*. They boarded her unopposed, to find that Lucas still would not strike his flag, despite casualties of 300 killed and 222 badly wounded out of his 643-strong crew.

With *Victory* once more under way, Hardy signalled the six undamaged and four still fully combat-worthy ships of the weather division to follow him against a group of seven ships from the enemy van as it belatedly entered the battle. He then went below to report to Nelson, whose earlier calls he had been obliged to disregard. The dying admiral took comfort from what he heard and Hardy returned to the deck to send a boat telling Collingwood that Nelson was wounded. At about 4 p.m. he again went below, to congratulate Nelson on having achieved a total victory, with fourteen or fifteen enemy ships captured. The admiral replied 'That is well, but I bargained for twenty' and then, 'Anchor, Hardy, anchor'. Hardy, aware that the command must soon change, tactfully answered 'I suppose, my Lord, Admiral Collingwood will now take upon himself the direction of affairs'. 'Not while I live, I hope, Hardy' said Nelson and then, struggling to raise himself, repeated the order to anchor. 'Shall *we* make the signal, sir?' asked Hardy. 'Yes', came the reply, 'for if I live, I'll anchor.' Hardy stayed with his chief for a few more minutes and then returned to the deck, where he soon afterwards learned that Nelson had died. He did not make the signal to anchor, nor did Collingwood when Hardy mentioned it on reporting to him at the end of the battle.

Victory, with fifty-seven officers and men dead or dying and 102 wounded, struggled hard to ride out the gales that began on the day after the battle. Her lower masts, yards and bowsprit, with their rigging, had all been badly damaged and the mizen mast had fallen shortly after the close of the engagement. Her carpenters were set to work repairing the numerous shot holes in her hull and various emergency measures were undertaken, including the replacement of the mizen mast by a spare jib-boom. On 24 October she was taken in tow by the 3rd-rate *Polyphemus* (64) but lost the tow and some of her sails two days later in the continuing storm. On 27 October she was taken in tow by the 2nd-rate *Neptune* which, despite losing her own fore topmast, brought her safely into Gibraltar the next day. Hardy, always noted as a martinet, then had several of his men flogged for contempt and disobedience.

On 4 November *Victory* sailed for home, reaching Portsmouth on 5 December and then moving to Sheerness, where Nelson's body was placed on board the yacht *Chatham* to be taken upriver to lie in state at Greenwich. Hardy then took *Victory* up the Medway to Chatham dockyard for a refit. Her marines went to their barracks while most of her seamen were turned over to the newly-completed 2nd-rate *Ocean* (98), under orders for the Mediterranean. A large contingent of them marched in Nelson's funeral procession on 9 January 1806, in which Hardy himself carried one of the banners. He left *Victory* on 15 January when the ship was decommissioned. Despite his sympathy for the wronged Lady Nelson, he faithfully delivered Nelson's personal effects to Lady Hamilton in accordance with his dying admiral's wishes.

After being created a baronet in February 1806, Sir Thomas Hardy was appointed to the 3rd-rate *Triumph* (74) in which he served on the North America station until 1809. While there, in Halifax, Nova Scotia, he married Anna Louisa, the spirited young daughter of his C-in-C, Sir George Cranfield Berkeley, in December 1807. When Admiral Berkeley was appointed C-in-C at Lisbon in 1809, Hardy became his flag-captain in the 2nd-rate *Barfleur* (98) and was made a commodore in the Portuguese Navy in 1811. In August 1812 he was appointed to the 3rd-rate *Ramillies* (74) in which he was deployed to the North America station following the outbreak of hostilities with the United States in the War of 1812.

With the US Navy consisting of only ten frigates and various minor combatants (it was said that the Royal Navy had more ships than the US Navy had guns), the Americans made great use of privateers for commerce raiding purposes. Well over 500 of these were commissioned, mostly from the New England seaports, and had considerable success in preying on British merchantmen on both sides of the Atlantic. Hardy, commanding a squadron off New London, Connecticut, captured an American schooner on 25 June 1813. Her crew declared her to be carrying provisions, before escaping in their boats. In fact, she was laden with gunpowder and her crew, expecting her to be taken alongside *Ramillies*, had set a clockwork fuse so that she would explode and destroy the flagship. Hardy, however, ordered her alongside another prize, where she blew up, killing the boarding lieutenant and ten seamen.

Hardy was awarded the KCB in January 1815, after Napoleon had gone into exile at Elba and peace had been signed with the United States. Sir Thomas Hardy returned home in June 1815 and was appointed to the royal yacht *Princess Augusta*, which he commanded from July 1816 until 1818. From August 1819 to early 1824 he was C-in-C and commodore on the South America station, with his broad pendant in the 3rd-rate *Superb* (74). During the Napoleonic Wars, British trade with Spanish America had increased fourteen-fold, while the local colonists had gained a large measure of self-government. Spanish attempts to re-establish control led to revolts that placed valuable British interests at risk. The British openly sympathized with the insurgents and in 1824 recognized Mexico, Columbia and Argentina as independent republics. A year earlier, President Monroe had declared that the United States would oppose any European power that tried to reconquer colonies that had declared their independence. It was, however, not the famous 'Monroe Doctrine' but Hardy's ships that would have prevented any Spanish troops from landing. He returned to the UK early in 1824 and was commended by the Admiralty and by public opinion (especially among the business community) for his diplomatic handling of all parties in the wars of independence.

Hardy was promoted to rear-admiral on 27 May 1825. At this time, the constitutionalist Portuguese Regency, ruling on behalf of the eight year old Queen Maria, was faced with the threat of a renewed revolt by her uncle, the absolutist Dom Miguel. Faced with anarchy in the streets of Lisbon and the threat of invasion by Dom Miguel and his army, the Regency invoked the Treaty of Alliance with the United Kingdom and called for British aid. In December 1826, with his flag in the 3rd-rate *Wellesley* (74), Hardy escorted a 4,000-strong British expeditionary force to Lisbon. The troops landed and restored order, and the Spanish government, which had armed and supplied Miguel's men, yielded to diplomatic pressure and ordered them to disband.

Hardy was subsequently given command of an experimental squadron in the Channel, with his flag first in the 5th-rate frigate *Sybille* (44) and then in the 5th-rate frigate *Pyramus* (36), until going ashore for the last time on 21 October 1827. Hardy became a lord commissioner of the Admiralty in November 1830 and governor of the Royal Hospital, Greenwich, in April 1834. Sir Thomas Hardy was promoted to vice-admiral on 10 January 1837 and died at Greenwich on 20 September 1839. He was buried in the mausoleum of the Hospital (later the Royal Naval College and now within the campus of Greenwich University). He left three daughters, but no sons, so that his baronetcy became extinct. His wife, who married again, survived him by thirty-seven years. An immense pillar was erected on Black Down, Portesham, Dorset, in his memory.

HARGOOD, Admiral Sir WILLIAM, GCB, GCH (1762–1839) **[18]**
William Hargood was born on 6 May 1762, the youngest son in a family of nine children of Hezekiah Hargood, a gentleman of independent means, descended from the Earls of Harcourt and residing at Blackheath, Kent. Hezekiah Hargood had previously served as a purser in the Navy. William Hargood entered the Navy in 1773 as a first-class volunteer carried on the books of the 2nd-rate *Triumph* (90) at the Nore and in January 1775 was appointed to the 3rd-rate *Mars* (74). On 11 March 1775 he joined the 4th-rate *Romney* (50), flagship of Rear-Admiral Robert Duff, under orders for deployment to Newfoundland. *Romney* sailed for Newfoundland in June 1775 and returned home five months later after being badly damaged in a storm off Nova Scotia. Hargood was then appointed midshipman in the new 4th-rate *Bristol* (50), pendant-ship of Commodore (later Admiral of the Fleet) Sir Peter Parker, a friend of his father, under orders for the North America station following the outbreak of the American War of Independence. He fought under Parker in the disastrous British attack on Charleston, South Carolina (28 June 1776) where *Bristol*'s casualties amounted to forty killed (including her commanding officer, Captain John Morris) and seventy-two wounded, including Parker himself. Hargood subsequently followed Parker to the 4th-rate *Chatham* (50) and served with him in the capture of Long Island, New York, in August 1776 and Rhode Island in December 1776. They returned to *Bristol* in December 1777, when Parker (a rear-admiral since the previous May) was appointed C-in-C, Jamaica. After France and Spain entered the war on the American side in 1778 Hargood remained in the West Indies in *Bristol* where his first lieutenants during 1788–89 were successively Horatio Nelson and Cuthbert Collingwood **[8]**. On 13 January 1780 Parker (by then a vice-admiral) promoted Hargood to lieutenant and appointed him second-in-command of the sloop *Port Royal* (18). In March

1781 the Spanish attacked Pensacola, Florida, ceded by them to the British in 1763 at the end of the Seven Years War. Hargood served ashore in the batteries with a party of fifty seamen and two midshipmen from *Port Royal* and lost twelve men and one midshipman killed before Pensacola surrendered on 8 May 1781. *Port Royal* was included in the terms of capitulation, but her crew and the rest of the British garrison were released and allowed to sail for New York on 4 July 1781.

Hargood returned home and in December 1781 was appointed fourth lieutenant of the 3rd-rate *Magnificent* (74) in which he went back to the West Indies during February 1782. As part of Sir George Rodney's fleet, he took part in an inconclusive fleet action off **Guadeloupe (9 April 1782)** and the subsequent **Battle of the Saintes (12 April 1782)**. On 19 April 1782 he was with Rear-Admiral Sir Samuel Hood's squadron at the capture of two French ships of the line that had gone into Guadeloupe for repairs after the action of 9 April. After the war ended in January 1783 *Magnificent* returned home and Hargood went ashore until May 1784, when he was appointed third lieutenant of the 5th-rate frigate *Hebe* (38). In June 1785 he became her second lieutenant and George III's third son, Prince William (later Duke of Clarence), was appointed third lieutenant. The two got on well and in April 1786, when the Prince was given command of the 6th-rate frigate *Pegasus* (28), he asked for Hargood as his second lieutenant.

Pegasus was deployed first to Nova Scotia and then to the Leeward Islands, where she was in a squadron under Captain Horatio Nelson, a friend and mentor of the Prince. William disliked *Pegasus*'s first lieutenant, Isaac Schomberg, an experienced officer of whom Nelson had a high opinion. Schomberg's attempts to ameliorate the harsh discipline imposed by William led to him being placed under arrest for insubordination. He was subsequently transferred to Hood's flagship *Barfleur*, where, to the Prince's irritation, he was made flag lieutenant. William also disliked his third lieutenant, William Hope, who left the ship after being harshly treated. Hargood, however, remained on good terms with his royal captain and, having become his first lieutenant, returned home with him at the end of 1787, when *Pegasus* was suddenly recalled from the North America station in consequence of an affair between William and the wife of a colonial official.

In March 1788, William assumed command of the 5th-rate frigate *Andromeda*, taking the crew of *Pegasus* with him. Hargood, at William's request, became his first lieutenant and in July 1788 the ship put to sea with the rest of their squadron for evolutions in the Channel. Meanwhile, George III learned of an affair between his son and the daughter of a naval victualling contractor, and ordered *Pegasus* to proceed immediately to Nova Scotia, despite William's protests that his ship's company, expecting to be away for only a few days, had not been able to make any provision for their wives and families. From Nova Scotia they went to Jamaica, where *Andromeda* was caught in a sudden squall and thrown onto her beam ends. Hargood was below at the time, but as he was of small stature, his messmates pushed him up through the gunroom skylight on their shoulders, so that, half-dressed, in an example of duty before decency, he was able to reach the quarterdeck and give the necessary orders for shortening sail. They returned home early in 1789, when William was recalled because the King had become seriously ill.

Hargood, after going ashore in April 1789 when *Andromeda* paid off, was promoted to commander on 24 June 1789. He commanded the sloop *Swallow* (16), off the coast of Ireland, from December 1789 to 22 December 1790, when he was promoted to post captain. Lacking a ship, he spent time in the company of his old friend the Duke of Clarence, and on one occasion used extreme measures to restrain him when, in his cups, he stood up in a Thames wherry and danced about, to the alarm of both Hargood and the boatman. The boatman, unaware of his passenger's identity, expressed himself freely and had to be given a guinea to prevent the episode reaching the King's ears. In April 1792 Hargood was appointed to the 6th-rate frigate *Hyaena* (24) in which he was serving in the West Indies when war with Revolutionary France broke out in the following February. He became seriously ill, probably with yellow fever, and was about to be stitched into a hammock prior to burial at sea when he showed signs of life and was revived in the nick of time. On 27 May 1793, *Hyaena*, still at her peace establishment with a crew of only 120 hands, was captured off Cape Tiburon, French Santo Domingo (Haiti) by the French frigate *Concorde* (44). Hargood and his officers were released on parole at the French port of Cape Francois (Cap Haitien) where they were caught up in the struggle for freedom of Afro-Caribbean slaves who, responding to the Declaration of the Rights of Man had, in 1791, risen against their French masters. On 20 June 1793, when the insurrection reached Cape Francois, Hargood and most of his officers escaped to the beach through the fire of both parties and swam out to *Concorde*, where they were released from parole and allowed to take passage to Jamaica. From there they returned home, where on 11 October 1793 they were tried by the customary court martial for the surrender of their ship and honourably acquitted.

From April 1794 to August 1796, Hargood commanded the 5th-rate frigate *Iris* (32) on convoy escort duty in the North Sea, on the coast of Africa and on the North America station. He then transferred to the 4th-rate *Leopard* (50) deployed on trade protection duties in the North Sea, where the Netherlands (as the French-controlled Batavian Republic) had been a British enemy since May 1794. On 29 May 1797, a fortnight after the outbreak of mutiny at the Nore, all but two ships of the line in the North Sea fleet, sailing to blockade the Dutch in the Texel, were seized by their crews and taken back to Great Yarmouth. Hargood was set ashore there on 31 May and the mutineers then sailed round to the Nore. In the face of Government countermeasures, the mutiny there began to weaken and, on 9 June, those officers still on board *Leopard* recovered control and escaped in company with the 3rd-rate *Repulse* (64) despite a cannonade from the mutineers.

After the collapse of the mutinies, Hargood was appointed to the 3rd-rate *Nassau* (64) on 12 July 1794 and returned to the North Sea, where the two loyal ships, supported by a small Russian squadron, had kept up the blockade of fifteen Dutch ships of the line and eight frigates. Early in October 1796 equinoctial gales drove the fleet to take shelter in Yarmouth Roads and the storm-damaged *Nassau* was ordered into Sheerness to refit, so missing the subsequent British victory at Camperdown (11 October 1797). In February 1798 Hargood was given command of the 3rd-rate *Intrepid* (64) and on 30 April 1798 sailed for China as convoy escort. On 27 January 1799, while waiting for a home-bound convoy, he encountered a squadron of six French and Spanish men-of-war off Macao and successfully drew them away from the assembling East Indiamen. He remained on the China station until 1802, when *Intrepid* was deployed to the west coast of India and carried troops to various stations as tension increased with the princes of the Maratha Confederacy. Hargood returned home in February 1803, during a brief period of peace with France and her allies, and the East India Company's Court of Directors awarded him 300 guineas in recognition of his efforts at Macao. War with France was renewed in May 1803 and Hargood was appointed in November 1803 to the 3rd-rate *Belleisle* (74) in Nelson's Mediterranean Fleet, and joined her off Toulon in March 1804. *Belleisle* remained there after Spain joined the war on the French side in December 1804 and, when Vice-Admiral Pierre Villeneuve escaped from Toulon on 30 March 1805, sailed in Nelson's pursuit of the Franco-Spanish Combined Fleet to the West Indies and back.

When both fleets returned to European waters in August 1805, *Belleisle* was sent into Plymouth to refit. On completion, she was ordered to Cadiz, where Villeneuve's fleet was under blockade. Hargood, determined to reach his station without delay, sailed from Hamoaze on 23 September, despite adverse wind conditions, and joined Nelson off Cadiz on 10 October 1805. Many years later, when Hargood was C-in-C at Plymouth, the lieutenant commanding a small brig asked for a steamer to tow him out into the Sound. Hargood answered that if he himself had not worked *Belleisle* out with the wind two more points against him, he would have been too late for the battle of Trafalgar.

At **Trafalgar (21 October 1805)**, *Belleisle* was the second ship in the lee column, immediately behind Vice-Admiral

Cuthbert Collingwood [8] in his flagship *Royal Sovereign* (100). Seeing his leader come under fire, Hargood ordered his upper-deck men to lie down while he himself, because of his own short stature, climbed onto a gun carriage to get a better view and give course corrections to the sailing master. *Belleisle* herself then came under fire, losing her mizen-topmast, having her ensign three times shot away and rehoisted, and suffering more than fifty casualties in the quarter of an hour or so before she could reply. Her first lieutenant asked Hargood if they could show their broadside and fire, if only to cover the ship with smoke but Hargood replied 'No, we are ordered to go through the line and go through she shall!' With their guns loaded with two round shot and grapeshot, they broke through the enemy line about three minutes behind *Royal Sovereign*, firing their port broadside into the stern of the Spanish flagship *Santa Ana* (112) as they passed. After firing his starboard broadside into the French *Fougueux* (74), Hargood then ordered his sailing master to place *Belleisle* close alongside the French *Indomptable* (80) but, with her speed reduced by damage to her sails, *Belleisle* was unable to reach her before being run into by *Fougueux*. These two ships, held together by their entangled rigging, then fought a prolonged gunnery duel at point-blank range until eventually drifting apart.

Belleisle was then engaged by several other enemy ships and, having already lost her mizen mast over the port quarter, lost her mainmast over the port side and foremast over the starboard bow, so that the ship could neither be moved nor, because the broken masts with their sails and rigging covered most of the gun-ports, make any effective reply. Guns were run out from the stern ports, and sweeps (long oars, normally used when a ship was becalmed) from the gunroom ports, but the enemy ships easily evaded these measures and continued to inflict damage until driven off by the 2nd-rate *Swiftsure* (98) and 3rd-rate *Polyphemus* (64).

At one point Hargood himself had been severely bruised from throat to thigh by a flying fragment of wreckage, but refused to leave the deck and continued to encourage his men by shouting, 'Let 'em come on, I'll be damned if I strike. No, never, to nobody whatever.' As the fight went on, he shared his stock of grapes with his officers (some had already helped themselves from the stock he kept in his cabin) and was glad to receive their reports that the men were doing nobly and the ship had greatly distinguished herself. With no masts left standing, they put up a Union Flag on a pike and fastened a white ensign to the broken remains of the mainmast. At the end of the battle, seeing the Spanish *Argonauta* flying the British flag (she had surrendered to the British 3rd-rate *Achille*) Hargood sent Captain John Owen of the Royal Marines and the sailing master, Mr Hudson, across in their last remaining boat to take possession. The senior unwounded Spanish officer on board offered his sword, but Owen said he should give it to Hargood and took him to *Belleisle*. There, Hargood accepted the sword and gave him, and *Belleisle*'s own officers, tea in his cabin.

In an engagement lasting some four hours, *Belleisle* lost her first and junior lieutenants, a midshipman and thirty men killed, with seven officers and warrant officers and eighty-six men wounded. At about 5 p.m. she was taken in tow by the frigate *Naiad* but in the subsequent storm the towing cable parted and left *Belleisle*, under jury rig, to be blown towards a lee shore. At the critical moment, *Naiad* reappeared and towed her away from the breakers, which were clearly visible a mile away. They headed for Gibraltar and on the way encountered a ship of the line that at first they took to be part of the French squadron that escaped from the battle. Hargood prepared to scuttle *Belleisle* and transfer her crew to *Naiad*, but an exchange of recognition signals revealed the stranger to be one of Rear-Admiral Louis's ships returning from replenishment at Tetuan. After making repairs at Gibraltar, *Belleisle*, with a main-topmast as mainmast, fore-topmast as foremast, bowsprit for mizenmast and a spare spar as bowsprit, sailed for home on 4 November 1805, in company with the 3rd-rate *Bellerophon* (74) and *Victory* as she carried Nelson's body to England.

With *Belleisle* refitted, Hargood resumed command in February 1806 and in the following May sailed from Plymouth for the West Indies, in a squadron under Sir

Richard Strachan. Off Bermuda, the squadron was scattered by a hurricane on 18–19 August, leaving Hargood to make his way northwards in the badly-damaged *Belleisle* to the mouth of Chesapeake Bay, where he was re-joined on 5 September by the 3rd-rate *Bellona* (74) and the 5th-rate frigate *Melampus* (36). On 14 September 1806 they encountered the French ship of the line *Impétueux*, which had been dismasted by the same hurricane and was proceeding under jury rig. Unable to escape, she ran aground and was captured but then set on fire while Hargood divided her crew between his own ships as prisoners of war. This was one of the many breaches of neutrality by the Royal Navy that preceded the American War of 1812, but on this occasion the United States government chose to ignore it and Hargood's action was approved by the Admiralty. He returned home with *Belleisle* in November 1806 and, after another refit, took her back to the West Indies where, in 1807, she became flagship of the C-in-C, Sir Alexander Cochrane. Hargood exchanged into the 3rd-rate *Northumberland* (74) and escorted a convoy back to England. They subsequently served in the blockade of Lisbon, occupied by the French in November 1807.

Hargood was made a colonel of Marines in April 1808. After Portugal and Spain rose against Napoleon in the summer of 1808, the British ended their blockade of the Iberian coasts and redeployed the Mediterranean fleet to Minorca from where, in March 1809, *Northumberland* sailed to join the blockade of Toulon. In April 1809 the Austrians declared war on Napoleon and, with British encouragement, marched to drive the French from German soil. Hargood was detached with *Northumberland* and two other ships of the line to support the Austrians in the Adriatic, but arrived just too late to save Trieste, which fell to the French on 20 May 1809. Napoleon's vigorous counter-offensive against Austria forced her to sign an armistice on 18 July, but in the meanwhile Hargood's squadron carried out a number of successful boat actions off the coasts of Trieste, Pesaro and Fiume (Rijeka). In October 1809 Austria made a humiliating peace that included the transfer to French rule of all her Adriatic provinces, including Trieste, Slovenia and Croatia. Without a base in the

Adriatic, Hargood's squadron rejoined the main fleet under Collingwood in October 1809.

On 28 March 1810 Hargood and the badly-leaking *Northumberland* were ordered home in company with the even more leaky 1st-rate *Hibernia* (110). On the way they were to collect the five Spanish ships of the line in Cartagena and take them to Gibraltar. The French under Marshal Suchet had seized Murcia, Cartagena's hinterland, and the Spanish nationalist government appreciated that the city, and the warships in its port, were in danger of being captured likewise. The local patriots, however, thought otherwise and their junta, by a majority of one, decided that the British could take out only two ships. Fearing that even this permission might be revoked, Hargood sent three lieutenants, his boatswain, gunner and 300 seamen into the dockyard and within two days both ships were serviceable and out of harbour.

Hargood was promoted to rear-admiral on 7 August 1810. From then until March 1811 he was second-in-command at Portsmouth, after which he became C-in-C, Guernsey, with his flag in the sloop *Vulture* (16). In May 1811 he married Maria, the forty year old daughter of Thomas Somers Cocks, a prominent banker. Maria's elder sister, Margaretta, was the wife of Hargood's old friend Captain James Morris [26], who had commanded *Colossus* at Trafalgar and was the son of Captain John Morris under whom Hargood had fought at Charleston. On 4 June 1814, after Napoleon's defeat and exile to Elba, Hargood was promoted to vice-admiral and went ashore, having been in active employment for thirty-nine out his previous forty-one years of service. In January 1815 he was awarded the KCB. In March 1831 Sir William Hargood was made a GCH, to mark the accession of the Duke of Clarence to the throne as William IV. The new king had maintained a friendly personal correspondence with his old shipmate and now, reminding him that he had saved his future sovereign's life by steadying him in the Thames wherry, singled him out for this award. He was promoted to admiral on 22 July 1831 and was awarded the GCB in September 1831. Between March 1833 and April 1836 he was

C-in-C, Plymouth. There, his unfavourable opinion of steamships was confirmed when the royal yacht *Emerald*, with Princess Victoria and her mother, the Duchess of Kent, on board, snagged her mast on a moored hulk while proceeding under tow by the paddle steamer *Messenger*. A dangerous accident seemed imminent, but Hargood told his flag captain to bring the admiral's barge alongside and the future Queen was handed across to safety. Sir William Hargood subsequently retired to Bath, where he died of congestion of the lungs on 11 September 1839.

HARVEY, Admiral Sir ELIAB, GCB (1758–1830) [19]

Eliab Harvey was born on 5 December 1758, the second son of William Harvey of Rolls Park, Chigwell, in south-east Essex. William Harvey died in 1763, but his eldest son succeeded to both his estate and parliamentary seat as a member for Essex and in 1771 secured an appointment for Eliab Harvey on the books of the royal yacht *William and Mary*. Harvey went to sea two years later, first in the new 5th-rate frigate *Orpheus* (32) and then in the sloop *Lynx* (10) in the West Indies. With the outbreak of the American War of Independence in 1776 he went to the North American station in the 6th-rate frigate *Mermaid* (28) and was appointed midshipman in the 3rd-rate *Eagle* (64), flagship of Vice-Admiral Lord Howe. In October 1778 he returned home, where he was promoted to lieutenant on 25 February 1779 and appointed to the 3rd-rate *Resolution* (74), but did not join the ship as his brother's death at this time brought him the family estate and a large fortune.

Harvey became a figure in London society and a noted gambler, on one occasion losing £100,000 at dice and putting up Rolls Park to cover the debt. His opponent generously took only £10,000 and offered to throw again for the balance, which Harvey then won. In 1780 he entered Parliament as MP for Maldon, Essex, but gave up the seat the following year and, with the war still in progress, returned to sea in August 1781 as lieutenant in the new 5th-rate frigate *Dolphin* (44). From there he briefly moved to the sloop *Fury* (14) in February 1782, before becoming commander of the new brig-sloop *Otter* (14) on 21 March 1782 and being deployed in the North Sea. On 20 January 1783 he was promoted to post captain and went ashore. In the same year he married Lady Louisa Nugent, younger daughter of the third marriage of the millionaire Irish peer Earl Nugent. The Earl refused to recognize Lady Louisa as his daughter, but her elder sister, Lady Mary Nugent, eventually succeeded to his barony in her own right and married Earl Temple, later created Marquis of Buckingham. In due course, Harvey and Lady Louisa had their own family of two sons and six daughters.

In May 1790, when a fleet was mobilized to meet the threat of war with Spain over the possession of Nootka Sound (Vancouver, British Columbia), Harvey was appointed to the 6th-rate frigate *Hussar*. Spain, with her former ally France in the throes of revolution, bowed to British naval pressure and the dispute was resolved by diplomacy, after which the fleet was demobilized and Harvey once more went ashore.   After the French Revolutionary War began in February 1793, he returned to sea in the 5th-rate frigate *Santa Margarita* (38). He served in the West Indies under Sir John Jervis and took part in the capture of the valuable French islands of **Martinique (February–March 1794)** and **Guadeloupe (April–May 1794)**. Harvey and *Santa Margarita* went home in the summer of 1794 and were deployed to the Channel, where on 23 August 1794, as part of a frigate squadron under Sir John Borlase Warren, they took part in an action that drove the French frigate *Felicité* and two corvettes ashore in the Bay of Audierne, Brittany.

Early in 1796 Harvey moved to the 3rd-rate *Valiant* (74) in which he served in the West Indies until returning home the following year on medical grounds. In 1798 he was given command of the Essex division of the Sea Fencibles, tasked with the local defence of creeks, landing places and shore installations of his native county against the threat of a French invasion. He was appointed to the 3rd-rate *Triumph* (74) in 1799 and served in the Channel, mostly blockading Brest, until peace with France was signed in March 1802. At the general election of 1802 Harvey re-entered parliament as MP for Essex, and retained this seat, previously held by his father and elder brother, until 1812.   The war with France was renewed on 18 May 1803 and in the following November Harvey was appointed to the 2nd-rate *Téméraire* (98), deployed to the Channel and the blockade of Brest. After Spain entered the war on the French side in December 1804 Harvey and *Téméraire* remained with the Channel Fleet, serving in the blockade of Brest and in the Bay of Biscay. On 30 August 1805, as part of a reinforcing squadron under Vice-Admiral Sir Robert Calder, they joined the blockade of Vice-Admiral Pierre Villeneuve and his Franco-Spanish Combined Fleet in Cadiz.

At **Trafalgar (21 October 1805)** *Téméraire* was immediately behind Nelson's flagship, the 1st-rate *Victory*, leading the weather column of the British fleet. At one point, making all possible sail in accordance with Nelson's order to the whole fleet, she came up with the flagship, but Nelson, who earlier had seemed inclined to accept his officers' advice to allow her to take the lead, hailed Harvey and ordered him to assume his appointed station astern of *Victory*. Harvey came under fire from six enemy ships as he approached their line and altered course, hoping to pass astern of the French *Redoutable* (74) as she lay along *Victory*'s starboard side. He lost sight of *Victory* in the smoke and, when he did find *Redoutable*, was unable to avoid a collision.

This left *Redoutable* between *Victory* on one side and *Téméraire* on the other. *Redoutable*'s captain had trained his men to fight as much by boarding as by gunnery, and tried to board *Victory*, despite his ship's impossible position as a two-decker overhung by the British three-deckers either side of her. Harvey fired a broadside that wiped out most of the boarders and then called on the French captain to surrender rather than prolong a useless resistance. He was answered by a hail of musketry and grenades that drove most of *Téméraire*'s upper deck crews below and a fireball exploded on her main deck, with flames threatening to reach her aft magazine. Heavy fire from the French *Neptune* (84), some distance away on *Téméraire*'s starboard side, did severe damage to her masts and yards and encouraged the French *Fougueux* (74), previously engaged with the 3rd-rate *Belleisle* (74), to close on *Téméraire*.

Harvey met her with a series of broadsides from his starboard batteries and, for lack of wind, she then drifted alongside so that, for a time, the four ships *Victory, Redoutable, Téméraire* and *Fougueux* were locked together, all lying in the same direction. *Redoutable*'s mainmast and foremast fell across her starboard side onto *Téméraire*, while *Téméraire*'s topmasts fell across her port side onto *Redoutable*.

Having repulsed an attempt by *Redoutable* to board *Téméraire* across the fallen masts, Harvey now ordered his own boarders across to *Fougueux*. After they had fought their way to his poop deck, her captain surrendered and was taken to *Téméraire* to hand his sword to Harvey. The fiery Captain Lucas of *Redoutable*, with his ship sinking beneath him, hailed *Téméraire* to ask for help with the pumps and threatened to burn both ships together if his request was denied. A boarding party from *Téméraire* prevented him and he surrendered his ship to *Victory* at much the same time as *Fougueux* struck her colours. The two British ships then began to clear away their wreckage and set what sail they could, enabling them to fire at the ships of the enemy van division that had belatedly turned back to join a battle already lost. *Téméraire*'s casualties amounted to two Royal Marine officers, a midshipman and the carpenter killed and another five officers and warrant officers wounded, with forty-three men killed and seventy-one wounded. She was taken in tow by a frigate and survived the subsequent storm to reach Gibraltar in safety. Though so close to Nelson in the battle, Harvey and his officers did not learn of their admiral's death until some days later for although they saw the flag had been shifted into the frigate *Euryalus*, they had no immediate way of knowing that it was that of Vice-Admiral Collingwood **[8]** from the dismasted *Royal Sovereign* rather than Nelson's from *Victory*.

In his dispatches, Collingwood (who always remembered being the only captain not to have been mentioned in dispatches after **The Glorious First of June**) departed from his principle of not singling out anyone for special praise and mentioned Harvey and *Téméraire* for 'a circumstance ... which so strongly marks the invincible spirit of British seamen, when engaging the enemies of their country, that I cannot resist the pleasure I have in making it known to their Lordships'. Some other captains felt that Harvey, who was one of the first to meet Collingwood after the battle, had given him too glowing an account of *Téméraire*'s part in it. Fremantle [15] wrote to his wife Betsey that 'never having been in action before, he thinks every Ship was subdued by him and he wears us all to Death with his incessant jargon'. Similarly, Codrington [7] wrote 'He is become the greatest bore I ever met with'. This criticism was not entirely fair, as Harvey had indeed seen action, albeit as a frigate captain, nine years previously. Certainly, Collingwood, an experienced officer who did not bestow praise lightly, wrote privately to Harvey congratulating him on 'the noble and distinguished part that *Téméraire* took in the battle; nothing could be finer. I have not words in which I can sufficiently express my admiration of it.' From Gibraltar *Téméraire* was sent home for repair, with Harvey being promoted to rear-admiral on 9 November 1805.

In the spring of 1806 Harvey joined the Channel fleet, with his flag in the 3rd-rate *Tonnant* (80). In May 1807 command of this fleet passed from Earl St Vincent (the former Sir John Jervis) to Lord Gambier, whose second-in-command Harvey subsequently became. In March 1809 the French fleet in Brest slipped past Gambier's blockade and was discovered, a few days later, in the Basque Roads, covering the approaches to Rochefort. Captain Lord Cochrane, one of the most daring frigate captains of his day, submitted to the Admiralty a plan for a night attack with fireships, using incendiary devices he had designed himself. Somewhat to his astonishment, the plan was accepted with such enthusiasm that he was ordered to proceed to the Basque Roads immediately and put it into action. He protested that there were many officers senior to him in the blockading squadron already on station there, but was overruled. He reached Gambier's flagship to find him being subjected, on his own quarterdeck, to a violent protest from Harvey, who had already offered to lead such an attack and had prepared a list of officers and men who had volunteered to accompany him. Having just learned that

Cochrane had been dispatched with special orders from the Admiralty for this task, Harvey declared that, if passed over in such a way, he would strike his flag.

Gambier, a man of strong religious convictions (he was known in the fleet as 'Dismal Jimmy') had no enthusiasm for an attack with infernal machines on anchored ships, and was as offended as Harvey himself by the Admiralty's decision to place the operation in Cochrane's hands. Nevertheless, he insisted that orders must be obeyed, after which Harvey went below to the flag captain's cabin, where he shook hands with Cochrane and assured him that his objections were not the result of any personal animosity towards himself. He added, however, that he had never served under anyone so unfit for command as Gambier, who (he said) had made no attempt to sound the shoals around the French fleet and had instead occupied the time with pointless musters. Nelson, he continued, would already have followed the French in to attack them at their moorings. He told Cochrane that he had already expressed these opinions to Gambier himself, with the same degree of moderation that he was using towards Cochrane. 'You have a strange notion of prudence' said Cochrane, who himself often freely spoke his mind to those in authority.

Harvey then returned to his own ship, shouting that this was not the first time he had been lightly treated and that it was because 'I am no canting Methodist, no hypocrite, no psalm-singer and do not cheat old women out of their estates by hypocrisy and canting'. It was indeed widely believed in the fleet that Gambier showed preference to officers who shared his religious views, but Harvey had gone too far and was sent home in disgrace. At his subsequent court martial for insubordination, held at Portsmouth on 22–23 May 1809, he called no witnesses in his defence and made a full apology, but was nevertheless dismissed the service. A year later, an Order in Council dated 21 March 1810 restored him to his rank and seniority 'in consideration of his long and meritorious services' though the decision may also have owed something to his influential political connections and his continued parliamentary support for the Government. He was never given another naval appointment, though he became a vice-admiral on 31 January 1810 and was awarded the KCB in January 1815. Sir Eliab Harvey was promoted to admiral on 12 August 1819.

Harvey returned to Parliament as a member for Essex after an eight year break, in the General Election occasioned by the death of George III in 1820. Awarded the GCB in 1825, he was re-elected in 1826 and retained his seat until his death. As one of the leading men in his neighbourhood, though with a reputation for irascibility, he played his part in local affairs and served as a verderer of Epping Forest, a trustee of the Ongar Hundred Savings Bank and a governor of Chigwell School. He died on 20 February 1830 and was buried in St Andrew's parish church, Hempstead, north Essex. Of his two sons, the elder, an officer in the Coldstream Guards, was killed in action during Wellington's unsuccessful siege of Burgos in October 1812, and his younger predeceased him in 1823. Lady Louisa Harvey outlived her husband and continued to reside at Rolls Park. The mansion and its surrounding estate were inherited by their eldest daughter, Louisa, who married William Lloyd of Aston, Shropshire.

HOPE, Rear-Admiral Sir GEORGE JOHNSTONE, KCB
(1767–1818) **[20]**
George Hope, a son of the Honourable Charles Hope-Vere and a grandson of the 1st Earl of Hopetoun, was born on 6 July 1767. He joined the Navy in 1782, at the end of the American War of Independence. He was promoted to lieutenant on 29 February 1788 and commander on 22 November 1790 and, after the beginning of the French Revolutionary War in February 1793, was appointed to the sloop *Bulldog* (16) on convoy protection duties in the Mediterranean. He was promoted to post captain on 13 September 1793 and commanded the 5th-rate frigate *Romulus* (36) at **Leghorn (13–14 March 1795)**. Hope was later appointed to the 5th-rate frigate *Alcmene* (32) in which he joined Rear-Admiral Sir Horatio Nelson's fleet in Aboukir Bay on 13 August 1798, eleven days after **The Nile (1–2 August 1798)**. Nelson himself sailed for Naples on 19 August,

leaving Captain Samuel Hood with three 3rd-rates and three frigates, including *Alcmene*, to blockade the surviving French ships (two small ships of the line, eight frigates, and four brig-corvettes) in Alexandria. On 22 August *Alcmene* intercepted the French gunboat *Légère*, whose captain was seen to throw documents overboard just as the frigate approached her. Two of *Alcmene*'s seamen, John Taylor and James Harding, jumped overboard to retrieve them, at some risk to their lives, as the ship was then making over five knots. They recovered all the papers, which proved to be dispatches intended for General Napoleon Bonaparte and the French army in Egypt, and the two seamen were in due course rewarded by the Corporation of the City of London with a life pension of twenty pounds annually.

Hope returned to Egypt in March 1801, commanding the new 5th-rate frigate *Leda* (38). As part of the fleet under Lord Keith he supported the landing on 1 June 1801 of 15,000 British troops on an open beach under heavy fire from the French in Aboukir castle. The army, with its flanks protected by the fleet, then marched the twelve miles along a narrow isthmus to Alexandria and after a battle in which the veteran British commander, General Sir Ralph Abercromby, was killed, the French retired behind the city's defences. The rest of the French army in Egypt (isolated there since the Battle of the Nile) surrendered at the end of June 1801, but Alexandria held out until the war ended in March 1802.

War with France was renewed on 18 May 1803. Hope returned to sea and was appointed to the 3rd-rate *Defence* (74). Spain, which at first remained neutral, declared war in December 1804 and *Defence*, as part of a newly established 'Spanish squadron' of six ships of the line under Vice-Admiral Sir John Orde, was then deployed to the blockade of Cadiz. There, with the rest of Orde's squadron, she was engaged in revictualling and replenishment when Vice-Admiral Pierre Villeneuve's fleet, having evaded Nelson's blockade of Toulon, arrived there on 8 April 1805. Orde hastily cast off his store-ships and formed a line of battle to cover their departure, but Villeneuve, with eleven ships of the line and six frigates, made no attempt to force an engagement and allowed the

1. A 1st-rate ship of the line, 104 guns, HMS *Victory*, Nelson's flagship at Trafalgar.

(Lithograph after Arthur Burgess)

2. Vice Admiral Sir Thomas Masterman Hardy.

W. Fred Mitchell

(Lithograph after W. F. Mitchell)

3. A 3rd-rate ship of the line, 74 guns.

4. Vice Admiral Cuthbert, Lord Collingwood. Engraving with facsimile signature.

5. Admiral Sir Edward Codrington. Engraving with facsimile signature.

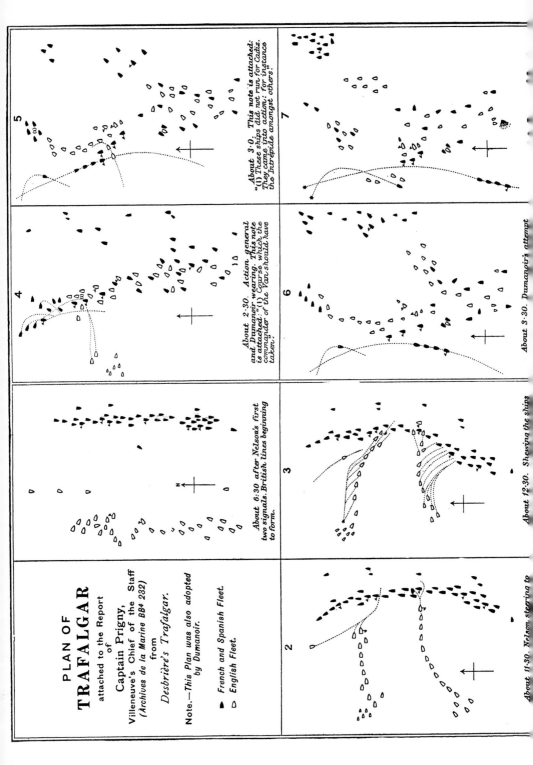

PLAN OF
TRAFALGAR
attached to the Report
of
Captain Prigny,
Villeneuve's Chief of the Staff
(Archives de la Marine BB4 282)
from
Desbrière's Trafalgar.

Note.—This Plan was also adopted
by Dumanoir.

▲ French and Spanish Fleet.
◊ English Fleet.

About 6.30 after Nelson's first two signals. British lines beginning to form.

About 2.30. Action general and Dumanoir wearing. This note is attached: "(1) Course, which the commander of the Van should have taken."

About 3.0. This note is attached: "(1) These ships did not run, for Cadiz. They came into action: for instance the Intrépide amongst others".

About 11.30. Nelson steering to

About 12.30. Shewing the ships

About 3.30. Dumanoir's attempt

6. Captain Prigny's Plan of Trafalgar 1805.

7. Plan of Trafalgar from the Naval Chronicle, Volume XIV, 1805.

8. A 5th-rate frigate, 42 guns.

(Lithograph after W. F. Mitchell)

British to retire towards Lagos Bay. When Orde learnt that Villeneuve had picked up those Spanish ships that were ready for sea and had sailed after a mere six hours in Cadiz, he decided that the enemy fleet was en route to cover the long-expected French invasion of the United Kingdom. Accordingly he abandoned the blockade and sailed north to join forces with the Channel fleet, searching for Villeneuve as he went, but failing to find him, as the Franco-Spanish Combined Fleet was en route for the West Indies.

Defence remained with the Channel fleet until the end of August 1805 when, as part of a squadron led by Vice-Admiral Sir Robert Calder, she went back to Cadiz, where Villeneuve, having returned from the West Indies, was under blockade. Vice-Admiral Viscount Nelson arrived there on 29 September with the 1st-rate *Victory* (104) to take over command from Vice-Admiral Cuthbert Collingwood [8] and moved his main force further out to sea, so as to tempt Villeneuve to sail. When Villeneuve eventually began to do so, on 19 October 1805, *Defence* was fifth in the chain of four frigates and three ships of the line that passed the signal 370 'Enemy ships are coming out of port or getting under sail' from the edge of Cadiz to Nelson, forty-eight miles away to the west. In the subsequent chase, *Defence*, along with the 3rd-rates *Mars* and *Colossus*, took station on the port side of the main fleet, so as to keep contact with the frigates.

At **Trafalgar (21 October 1805)** *Defence* was stationed in the rear of the British lee column led by Collingwood, so that she entered the action more than two hours after it had begun, with most of the enemy ships either so badly damaged or so demoralized as to offer little resistance. After engaging the French *Berwick* (74), *Defence* encountered the Spanish *San Ildefonso* (74), whose captain, Commodore Don Juan de Varga, with heavy losses among his men and his ship already severely damaged, surrendered to Hope after an hour's fighting. *Defence* suffered relatively light casualties, amounting to seven men killed and twenty-nine wounded, and damage to her mainmast, gaff and rigging.

At the end of the battle, Hope, acting on his own initiative, anchored off Cape Trafalgar in company with three prizes, including *San Ildefonso* and rode out the ensuing gale. These, with one other, were the only prizes to remain in British hands. After Hope rejoined the fleet, he was one of the five captains selected by Collingwood (who had succeeded to the command on Nelson's death) to sink the remaining prizes to prevent them being retaken, and to take off their crews, a mission that Collingwood described as 'an arduous task in the high sea which was running', when mentioning Hope in dispatches.

In 1809, Hope became captain of the fleet deployed to the Baltic under Vice-Admiral Sir James Saumarez, with his flag in *Victory*. Their mission was the defence of British trade with the Baltic, a vital source of naval stores, and the blockade of north German ports under French control. They also blockaded the Russian Baltic fleet until Tsar Alexander I reopened his ports to British trade. In November 1810, Sweden, under French pressure, declared war on the United Kingdom, but Saumarez respected her shipping, correctly appreciating that the Swedes would eventually follow the example of their Russian neighbours and defy Napoleon. Denmark, another French satellite, had also to be watched, until 1814, when it was overrun by a Swedish army led by their new Crown Prince, the former French Marshal Bernadotte.

Hope remained Saumarez's chief of staff in *Victory* and in July 1810 was made a major general of Royal Marines. He returned home with the fleet each winter to refit until promoted to rear-admiral on 12 August 1811. Between March 1812 and May 1813 he served as a lord commissioner of the Admiralty. In June 1812 Napoleon, enraged at Tsar Alexander's refusal to cease trading with the British, invaded Russia with half a million men. Russia became a British ally and, as French troops approached her Baltic coasts, Hope was sent to help the Russian fleet escape to England. He returned to the Admiralty in October 1813 where he remained until after Napoleon's final defeat and was awarded the KCB in January 1815.

Sir George Hope, who also sat as MP for East Grinstead, Sussex, died in harness at the Admiralty on 2 April 1818. In

1803, in the intricate web of marriage alliances that bound together the landed families of his day, Hope married Lady Jemima Johnstone Hope, younger daughter of his cousin James, third Earl of Hopetoun. Her elder sister, Lady Anne, married Hope's nephew, William Johnstone Hope, a naval captain and future admiral, in 1792. Their mother (the third Earl of Hopetoun's countess) was the daughter of Admiral the sixth Earl of Northesk, and her nephew became the seventh Earl of Northesk [6] who served at Trafalgar as a rear-admiral. Lady Jemima Hope died in 1808, leaving her husband with two young children. Their son entered the Navy and, encouraged by Northesk (his mother's cousin), eventually rose to the rank of admiral of the fleet. Hope was married again in 1814, to Georgiana, daughter of the seventh Lord Kinnaird, with whom he had another daughter. He was buried in Westminster Abbey, London.

KING, Vice-Admiral Sir RICHARD, 2nd Baronet, KCB
(1774–1834) **[21]**
Richard King, born in 1774, was the only son of Captain (later Admiral Sir) Richard King, a then forty-four year old experienced sea officer who went on to distinguish himself in the East Indies during the American War of Independence. The young Richard King joined the Navy in 1788 on appointment to the 3rd-rate *Crown*, pendant-ship of Commodore the Honourable (later Admiral Sir) William 'Billy Blue' Cornwallis as C-in-C, East Indies. He was promoted to lieutenant on 14 November 1791, commander in 1793 after the outbreak of war with Revolutionary France, and post captain on 14 May 1794. After returning home in November 1794 he was appointed to the 6th-rate frigate *Aurora* (28) deployed in the Channel. When the Batavian Republic (the Netherlands) became a French satellite in May 1795, its navy posed a threat to the British in the North Sea. The mutiny of the fleet at the Nore in 1797 was on that account all the more dangerous and King was a member of the court martial that tried and condemned its leader, Richard Parker.

In 1797 King was given command of the new 5th-rate frigate *Sirius* (36). On 24 October 1798, deployed off the Texel,

he encountered two Dutch warships, *Furie* (36) and
Waakzaamheit (24) about two miles apart from each other.
Steering between the two, he captured *Waakzaamheit* without
a fight and then pursued *Furie*, which he overtook after a
chase lasting eight hours. In a running fight, the weaker *Furie*
suffered considerable damage to her hull, masts and rigging
before surrendering to *Sirius*, whose total casualties
amounted to a shot through her bowsprit and one man
wounded by a musket ball. The two Dutch ships were found
to be carrying troops and arms intended to support
insurgents (or patriots) in Ireland, where a major rising had
been suppressed by General Lord Cornwallis the previous
month. Both ships were bought by the Admiralty for the
British service, providing King and his crew with welcome
prize money. Later that month, off the coast of France, they
captured the French minor combatant *Favorie* (6) and a
Spanish brig. On 27 January 1801, in company with the 5th-
rate frigate *Oiseau* (36), *Sirius* captured the French frigate
Dédaigneuse (36), inward bound for Rochefort with dispatches
from Cayenne, French Guiana.

After the war ended in March 1802 *Sirius* was paid off and
King went ashore. In 1803 he married Sarah Anne, daughter
of the future Admiral Sir John Duckworth. The war with
France was resumed in May 1803 and King returned to sea
in April 1804 on appointment to the 3rd-rate *Achille* (74), a
ship that, although launched at Gravesend in 1798,
commemorated the name of a French prize taken at **The
Glorious First of June** four years earlier. Spain entered the
war on the French side in December 1804 and *Achille* was
assigned in March 1805 to a small squadron being assembled
under Vice-Admiral Cuthbert Collingwood **[8]**. Soon
afterwards Vice-Admiral Pierre Villeneuve escaped from the
blockade of Toulon and reached Cadiz whence, after picking
up such Spanish ships as were ready for sea, he disappeared
from British view. Collingwood was dispatched to the south-
west coast of Spain, where he learned that Villeneuve had
gone to the West Indies, with Vice-Admiral Viscount Nelson
and his Mediterranean fleet in pursuit. After sending two
ships to reinforce Nelson, Collingwood divided the rest of

his squadron between the blockades of Cartagena and Cadiz. *Achille* was with Collingwood and two other ships of the line outside Cadiz when Villeneuve's Franco-Spanish Combined Fleet, after returning to European waters, appeared there on 20 August 1805. Pursued by sixteen enemy ships, Collingwood retired towards Gibraltar but when the enemy turned back to Cadiz, he followed and kept watch there while reinforcements gathered to his support. *Achille* remained with him in the subsequent blockade and, with the rest of the fleet, came under Nelson's command when the latter arrived to take over from Collingwood on 28 September 1805.

When Villeneuve again put to sea and the two fleets met at **Trafalgar (21 October 1805)**, *Achille*'s lookouts, in the early dawn, were the first to see the enemy, and King signalled to Nelson 'Have discovered a strange fleet'. In the ensuing battle, *Achille* was stationed five ships astern of Collingwood's flagship, the 1st-rate *Royal Sovereign*, leading the lee column, and was thus among those most heavily engaged. On reaching the enemy line, King passed astern of the Spanish *Montanez* (74), then luffed up into the wind and engaged her from the leeward side. After about twelve minutes *Montanez* broke off the engagement and King then steered to help the 3rd-rate *Belleisle* (74) but, before reaching her, encountered the Spanish *Argonauta* (80). After almost an hour's fighting with *Achille* stationary on her port beam, *Argonauta* tried to make sail but, unable to escape, closed her lower gun-ports and ceased firing. Before King could send a party to take possession, *Achille* came under fire from her namesake the French *Achille* (74) while the French *Berwick* (74) got between him and *Argonauta*. The Spanish ship drifted to leeward and, after hoisting British colours above her own, was eventually captured by a boat from *Belleisle*.

Achille then closed with *Berwick* which, with her captain killed and another 250 dead or wounded, surrendered following an hour-long combat. King sent one of his lieutenants with a prize crew to take over the ship and hove sixty-seven butts overboard from *Achille*'s fore-hold to make room for his prisoners of war. *Achille* lost one midshipman and twelve men killed, with two lieutenants, two officers of Royal Marines, a master's mate, two midshipmen, a 1st-class volunteer and fifty-one men wounded, and much damage to her masts, bowsprit and hull.

Sir Richard King succeeded to his father's baronetcy on 7 November 1806. He remained in *Achille* and was deployed until 1811 off the west coasts of Spain (which became a British ally in the summer of 1808, when Spanish patriots rose against French occupation) and France. He was then appointed captain of the fleet under Vice-Admiral Sir Charles Cotton, with whom he served first in the Mediterranean and then in the Channel until promoted to rear-admiral on 12 August 1812. During the remainder of the Napoleonic Wars, King, with his flag in the 1st-rate *San Josef* (114), served in the Mediterranean, under Admiral Sir Edward Pellew, later Lord Exmouth. He was awarded the KCB on 2 January 1815 and served as C-in-C, East Indies, from 1816 to 1820. Promoted to vice-admiral on 19 July 1821, and having previously been left a widower, he married a second time in 1822, to Maria Susanna, daughter of his old chief Sir Charles Cotton. In 1833 he was appointed C-in-C at the Nore, where he died of cholera at Admiralty House, Sheerness, on 5 August 1834. He had children from both of his marriages. His eldest son succeeded to the baronetcy and was in turn succeeded, in 1847, by the second son, the future Admiral Sir George St Vincent Duckworth King.

LAFOREY, Admiral Sir FRANCIS, 2nd Baronet, KCB (1767–1835) [22]

Francis Laforey, born in Virginia in 1767, was the son of Admiral Sir John Laforey and his wife Eleanor, the daughter of an artillery officer, Lieutenant-Colonel Francis Farley, judge advocate at Antigua, where the couple were married. The admiral's grandfather, Louis Laforey, was a French Huguenot who had come to England as an officer in the army of William of Orange at the time of the Glorious Revolution of 1688. Louis's son John (Sir John Laforey's father) also served in the British Army and rose to become a lieutenant-colonel and governor of Pendennis Castle. Francis Laforey joined the Navy in 1780, during the American War of Independence, when his father was commissioner of the Navy at Barbados and the Leeward Islands. He was promoted to lieutenant on 26 August 1789 and commander on 22 November 1790, when his father, newly created a baronet, was C-in-C, Leeward Islands. Between 1791 and 1793 he commanded the newly- rebuilt sloop *Fairy* (14) in the West Indies. When news reached Sir John Laforey that war with Revolutionary France had begun in February 1793, he immediately prepared an expedition against the rich sugar island of Tobago, in the Windward Islands, which had been held by the French since the American War of Independence. The expedition, which included *Fairy*, proved successful and Tobago capitulated on 15 April 1793. Commander Francis Laforey was sent home with the dispatches as a mark of distinction and was promoted to post captain on 5 June 1793.

On 29 May 1794 Laforey, patrolling off Land's End in the 6th-rate frigate *Carysfort* (28), met the 5th-rate frigate *Castor* (32) which, along with her captain (the future Rear-Admiral Sir Thomas Troubridge) and most of the convoy she was escorting from Newfoundland, had been captured by a French squadron almost three weeks earlier. *Castor*, hastily remanned by individuals transferred from her captors, pursued and captured a Dutch brig, which she had under tow when Laforey appeared. Abandoning her prize, she then fought a one and a quarter hour's duel with *Carysfort* before striking her colours. Laforey manned her with a master's mate and eighteen men from her original crew, left behind as prisoners of war when Troubridge and the rest of the ship's company was taken into captivity aboard other ships.

The Admiralty at first refused to pay anything more for *Castor* than salvage money, on the grounds that she had not reached a French port before being recaptured and was therefore not a prize in the legal sense. Laforey appealed to the High Court of Admiralty, where the case was heard by the eminent judge Sir James Marriot. *Castor*'s French commander, Captain L'Huillier, gave evidence that, after her capture from the British, she had been taken into the navy of the French Republic on the authority of his squadron commander, Rear-Admiral Nielly, and had full powers to wage war as such. Marriot found that this amounted to 'setting forth as a ship of war' and so made her a lawful prize. *Castor* was then purchased back by the Navy, and Laforey and his men were awarded their full prize money.

Laforey was subsequently appointed to the 5th-rate frigate *Aimable* (32) in which, in May 1795, he carried his father to resume the post of C-in-C, Leeward Islands. There, encouraged by the principles of human rights expounded by the French Revolutionary government, many Afro-Caribbean slaves had risen in rebellion against their British masters. In the Windward Islands, many planters and their families were murdered and the fever stricken British garrisons, faced with a guerrilla war, were forced back into coastal defences where they could be supplied by the Navy. French troop transports and frigates continued to escape the blockade of their home ports and reach the West Indies, where they delivered arms and men to aid the insurgents.

In the spring of 1796 General Sir Ralph Abercromby was dispatched to suppress the slave rebellion. The first of his reinforcements reached Barbados on 1 April 1796, where they were joined three days later by Admiral Laforey. Meanwhile the planters of Dutch Guiana, with their homeland occupied by the French and renamed the Batavian Republic, had asked for British protection. The British Cabinet, influenced by the powerful West India lobby, ordered three regiments to Dutch Guiana, where the troops, supported by their frigate escorts and the 3rd-rate *Scipio* (64) under Captain Laforey, captured Demerara, Berbice and Essequibo by the end of April 1796. These all proved profitable conquests apart from the toll taken by tropical diseases which, during the years from 1794 to 1796, killed over 40,000 British servicemen in the West Indies. Among them was Admiral Laforey who, having escorted Abercromby and his army to St Anne's Bay, Martinique, en route to St Lucia, handed over his command on 24 April 1796. He then sailed for England only to die of yellow fever at the age of seventy-six, two days before reaching Portsmouth, where he was buried in the Royal Garrison Church.

Sir Francis Laforey, succeeding to his father's baronetcy on 14 June 1796, also returned home, and was subsequently appointed to the 5th-rate frigate *Hydra* (38). On 8 April 1798, in company with Captain Richard Strachan in the 5th-rate frigate *Diamond* (38), he intercepted a force of thirty-three flat-bottomed invasion barges, escorted by gun-brigs, taking troops from Le Havre to the St Marcouf islands, four miles off the coast of Normandy and under British occupation since July 1795. The French flotilla formed a line and anchored in shoal water, where *Diamond*, after a few broadsides, went aground while attempting to wear. Both frigates came under fire from the French brigs and shore batteries until the onset of darkness, after which *Hydra* helped *Diamond* refloat herself. During the next day they stood off and watched the progress of the flotilla along the coast to Bernie, where they were joined by the 4th-rate *Adamant* (50). The flotilla then went back to the estuary of the River Caen, with the two British frigates exchanging fire with the French brigs and coast artillery until forced to stand out to sea to resume their blockade.

On 30 May 1798 Laforey and *Hydra*, in company with the bomb vessel *Vesuvius* (12) and the cutter *Trial* (12), sighted the French frigate *Confiante* (36), corvette *Vésuve* (20) and an armed cutter en route from Le Havre to Cherbourg. Well ahead of his consorts, Laforey returned *Vésuve*'s fire and drove her inshore, leaving the shallow draft *Vesuvius* and *Trial* to follow her while he went in pursuit of *Confiante*. After a running fight of over an hour, the French frigate ran aground and Laforey backed his sails to allow *Hydra* to stand off and maintain continuous fire at close range for another two hours, at the end of which *Confiante* lost her mizen mast.

Meanwhile, about five miles away, *Vésuve* had also gone aground and, as a stationary target, come under fire from *Vesuvius* and *Trial*. When the falling tide forced *Hydra* to move into deeper water, Laforey ordered them away and then sent *Trial* to investigate the state of *Confiante*. The cutter reported that her crew had hauled her further inshore, but that her guns were still in action and troops had arrived to counter any threat of boarding from British boats. The next morning

Laforey sent *Hydra*'s boats, covered by *Trial*, to set fire to *Confiante*, whose crew had by this time been withdrawn ashore. While the British were engaged in this task, *Vésuve* managed to escape into the River Dive, where she was protected by the troops and guns of the invasion flotilla that *Hydra* and *Diamond* had encountered previously, and eventually returned with them to Le Havre.

The war with France ended in March 1802 but was renewed in May 1803, with Spain re-entering the war on the French side in December 1804. On 11 January 1805 a French squadron under Rear-Admiral the Comte de Missiessy escaped from Rochefort and sailed for the West Indies with orders to wait there for Vice-Admiral Pierre Villeneuve's Franco-Spanish Combined Fleet. Rear-Admiral the Honourable (later Admiral Sir) Alexander Cochrane, thereupon abandoned his blockade of Ferrol and set off in pursuit of Missiessy, with the blockade of Ferrol being passed to Vice-Admiral Sir Robert Calder. Laforey, in the 3rd-rate *Spartiate* (74), formed part of Cochrane's squadron in the West Indies, where Cochrane became C-in-C, Leeward Islands, and hunted for Missiessy, who had reached Martinique on 20 February 1805. Six weeks later Missiessy received orders from Napoleon, informing him that Villeneuve had been forced back by bad weather and that Missiessy was to return to France at once. Fresh orders saying that Villeneuve was, after all, on his way to the West Indies and that the recall was countermanded, did not reach Missiessy in time, and he re-entered Rochefort a week after Villeneuve had finally arrived at Martinique on 14 May 1805. Vice-Admiral Viscount Nelson and the Mediterranean fleet, pursuing Villeneuve, joined Cochrane at Barbados on 4 June 1805. Villeneuve, learning of his arrival, sailed for Europe on 10 June, followed by Nelson's fleet, now including *Spartiate*, five days later.

After refitting in England, Laforey and *Spartiate* formed part of the squadron with which on 30 August 1805 Calder reinforced Vice-Admiral Cuthbert Collingwood **[8]** blockading Villeneuve in Cadiz. Nelson arrived to take over from Collingwood on 28 September 1805 and withdrew his fleet beyond the horizon to tempt Villeneuve out. At **Trafalgar (21**

October 1805) *Spartiate* (said to have been built of stolen timber, as she was difficult to handle and allegedly sailed faster by night than by day) was one of the two slow sailers bringing up the rear of the weather column led by Nelson in the 1st-rate *Victory* (104). Together with Captain Mansfield **[24]** in the 3rd-rate *Minotaur* (74), Laforey came into action late in the day, when they met four French ships of Rear-Admiral Dumanoir's van division that had belatedly turned back to join the battle.

As *Spartiate* was faster than *Minotaur*, Laforey asked Mansfield, who was senior to him in the Navy List, for permission to overtake, so as to prevent Dumanoir from cutting these two ships off from the rest of the British fleet. Mansfield agreed and *Spartiate*, sailing on an easterly course as the French came down from the north, went ahead to pass immediately in front of Dumanoir's flagship *Formidable* (80), firing a broadside into her bows at close range as she did so. Then, with Mansfield following, Laforey turned to port and hove to, firing further broadsides into each French ship in succession as they passed. *Formidable*, holed at the waterline as she heeled over, began to take in water at a dangerous rate and, with her rigging so badly damaged that she could no longer turn into the wind, continued on a south-westerly course and so out of the battle, followed by her three consorts.

Spartiate and *Minotaur* then went alongside the Spanish *Neptuno* (80) which, though part of Dumanoir's division, had become separated from it in an attempt to go to the aid of the Spanish flagship *Santisima Trinidad* (130). After an hour's close combat, with the battle almost over, *Neptuno* struck her flag to *Minotaur* at about 5.15 p.m. *Spartiate* lost three men killed and two midshipmen, a boatswain and seventeen others wounded. She suffered considerable damage to her masts, yards and rigging and had her fore topsail yard shot away, but was in a better state than ships that had been more heavily engaged and, after the battle, was able to tow the 3rd-rate *Tonnant* (80) to Gibraltar. They were then sent home, where Laforey carried the standard in the first barge in Nelson's funeral procession from Greenwich to London.

Laforey remained in command of *Spartiate* in which, during 1807–08, he served under Rear-Admiral Sir Richard Strachan blockading Vice-Admiral Allemand and five French ships of the line in Rochefort. In January 1809, when Strachan left his station in order to revictual and replenish his ships, Allemand escaped and made for the Mediterranean where, early in March 1809, he joined the French Toulon squadron. Strachan, with Laforey and *Spartiate* in company, pursued him into the Mediterranean and joined the fleet there under Collingwood. The French, however, avoided contact and, after two months at sea, returned to Toulon on 10 April 1809. Laforey remained in the Mediterranean with *Spartiate* and in June 1809 covered the landing of British troops from Sicily to recover the Neapolitan islands of Ischia and Procida for the Bourbon King Ferdinand IV of the Two Sicilies, a British ally whom the French had driven from the mainland part of his kingdom.

Laforey was promoted to rear-admiral on 31 July 1810 and returned to the Caribbean as C-in-C, Leeward Islands, from 1811 to 1814. The last of the French West Indian colonies had surrendered to the British during the winter of 1810, so that the wealth of the sugar islands now flowed directly to English merchants and the British exchequer without the Navy taking any of it as prize money from captured French ships. Only the policing of the African slave trade, abolished for British-registered ships in 1807, offered a modest source of reward, in the form of head-money for African slaves intercepted and liberated on passage to America. The American War of 1812 made United States vessels liable to capture by British cruisers and offered the prospect of prize money, but at the same time, Laforey had to protect British merchantmen in the West Indies against numerous Yankee privateers. After the end of the American War he was awarded the KCB in 1815. In the same year, Napoleon was exiled to St Helena and the long war with France came to an end. Laforey became a vice-admiral on 12 August 1819 and an admiral on 22 July 1830 and died, unmarried, at Brighton, Sussex, on 17 June 1837, when his baronetcy became extinct.

LAPENOTIERE, Captain JOHN RICHARDS (1780–1834) **[23]**
John Lapenotiere, descended from a Huguenot officer who

served in the army of William of Orange (William III) and settled in England after the Glorious Revolution of 1688, was born on 22 June 1770 at Ilfracombe, Devon. His father, Lieutenant Frederick Lapenotiere, had joined the Navy under the patronage of the Earl of Winchilsea, First Lord of the Admiralty from 1742 to 1744. Lapenotiere was distantly related to the Countess of Winchilsea, but the earl's premature death left him without a patron and his career languished. John Lapenotiere nominally entered the Navy in 1780, during the American War of Independence, was held on the books of a series of warships, but his first long period at sea was between 1785 and 1788 when, through his great-uncle, Samuel Salt, an influential lawyer, member of parliament and deputy governor of the South Sea Company, he became a volunteer in the hired merchantman *King George* under Lieutenant Nathaniel Portlock. In an expedition financed by the King George's Sound Company, they circumnavigated the globe, exploring the waters around the Sandwich Islands and then carrying sea-otter pelts and other furs from the north-western coast of America to China. After returning to England, Lapenotiere was appointed midshipman in 1788 and served on the home station first in the brig *Scout* (14) and then the 3rd-rate *Magnificent* (74). In 1791, once more under Portlock he sailed for the South Pacific in the transport *Assistance*, held on the books as an able seaman. In company with the sloop *Providence* (12) in which Lieutenant William Bligh was making his second attempt to collect breadfruit plants, he circumnavigated the world a second time before returning home in 1793 after the outbreak of war with Revolutionary France. He was then appointed master's mate in the 5th-rate frigate *Santa Margarita* under Captain Eliab Harvey **[19]** in Vice-Admiral Sir John Jervis's fleet in the West Indies. During 1794, as a midshipman in Jervis's flagship, the 2nd-rate *Boyne* (98), he served at **Martinique (February–March 1794)**, where he took part in the capture of the French frigate *Bienvenue* in Fort Royal Bay, **St Lucia (1–4 April 1794)** and **Guadeloupe (April–May 1794)**. Lapenotiere was promoted to lieutenant in April 1794 (confirmed on 29 August 1794) and given command of the schooner *Berbice* (8). During 1795 he served as first lieutenant of the 6th-rate frigate *Resource* (28). From 1797 to 1798 he was in the 3rd-rate *Ganges* (74), deployed to the North Sea, and from 1798 to 1799 in the 5th-rate frigate *Inconstant* (36), deployed to the Channel. In 1800 he was given command of the hired cutter *Joseph* (8), in which he was involved in several actions first while supporting the blockade of Brest and then on trade protection duties in the Mediterranean, and was officially commended. After peace with France was signed in March 1802, *Joseph* was paid off but on 24 May 1802 Lapenotiere was given command of the schooner *Pickle* (10), in which he was serving on the home station when hostilities with France were renewed in May 1803. In October 1803 he had to deal with a suspected mutiny, led by the boatswain's mate, who was acquitted of this charge but flogged for insolence and desertion. Off Ferrol in March 1804 a group of malcontents swore an oath (on *The Rights of Ireland*) to desert to the French but once more discipline was preserved, though Lapenotiere subsequently submitted an unsuccessful request to the Admiralty for a file of marines in lieu of seven seamen. Despite her troubles, *Pickle* remained in commission and played a valuable part in rescuing the crew of the 3rd-rate *Magnificent* (74), wrecked off Brest on 25 March 1804.

Spain entered the war on the French side in December 1804, and *Pickle* was sent to the West Indies. On 10 March 1805 Lapenotiere was ordered to sail from Jamaica as convoy escort to the Bahamas and thence to Plymouth via Bermuda 'without a moment's loss of time'. From Plymouth the ship was ordered to Gibraltar and, on 19 July 1805, on passage to her new station, was attacked by Spanish gunboats while becalmed in the Straits. The gunboats, propelled by oars, used their favourite tactic of lying off the schooner's stern where she could not bring a gun to bear, but when the wind returned Lapenotiere was able to draw away and head for Tangier. The wind failed again and the gunboats caught up with *Pickle*, which sailed badly in light airs, but a steady breeze then sprang up and allowed Lapenotiere to escape out of range.

After returning to Plymouth in August 1805, *Pickle* sailed again on 21 September carrying men for the ships gathered outside Cadiz in the blockade of Vice-Admiral Pierre Villeneuve's Franco-Spanish Combined Fleet. There Lapenotiere made one of his few prizes, a Portuguese merchantman loaded with bullocks from Tangiers for Cadiz, where provisions were running low and fresh meat brought a good price. On 19 October 1805, when Villeneuve began to put to sea, *Pickle* was close inshore with the 36-gun frigates *Euryalus* and *Sirius* and the brig-sloop *Weazle* (18). Captain Blackwood [3] of *Euryalus* hailed *Weazle* and *Pickle* and ordered them to sail south to alert the British ships revictualling at Gibraltar and Tetuan, and any others they might meet en route, while *Euryalus* passed the information along a chain of ships to Vice-Admiral Viscount Nelson in the main fleet. His final messages to them, by flag as they parted company, were the conventional one 'Make all sail possible with safety to the masts', followed, lest there be any doubt as to the urgency of their mission, by 'Let one reef out of your topsails'.

Pickle subsequently joined the main fleet and was at **Trafalgar (21 October 1805)** stationed with the frigates and the cutter *Entreprenante* on the port or windward side of the weather column, led by Nelson in the 1st-rate *Victory*. In the closing stages of the battle, she went with others to rescue the crew of the burning French *Achille* (74), which eventually blew up when the flames reached her magazine. One hundred and sixty survivors (outnumbering her own crew by four to one) were taken on board *Pickle*. Among these was a young Frenchwoman who had stowed away in *Achille* to be near her husband, a main-topman, and had been driven overboard by the flames. Her British captors gallantly provided her with a variety of materials from which she was able to replace her lost clothes and she was eventually reunited with her husband after reaching Gibraltar.

The next morning, 22 October 1805, Vice-Admiral Collingwood [8], who succeeded to the command on Nelson's death, sent *Pickle* and *Entreprenante* to round up as many of his scattered fleet as were within sight. On 26 October he gave Lapenotiere his dispatches and ordered him to take them home. This was normally regarded as a particular mark of distinction, but in this case it may simply have been that Collingwood, in his practical way, wanted to send a fast message, and was unwilling to weaken his continuing blockade by detaching any unit more powerful than a schooner. Lapenotiere sent his prisoners across to the 3rd-rate *Revenge* (74) and sailed at noon the same day. On 28 October *Pickle* was pursued and overtaken by an unidentified vessel that, when challenged, proved to be the new British sloop *Nautilus* (18) under Captain John Sykes. After boarding *Pickle* and hearing her news, Sykes decided to inform the British Embassy in Lisbon, where he arrived early the next day. From there he sailed at once for England with dispatches from the ambassador and sighted *Pickle* again on 30 October.

Early on 31 October both ships encountered a strong gale off Finisterre, and *Pickle* sustained damage to her spars and rigging. The next day, with water gaining on the pumps, Lapenotiere jettisoned four of his guns and this, together with the weather easing, allowed the schooner to make its way safely into the Channel. After being delayed by calms on 2 November, when Lapenotiere's exhausted men used sweeps to keep their vessel moving, they met the 3rd-rate *Superb* (74), flagship of Sir John Duckworth, and passed on their news. *Pickle* reached Falmouth on the morning of 3 November 1805. Lapenotiere went ashore by boat and left the town at noon. After travelling 265 miles by post-chaise with twenty-one stops to change horses, he arrived at the Admiralty in Whitehall thirty-seven hours later, at 1 a.m. on 5 November 1805. Sykes, having followed him across southern England, arrived about an hour later. Lord Barham, First Lord of the Admiralty, was awoken to read the dispatches and learn of Nelson's victory and death. The Prime Minister, William Pitt the Younger, was given the news two hours later and George III, at Windsor, later the same day. London newspapers were able to print Collingwood's dispatches on 7 November 1805.

In the subsequent distribution of honours and awards, Lapenotiere was promoted to commander with effect from 6 November 1805 and (after petitioning for it three times) awarded the £500 gratuity customarily given to officers delivering important dispatches. In his second petition he stated that he had been twenty-seven years in the service, had no other income but his pay, and was a family man (earlier in the year he had married Mary Ann, the daughter of the late Lieutenant John Graves, Royal Navy). He was subsequently appointed to the new brig-sloop *Orestes* (16) in which he formed part of the British fleet operating off **Copenhagen (16 August–7 September 1807)**. *Orestes* was not present at the bombardment of the city, but remained in the Baltic on trade protection duties after the armistice with Denmark. Lapenotiere was badly injured when one of his after-guns was fired to warn away a merchantman and a trail of powder exploded the charges in the nearby ready-use locker. He suffered burns around his head and neck and thought he might lose the sight of an eye where he had been hit by a flying plank. He recovered well enough to be redeployed with *Orestes* to the Channel where, during the following three years, he took a number of prizes, including the privateers *Concepcion* (12), *Dorade* (10) and *Loup Garou* (16) and recaptured an American merchantman carrying timber into Plymouth. His last combat, the taking of *Loup Garou*, was on 27 October 1810. He was at last promoted to post captain on 1 August 1811 but never given another ship. He remained ashore and survived the Napoleonic Wars to die in 1834 at Fanny Vale, near Liskeard, Cornwall. With his wife he had a family of seven children of whom one, John Good Lapenotiere, became a lieutenant in the Navy. His part in the Trafalgar story is not forgotten by the modern Navy in which, when the officers hold their Trafalgar Night dinners, the ratings celebrate with Pickle Night.

MANSFIELD, Captain CHARLES JOHN MOORE, (c.1757–1813) [24]

Charles Mansfield joined the Navy at an early age and became a lieutenant on 25 November 1778, during the American War of Independence. He was promoted to commander on 19 July 1793, some five months after the outbreak of the French Revolutionary War, and became a post captain on 4 October 1794. He was appointed to the 5th-rate frigate *Andromache* (32), deployed to the Mediterranean where on 31 January 1797 he was in a frigate squadron that sighted and gave chase to an unidentified vessel. *Andromache* outpaced the rest of the squadron and, far ahead of her consorts, came up with the strange ship and challenged her. When Mansfield's hail was answered in Spanish, he assumed that he was dealing with a ship belonging to Spain, which had entered the war on the French side in the previous December. He opened fire and after an engagement lasting over forty minutes, during which the enemy made an unsuccessful attempted to carry *Andromache* by boarding, found that he had captured a 24-gun corsair operating from the North African pirate stronghold of Algiers. Each of the combatants had failed to recognize the other's colours, and the corsairs thought they had been challenged by a frigate of the Portuguese Navy. The mistake cost them sixty-six killed and fifty wounded, mostly in the unsuccessful attempt to board *Andromache*, whose own casualties amounted to three killed and six wounded.

The war ended in March 1801, but hostilities with France were renewed on 18 May 1803. Mansfield, serving in the Channel in command of the 3rd-rate *Minotaur* (74) was in action two days later, on 20 May 1803, when in company with the 3rd-rate *Thunderer* (74) and armed ship *Albion* (22), he captured the French frigate *Franchise* (40). Mansfield remained in *Minotaur* after Spain joined the war on the French side in December 1804. In March 1805 *Minotaur* became part of a flying squadron under Vice-Admiral Cuthbert Collingwood [8], subsequently deployed to the south-western coasts of Spain in the hunt for Vice-Admiral Pierre Villeneuve and his Franco-Spanish Combined Fleet. After being pursued to the West Indies and back by Vice-Admiral Viscount Nelson and the Mediterranean fleet, Villeneuve entered Cadiz on 20 August 1805, brushing away the ships with which Collingwood had been watching that port. *Minotaur* was one of four ships of the line under Rear-Admiral Sir Richard Bickerton that Collingwood had detached to blockade Cartagena. They rejoined Collingwood off Cadiz on 22 August and large-scale reinforcements under Vice-Admiral Sir Robert Calder arrived eight days later. By 8

September, when Lieutenant Nathaniel Fish was dismissed from *Minotaur* and placed at the bottom of the lieutenants' list for insolence to Mansfield, some twenty captains were available to make up the court martial.

At **Trafalgar (21 October 1805)** *Minotaur* was behind the 3rd-rate *Spartiate* (74) under Captain Laforey **[22]**, at the rear of the weather column led by Nelson in the 1st-rate *Victory*. Mansfield addressed his men, telling them to keep silent, pay attention to their officers and not to waste ammunition, and promising he would stay with any enemy ship he got alongside until she struck, or one or other of them sank. *Minotaur* and *Spartiate*, both ships noted as slow sailers, came into action late in the day, when they met four French ships of Rear-Admiral Dumanoir's van division which had belatedly turned back to join the battle. As *Spartiate* was faster than *Minotaur*, Laforey asked Mansfield, who was senior to him in the Navy List, for permission to overtake so as to prevent Dumanoir getting between them and the rest of the British fleet. Mansfield agreed and allowed *Spartiate*, sailing on an easterly course as the French came down from the north, to go ahead and pass immediately in front of Dumanoir's flagship *Formidable* (80). Then, following *Spartiate*, he turned to port and hove to, firing broadsides into each French ship in succession as they passed. *Formidable*, holed on the waterline, began to take in water at a dangerous rate and, with her rigging so badly damaged that she could not turn into the wind, continued on a south-westerly course and so out of the battle, followed by her three consorts. *Minotaur* and *Spartiate* then went alongside the Spanish *Neptuno* (80) which, though part of Dumanoir's division, had become separated from it while attempting to go to the aid of the Spanish flagship *Santisima Trinidad* (130). After an hour's close combat and with the battle almost over, *Neptuno* struck her flag to *Minotaur* at about 5.15 p.m. *Minotaur* suffered minor damage to her spars, and lost three men killed with a midshipman, a boatswain and twenty others wounded. Mansfield's light casualties enabled him to find an exceptionally large prize crew, under a second lieutenant of Royal Marines, for the disabled *Neptuno*, but in the worsening weather she was recaptured, along with the Spanish *Santa Ana* (112) by a sortie from Cadiz on 23 October.

Mansfield continued in *Minotaur* and served with her in Admiral Lord Gambier's fleet in the expedition against **Copenhagen (16 August -7 September 1807)** where *Minotaur* was flagship of Gambier's third-in-command, Rear-Admiral William Essington. This was Mansfield's last major operation. He subsequently left *Minotaur* and went ashore, where he died, with the war still in progress, in May 1813.

MOORSOM, Admiral Sir ROBERT, KCB (1760–1835) **[25]**
Robert Moorsom, the second son of a country gentleman, Richard Moorsom of Airy Hill near Whitby, North Yorkshire, was born in June 1760. In 1774 he became a midshipman in the 3rd-rate *Ardent* (64) under Captain the Honourable Constantine Phipps (later Admiral Lord Mulgrave) before following him to the 3rd-rate *Courageux* (74). During the American War of Independence he served in *Courageux* at the battle of Ushant (27 July 1778), the first major fleet action fought after the entry of France into the war. The Spanish also entered the war and laid siege to Gibraltar which was first relieved by Admiral Sir George Rodney after **The Moonlight Battle, Cape St Vincent (16 January 1780)**. Moorsom served in the second relief, carried out in April 1781 by the Channel fleet under Vice-Admiral George Darby, and took part in the action off **Ushant (12 December 1781)** in which Rear-Admiral Richard Kempenfelt captured a large French convoy carrying stores and reinforcements to the West Indies. Moorsom then served in the 5th-rate frigate *Success* (32) in a successful action off Cape Spartel (16 March 1782), while escorting a supply ship to the Gibraltar garrison, and was with Lord Howe's fleet in the third and final relief of Gibraltar in October 1782. Moorsom was promoted to lieutenant on 5 January 1784, a year after the end of the war, and became a post captain on 22 November 1790.

The French Revolutionary War began in February 1792 and during the next ten years Moorsom commanded at various periods the elderly 5th-rate frigate *Niger* (32), the much newer 5th-rate frigate *Astraea* (32) and a converted East Indiaman, the 4th-rate *Hindostan* (54). The war with France ended in March 1802 but when it was renewed in May 1803, Moorsom was appointed to the 3rd-rate *Majestic* (74), in which he served during 1803 and 1804. Spain entered the war on the French side in December 1804 and Moorsom was given command of the newly-completed 3rd-rate *Revenge* (74) in April 1805. After fitting out, she was deployed to the Channel and formed part of the squadron under Vice-Admiral Sir Robert Calder that on 30 August 1805 joined the blockade of Villeneuve's Franco-Spanish Combined Fleet in Cadiz. When Villeneuve came out and gave battle to Vice-Admiral Viscount Nelson's fleet at **Trafalgar (21 October 1805)** *Revenge* was the eighth ship in the British lee column led by Vice-Admiral Collingwood **[8]**.

Moorsom steered to break through the enemy line between the Spanish *San Ildefonso* (74), sixth ship from the enemy rear, and the French *Achille* (74) immediately astern of her. Like the other leading ships in Collingwood's column, *Revenge* began to suffer from enemy fire in the slow approach to the enemy line, and some of her men murmured in favour of returning it. Moorsom told them that they would need all their shot when they came to close quarters and, in the meanwhile, to pay no attention to the enemy's firing. The signal for them to begin, he said, would be when he fired a carronade (a heavy close-action gun) from the quarterdeck, and he knew they would then 'do their duty like Englishmen'. He opened fire a few minutes later, with *Revenge* firing two broadsides into a French opponent with which she became briefly entangled when breaking the enemy line. *San Ildefonso* and *Achille* then both attempted to board her, as did the Spanish flagship *Principe de Asturias* (112). Engaged by a 74-gun ship on each side and a three-decker on her lee quarter, *Revenge* suffered heavy damage in a fight lasting for about an hour before the 2nd-rate *Dreadnought* (98) and 3rd-rate *Thunderer* (74) came to her aid. Her three topsail yards were carried away by collision and her bowsprit, three lower masts, main topmast and gaff were all damaged, with the braces shot away so that it was impossible to manoeuvre the ship. Further damage was sustained by the hull, with nine hits along the waterline as the ship heeled over, and three gun carriages destroyed.

Her casualties amounted to two midshipmen (one of them a teenage sadist whom no one on board mourned) and twenty-six men killed, with four officers and forty-seven men wounded. Moorsom himself was among the wounded, but remained in command while his ship made repairs at Gibraltar after the battle. After he sailed her home to Portsmouth, he carried the great banner in Nelson's funeral procession in London.

In 1807 Moorsom was appointed private secretary to Lord Mulgrave (a younger brother of his old captain), First Lord of the Admiralty in the new Tory government that came into office at the end of March that year. Mulgrave remained at the Admiralty until April 1810 when he became Master General of the Ordnance. Moorsom, who was made a colonel of Royal Marines on 28 April 1808, served as a lord commissioner of the Admiralty from 30 March 1809 to 3 July 1810 and was promoted to rear-admiral on 31 July 1810. He left the Admiralty in 1810 on appointment as Surveyor-General of the Ordnance under Mulgrave. On 15 January 1812 he was elected Member of Parliament for the Admiralty-controlled borough of Queenborough, Isle of Sheppey, and retained this seat until 1820. Moorsom was promoted to vice-admiral on 4 June 1814 and was awarded the KCB in 1815.

Sir Robert Moorsom was C-in-C, Chatham, from 1824 to 1827 and was promoted to admiral on 22 July 1830. He died in 1835 at Cosgrove Priory, near Milton Keynes. He was married to Eleanor, daughter of Thomas Scarth, Esquire, of Stakesby, near Whitby, Moorsom's native town. Of their sons, one, Commander Robert Moorsom, died in 1826 while in command of the brig-sloop *Jasper* (10), and another, Constantine Richard Moorsom, became a vice-admiral.

MORRIS, Vice-Admiral Sir JAMES NICOLL, KCB (c.1763–1830) [26]
James Morris was born in about 1763, the son of Captain John Morris who was later mortally wounded commanding the 4th-rate *Bristol* in the unsuccessful British attack on Charleston, South Carolina (28 June 1776) during the American War of Independence. James Morris had entered

the Navy under his father's command, but was not in *Bristol* at Charleston. He was appointed a midshipman in the 3rd-rate *Prince of Wales* (74), flagship of the then C-in-C in the West Indies, Rear-Admiral the Honourable Samuel Barrington, and served with him at St Lucia (December 1778) and **Granada (6 July 1779)**. He was promoted to lieutenant on 14 April 1780 and was in the 2nd-rate *Namur* (90) in **The Battle of the Saintes (12 April 1782)**, the last major naval action in the Caribbean during this war. Morris again served under Barrington in 1790, in the fleet mobilized in the Channel when there was a threat of war with Spain over the disputed possession of Nootka Sound (Vancouver Island). With Barrington's patronage, he was promoted to commander on 21 September 1790 and in the following year was appointed to the fireship *Pluto* (14), deployed to Newfoundland.

On the outbreak of the French Revolutionary War in February 1792, Morris was still in *Pluto* on the North American station, where he made his first prize, the French sloop *Lutine*, on 23 July 1793. He was promoted to post captain on 7 October 1793 and appointed to the 5th-rate frigate *Boston* (32), whose previous captain had been killed in a single-ship action with the French frigate *Embuscade* off Long Island, New York. Morris returned home with *Boston*, which he commanded during the next four years, serving in the Channel, the Bay of Biscay and, after Spain became a French ally in October 1796, the Spanish coast. In 1797, having captured several enemy privateers and merchantmen, he moved to the 5th-rate frigate *Lively* (32) in which he served until she was wrecked at Rota Point, near Cadiz, on 21 April 1798. He succeeded in saving his entire crew and, in 1799, was given a new command, the 5th-rate frigate *Phaeton* (38).

In the autumn of 1799 *Phaeton* joined the Mediterranean fleet and was deployed to Genoa as part of a squadron under Lord Keith. The republic of Genoa had been under French control since 1797, but in the spring of 1800 a major Austrian offensive forced the French troops to retire into the capital city, harassed by *Phaeton*'s guns as they retreated along the coast at Loano and Alassio. Besieged by the Austrians and blockaded by Keith's warships, Genoa was starved into surrender on 6 June 1800 and most of its garrison was given passage home to Antibes by the British Navy. Bonaparte's brilliant counter-offensive and his decisive defeat of the Austrians at Marengo (14 June 1800) was followed by the French recapture of Genoa and the withdrawal of the British fleet from north Italian waters. *Phaeton* was redeployed to the coast of Spain where, on 28 October 1800, her boats cut out a heavily-armed polacca from under a 5-gun shore battery at Malaga. Morris remained on this station until returning with *Phaeton* to England after an armistice on 1 October 1801.

With peace confirmed by the Treaty of Amiens in March 1802, Morris went ashore and in October 1802 married Margaretta Somers Cocks, the daughter of a wealthy banker. Her younger sister, Maria, later married Morris's old friend William Hargood [18]. War was renewed with France in May 1803 and with Spain in December 1804. Morris returned to sea in command of the 4th-rate *Leopard* (50) from which he soon moved to the new 3rd-rate *Colossus* (74) and joined the blockade of Brest. On 23 May 1805 *Colossus* was detached as part of a flying squadron formed under the command of Vice-Admiral Cuthbert Collingwood [8] and was present with him at Cadiz with two other ships of the line when Vice-Admiral Pierre Villeneuve and his Franco-Spanish Combined Fleet arrived there on 20 August 1805. She remained off Cadiz as part of the rapidly reinforced British blockade and, when Villeneuve began to put to sea early on 19 October 1805, was between the 3rd-rates *Defence* and *Mars* in the chain of ships that passed the news to Vice-Admiral Viscount Nelson and the main fleet. During the rest of 19 October, while Nelson headed south-eastwards with the aim of preventing Villeneuve from reaching the Mediterranean, *Colossus* was stationed with *Defence* and *Mars* on the port side of the fleet, to maintain contact with Nelson's scouting frigates.

At **Trafalgar (21 October 1805)** *Colossus* was seventh in the British lee column led by Collingwood. This placed her in one of the most fiercely-contested parts of the battle during which, in the course of two hours' fighting, she first ran into the Spanish *Argonauta* (80) and then successively closed with and captured two 74-gun opponents, the French *Swiftsure* and the Spanish *Bahama*. *Colossus* herself sustained heavy damage, with her foremast shot through in several places and her mainmast so weakened that, after the battle, it had to be cut away. Every part of her hull had been hit, with the loss of various boats and anchors, several guns put out of action, and four lower deck gun-ports lost in the collision with *Argonauta*. Her casualty list was the highest in the British fleet. Her master was killed, as were thirty-eight ratings. The wounded amounted to four of her eight lieutenants, one of whom subsequently died of wounds, one of her three officers of Royal Marines, one of the three master's mates, five of her fourteen midshipmen, a volunteer 1st Class and the boatswain, together with 146 ratings and Morris himself. Badly wounded in the thigh, he remained on deck with the aid of a tourniquet until the close of the engagement, when he fainted from loss of blood and was taken below. Earlier in the battle, *Colossus'* chicken coop was smashed and a cockerel escaped and perched on Morris's shoulder, where it crowed loudly to the delight of his crew, who cheered it while they went on with the fight. Afterwards, *Colossus* was towed to Gibraltar by the 3rd-rate *Agamemnon*.

Morris recovered from his wound and served in *Colossus* on the home station and in the Mediterranean until 1810, when he transferred to the 2nd-rate *Formidable* (90). He was made a colonel of Royal Marines on 31 July 1810 and promoted to rear-admiral on 1 August 1811. He then remained ashore until the next year, when he was appointed third in command of the British fleet in the Baltic at the request of the commander there, Vice-Admiral Sir James Saumarez. Sweden, under pressure from Napoleon, had declared war on the United Kingdom in November 1810 but Saumarez appreciated that the Swedes were reluctant opponents and respected their shipping. In April 1812 Sweden agreed with Russia that each would aid the other if attacked. When Napoleon invaded Russia in the following June, the Swedes opened their ports to British trade. In March 1813, after Napoleon's retreat from Moscow and with the Cossacks at the gates of Berlin, Sweden formally signed an alliance with the British and agreed to send an army, escorted by Saumarez's fleet, to North Germany. Napoleon was forced to abdicate in April 1814 and Morris was awarded the KCB on 2 January 1815. Sir James Morris was promoted to vice-admiral on 12 August 1819 and died at his house in Great Marlow, Buckinghamshire, on 15 April 1830.

PELLEW, Admiral Sir ISRAEL, KCB (1758–1832) **[27]**

Israel Pellew was born in 1758, the third son of Samuel Humphrey Pellew, captain of a Channel packet based at Dover, and his wife Constance. In 1771 he entered the Navy following his elder brother Edward, who would later become a famous frigate captain, and end his career as 1st Viscount Exmouth, C-in-C in the Mediterranean. Israel Pellew served in the newly-built sloop *Falcon* (14) in the West Indies until 1774, when he was appointed to a guard-ship, the 3rd-rate *Albion* (74). In 1775 he joined the 5th-rate frigate *Flora* (32), in which he served during the American War of Independence that began the following year. On 7 August 1778 *Flora* was scuttled in the harbour of Newport, Rhode Island, to prevent her being captured by the French and American forces besieging the town, but Newport was relieved by Lord Howe later in the month and Pellew remained available for duty. He passed his examination for promotion to lieutenant on 4 February 1779 and was promoted on 1 April 1779, appointed to the new brig-sloop *Drake* (14) and deployed to the West Indies.

After serving in the 5th-rate frigate *Apollo* (32) during 1781, Pellew was, in 1782, given command of the cutter *Resolution* (14) in the North Sea where, on 20 January 1783, he captured a Dutch privateer. The Treaty of Versailles, ending the war, was signed on the same day so that, with the consequent reduction in the number of ships in commission, the promotion that Pellew might otherwise have expected was not forthcoming. Nevertheless, he at least remained in command of *Resolution*, deployed to the coast of Ireland, until 1787. He was then appointed to the 4th-rate *Salisbury* (50), in which he served on the Newfoundland station until his promotion to commander on 22 November 1790. In 1792 he married Mary, daughter of George Gilmore, Esquire.

War with Revolutionary France began on 1 February 1793 and Pellew, unable to obtain a ship of his own, sailed as a volunteer under his brother, Captain Edward Pellew, in the 5th-rate frigate *Nymphe* (32). On 19 June 1793 they encountered the French frigate *Cleopatre* (40), off Prawle Point, the southernmost tip of Devon. Captain Pellew, after doffing his hat to his French opposite number, replaced it on his head as the pre-arranged signal for his guns to open fire. Commander Pellew sited one of the guns and with his first shot killed *Cleopatre*'s steersman. His following rounds killed or wounded the three others who in succession took the wheel, and then smashed the wheel itself and brought down *Cleopatre*'s mizen mast. The French frigate, now unmanageable, collided with *Nymphe* but continued to be hit by Captain Pellew's broadsides until a boarding party hauled down her flag. With British casualties of fifty-two against *Cleopatre*'s sixty, including her captain mortally wounded, the two ships entered Portsmouth in triumph two days later to the cheers of the fleet. In London, George III rose from his seat at the opera to announce the victory. Edward Pellew was knighted and Isaac Pellew was promoted to post captain on 25 June 1793. Both received their due share of prize money and *Cleopatre*, renamed *Oiseau*, was taken into the British fleet.

Pellew's first command in his new rank was the 6th-rate frigate *Squirrel* (24) in which he served in the North Sea. In 1795 he was given command of the 5th-rate frigate *Amphion* (32), deployed successively to Newfoundland and the North Sea, from where in September 1796 he was ordered to join his brother's frigate squadron in the Channel. On 22 September 1796, after getting ready for sea, the ship was at Hamoaze, Plymouth, when she suddenly blew up. About 300 people perished with her, among them a large number of local men, women and children who had come to see off friends and relatives among her crew. The few survivors included Pellew and his first lieutenant who, dining aft in his cabin, were thrown against the side of the ship by the explosion, but, badly bruised, managed to get out of a stern window onto a hulk moored alongside. The cause of the disaster was never established, though it was said that the ship's gunner, in the process of fraudulently selling some of her gunpowder, had left a trail of powder from the forward magazine where the explosion occurred.

Pellew returned to sea in the spring of 1797, appointed to the 5th-rate frigate *Greyhound* (32). At the end of April 1797, when the fleet mutinied at Spithead, he was one of the captains put ashore by their own men with allegations of brutality. After the mutiny, he did not return to *Greyhound* and was instead appointed to the 5th-rate frigate *Cleopatra* (32) in which he served in the West Indies and North America station until the war was formally ended in March 1802. Hostilities with France were renewed in May 1803 and eleven months later Pellew was appointed to the 3rd-rate *Conqueror* (74), a new ship less than a year into her first commission. Spain entered the war as an ally of France in December 1804 and *Conqueror* was deployed to the Mediterranean Fleet under Vice-Admiral Viscount Nelson. She sailed with Nelson in the pursuit of Vice-Admiral Pierre Villeneuve and his Franco-Spanish Combined Fleet to the West Indies and back during the summer of 1805 and was then deployed to the Channel. When Villeneuve's Combined Fleet was located in Cadiz, she formed part of the squadron under Vice-Admiral Sir Robert Calder that arrived to reinforce the blockade there on 30 August 1805.

After Villeneuve put to sea, *Conqueror* was at **Trafalgar (21 October 1805)** as the fifth ship in the weather column led by Nelson in the 1st-rate *Victory*. After passing through the enemy line, Pellew positioned *Conqueror* on the lee quarter of Villeneuve's command ship *Bucentaure* (80) and, with the 3rd-rate *Leviathan* (74) on *Bucentaure*'s lee bow, maintained a rapid fire to which the French ship was unable to make any effective reply. At about 1.40 p.m. *Conqueror*'s gunfire brought down *Bucentaure*'s main and mizen masts together. Out of control, *Bucentaure* then collided with the Spanish flagship *Santisima Trinidad* (130) directly ahead of her and lost her foremast. With *Bucentaure* thus completely dismasted, her guns masked by fallen wreckage, and over 400 of her officers and men dead or wounded, Villeneuve tried to move to another ship, but with all the boats lost and no other French ship within hail, was left with no choice but to surrender.

Pellew sent a boat over with a prize crew of five men under his senior officer of Royal Marines, Captain Atcherley, to whom Villeneuve offered his sword, asking the name of the officer to whom he was surrendering. The marine replied, formally, 'To Captain Pellew of the *Conquerer*'. Villeneuve responded that he was content to have surrendered to Sir Edward Pellew, whose exploits had made him an object of respect among the French Navy. When Atcherley answered, 'It is his brother, sir', the Admiral said, 'His brother? Are there two of them? *Helas*'. Thinking that it would be more correct for so senior an officer to surrender directly to Pellew, and after locking *Bucentaure*'s magazine and pocketing the key, Atcherley put Villeneuve and four other senior officers in his boat and set out to return to *Conqueror*. Pellew, however, had gone on to join *Leviathan* and the 2nd-rate *Neptune* (98) in attacking *Santisima Trinidad*, so that the boat could not find *Conqueror* in the smoke and eventually went alongside the 3rd-rate *Mars* (74). Her commanding officer, Captain Duff [12] had fallen earlier in the battle, so it was her first lieutenant who finally accepted the French officers' swords and subsequently gave them to Vice-Admiral Collingwood [8], to whom command of the fleet passed on Nelson's death. Pellew considered that, as the captain of the ship to which Villeneuve had surrendered, they should have been given to him, and thought Collingwood did wrong to keep them in his own possession, though he never actually claimed them from him.

Leaving *Santisima Trinidad*, Pellew turned to meet the French van division that had belatedly turned back to enter the battle. *Conqueror*, with much of her rigging shot away, was proving difficult to handle and, after receiving a heavy enemy fire, prepared to repel boarders. Two of her six lieutenants were killed and Pellew himself was knocked over and briefly stunned by the blast of a passing shot. Her Royal Marines lieutenant was also wounded, as was Lieutenant Philip Mendel, serving as a supernumerary volunteer, one of six officers of the Russian Navy present in the British fleet during the battle. As the weather column's rearmost ships, led by the Earl of Northesk [6] in his flagship the 1st-rate *Britannia* (100), came up to *Conqueror*'s support, Pellew in turn went to the aid of *Leviathan*, in action with two enemy 74-gun ships, the Spanish *San Agustin* and French *Intrépide*. He failed to close with *Intrépide* but opened a distant fire on her until other British ships came up. Meanwhile *Leviathan* boarded and captured *San Agustin*, with her men shouting across 'Huzza, *Conqueror*, she's ours!' In the closing stage of the battle, *Conqueror* intercepted a French ship attempting to make Cadiz with only a foresail. The French captain, holding the lower corner of his colours in one hand while securing the upper corner to the stump of the mizen mast with his sword, fired a few guns in token of resistance. Pellew chivalrously answered not with a broadside but with a single shot across his bows, so allowing the Frenchman to doff his hat and strike his flag with honour.

Despite the losses among her officers, *Conqueror*'s crew escaped lightly, losing only one man killed and nine wounded. Her mizen topmast and main topgallant mast were shot away, with the fore and main masts badly damaged, together with their rigging and several shot holes along the waterline on her port side. One shot cut away the head of the ship's figurehead, representing a hero from classical antiquity, but the crew asked the first lieutenant for Pellew's permission to replace it with a figure of Nelson. After towing the badly damaged 3rd-rate *Africa* to Gibraltar, *Conqueror* went home to Plymouth for a refit and was duly given a representation of Nelson as her new figurehead, which the crew then ornamented at their own expense. Pellew remained in command of *Conqueror* for another three years, serving in the blockade of Rochefort and then off the Tagus, where the presence of a British fleet encouraged the Portuguese to defy Napoleon and maintain their long standing alliance with the United Kingdom. *Conqueror* returned to the blockade of Cadiz, but in the summer of 1808 Spanish patriots rose against French occupation and turned Spain from an enemy into an ally. Pellew was able to take his ship home to pay off and became superintendent of the payment of ships at Chatham.

Pellew became a rear-admiral on 31 July 1810 and in the following year was appointed captain of the fleet to his brother, who had become C-in-C, Mediterranean. The two remained there until Napoleon's defeat and exile in the spring of 1814, after which Sir Edward Pellew was created Lord Exmouth and Israel Pellew was awarded the KCB. Sir Israel Pellew returned to the Mediterranean on his brother's staff early in 1815, but Exmouth decided not to employ him in the bombardment of Algiers by a multi-national fleet in August 1816, undertaken to rescue Christian prisoners and discourage further North African piracy. Pellew then went home, where he was promoted to vice-admiral on 12 August 1819. His only child, Edward, an officer in the 1st Life Guards, was killed in a duel on 6 October 1819 while serving with the Army of Occupation in Paris. Sir Israel Pellew, promoted to admiral on 22 July 1830, retired to Plymouth, where he died after a long and painful illness on 19 July 1832.

PILFOLD, Captain JOHN, CB (c.1776–1834) **[28]**
John Pilfold, second son of Charles Pilfold, Esquire and his wife Bathia, was born in about 1776 in Horsham, Sussex, where the families of both his parents lived. He entered the Navy in 1788 on appointment to the 3rd-rate *Crown*, pendant-ship of Commodore the Honourable (later Admiral Sir) William 'Billy Blue' Cornwallis and served in her as a midshipman on the East Indies station until the ship returned home in May 1792. Following the outbreak of war with Revolutionary France in February 1793, Pilfold became a master's mate in the 3rd-rate *Brunswick* (74) in which he served with distinction at **The Glorious First of June (1 June 1794)** and was recommended for early promotion. On 14 February 1795 he was promoted by Lord Howe as C-in-C of the Channel fleet to lieutenant in the 3rd-rate *Russell* (74), with the promotion officially confirmed with effect from 9 March 1795. He served in this ship in **Bridport's Action, Île de Groix, Lorient (23 June 1795)** and transferred in September 1795 to the brig-sloop *Kingfisher* (18), deployed to the Lisbon station, where she captured several enemy privateers. On 1 July 1797, responding belatedly to news of the mutinies at Spithead and

the Nore, some of *Kingfisher*'s crew attempted a violent mutiny of their own, but were faced down by her officers and loyal men, with Pilfold, then her first lieutenant, drawing his sword to maintain discipline. Soon afterwards, he moved to the 3rd-rate *Impétueux* (74), the former *Amérique* captured from the French on **The Glorious First of June**.

During May 1800 *Impétueux* formed part of a squadron deployed to the coast of Brittany in support of a rising by local French Royalists. The aim of the operation was to land 6,000 British troops on Belle Île, but the place proved too strongly held and the soldiers spent five weeks offshore in their transports waiting for further instructions. In the meanwhile, on 6 June 1800, Pilfold commanded a division of boats in a raid into the nearby Morbihan estuary led by the dashing frigate captain Sir Edward Pellew. This action left the French corvette *Insolente* (18) and various coast artillery installations destroyed, and a number of prisoners and small craft in British hands.

An armistice with France was agreed on 1 October 1801, followed by a formal peace treaty at Amiens on 27 March 1802. Pilfold went ashore and in 1803 married Mary Anne Horner, daughter of Thomas South, Esquire, of Donhead, near Shaftesbury, on the Dorset/Wiltshire border, and later had with her a family of two daughters. War was renewed with France in May 1803 and with Spain in December 1804 and Pilfold was first appointed to the 4th-rate *Hindostan* (54), a former East Indiaman then in use as a storeship. He soon moved to the 3rd-rate *Dragon* (74) and then to the 3rd-rate *Ajax* (74) in the Channel, where, as first lieutenant of *Ajax* he took part in **Calder's Action, Finisterre (22 July 1805)**. In this action Vice-Admiral Sir Robert Calder intercepted, but failed to destroy, the Franco-Spanish Combined Fleet under Vice-Admiral Pierre Villeneuve after its return from the West Indies. *Ajax* played a significant part in the engagement, and had her main yard and driver boom shot away, with eighteen casualties among her crew.

Most of Calder's squadron reached Cadiz with him on 30 August 1805, to join the blockade of Villeneuve's fleet there, but *Ajax* arrived later, on 29 September, in company with the 3rd-rate *Thunderer* (74) and Vice-Admiral Viscount Nelson in the 1st-rate *Victory*. Nelson brought with him orders for Calder to return home to face the court martial he had demanded in response to widespread public criticism of his indecisive encounter with Villeneuve off Finisterre. Nelson generously allowed Calder to sail home in his own flagship, and to take with him any officers who were willing to give evidence on his behalf. Among these was Captain William Brown of *Ajax*, so that Pilfold, as first lieutenant, became her acting captain and was still in command at **Trafalgar (21 October 1805)**.

In the approach to battle *Ajax* was seventh in line in the weather column headed by Nelson. Stationed immediately astern of the 1st-rate *Britannia* (100), flagship of the Earl of Northesk **[6]**, she was thus in the rear group that was unable to keep up with the five ships ahead of them and so came late into battle. As *Ajax* slowly neared the enemy line, her Royal Marines lieutenant noted that Nelson's signal 'England expects …' received a mixed reception on the gun decks, with several seaman murmuring in response that they always had done their duty, but cheering nevertheless out of regard for their admiral.

After catching up with their embattled leaders, *Britannia* and *Ajax* joined in the attack on Villeneuve's stricken command ship *Bucentaure* with a long-distance cannonade. Pilfold then followed Northesk to meet the enemy van division as it belatedly returned to Villeneuve's support. *Ajax* lost two men killed and nine wounded in the fighting, but otherwise suffered little damage. Afterwards, together with the 3rd-rate *Donegal* (76), which had come up from Gibraltar, and the 3rd-rate *Leviathan* (74) she was one of the British ships that anchored near Cadiz on the initiative of their captains and so rode out the storm that followed the battle.

Pilfold received the gold medal, thanks of Parliament and sword from the Patriotic Fund given to all the captains of major combatants at Trafalgar and was promoted to post captain on 25 December 1805. In 1808 he was granted an honourable augmentation to his coat of arms. In June 1815, the same month as Napoleon's final defeat, he was awarded the CB. From 1827 to 1831 he was captain of the Ordinary (ships held, in modern terms, in 'mothballs' or 'extended readiness') at Plymouth, where he died at Stonehouse on 12 July 1834.

PROWSE, Rear-Admiral WILLIAM, CB (1752–1826) **[29]**
William Prowse was born into a working-class Devon family in about 1752 and seems to have gone to sea as a boy in a merchant vessel. After joining the Navy he served between November 1771 and February 1776 as an able seaman in the 3rd-rate *Dublin* (74), guard-ship at Plymouth, and from November 1776 to June 1778 in the 3rd-rate *Albion* (74), deployed to North America in the early years of the American War of Independence. Early in 1778 *Albion* was given a new commanding officer, Captain (later Admiral Sir) George Bowyer, who noticed Prowse's potential and appointed him first a midshipman, on 31 August 1778, and subsequently a master's mate. Prowse served with Bowyer in *Albion* at **Grenada (6 July 1779)** and various inconclusive actions in April and May 1780, including **Martinique (17 April 1780)**, and was paid off with the ship on 21 December 1781. He passed his examination for promotion to lieutenant on 17 January 1782 and was promoted on 6 December 1782, appointed first to the new 2nd-rate *Atlas* (90) and then the 6th-rate frigate *Cyclops* (28), in which he served on the coast of North America until March 1784.

The end of the war in the previous year meant that there were limited prospects of employment with the Navy and Prowse seems to have returned to the Merchant Service. During 1787, when a fleet was briefly mobilized at a time of international tension in the Netherlands, his old patron, Captain Bowyer, secured Prowse a place with him in the 3rd-rate *Bellona* (74). In 1790 the fleet was mobilized again, during a dispute with Spain over the possession of Nootka Sound (Vancouver, British Columbia) and Prowse served successively in the 2nd-rate *Barfleur* (98) and 3rd-rate *Stately* (64) under Captain (later Admiral Sir) Robert Calder. Between August 1791 and January 1793 he served in the 2nd-rate *Duke* (90), flagship of Admiral Viscount Hood at Portsmouth.

A month after the beginning of the French Revolutionary

War in February 1793, Prowse was appointed to the 2nd-rate *Prince* (90) commanded by Captain Cuthbert Collingwood [8], flagship of the recently promoted Vice-Admiral Bowyer. In December 1793 he followed both of them to his old ship *Barfleur*, in which, as sixth lieutenant, he served at the **Glorious First of June (1 June 1794)** where Bowyer lost a leg. Prowse himself was among the wounded but in July 1794 was fit enough to leave the flagship and join Calder in the 3rd-rate *Theseus* (74), about to sail for the West Indies. They spent a year there, including minor actions against French shore batteries on Guadeloupe, until escorting a convoy home to Portsmouth in July 1795.

In October 1795 Prowse followed Calder to the new 5th-rate frigate *Lively* (32), deployed to the Mediterranean, where he subsequently transferred to the 1st-rate *Victory*, flagship of Sir John Jervis. On 26 October 1796 Jervis appointed Prowse commander of the new sloop *Raven* (14), and early in 1797 Calder became Jervis's captain of the fleet in *Victory*. After **Cape St Vincent (14 February 1797)**, *Raven* was with a group of four frigates and two sloops that pursued but eventually lost the Spanish four-decker *Santisima Trinidad*. On 6 March 1797, Jervis made Prowse a post captain, with command of the 1st-rate *Salvador del Mundo* (112), one of the prizes captured from the Spanish during the recent battle and subsequently taken into the Royal Navy. Prowse took this ship home to pay off in November 1797 but returned to sea in August 1800 as flag captain in the 2nd-rate *Prince of Wales* (90) under the recently promoted Rear-Admiral Calder and served there until April 1802.

Following a peace treaty with France and her allies in March 1802, much of the fleet was rapidly put out of commission but Prowse returned to sea in August 1802 in command of the 5th-rate frigate *Sirius* (36). After the war with France was renewed in May 1803, *Sirius* was deployed to the Channel and the Bay of Biscay where, in 1804, Vice-Admiral Sir Robert Calder assumed command of the squadron blockading Rochefort. Spain entered the war on the French side in December 1804 and Calder's squadron was subsequently redeployed from Rochefort to the blockade of

Ferrol. In July 1805 Calder was ordered to wait off Finisterre so as to intercept Vice-Admiral Pierre Villeneuve's Franco-Spanish Combined Fleet on its return from the West Indies. On 22 July Villeneuve was first reported in the area, taking a northerly course. Calder headed southwards and ordered his two frigates, *Sirius* and *Egyptienne,* to scout ahead and locate the enemy.

In poor visibility, *Sirius* found the French frigate *Sirène* astern of Villeneuve's fleet with a captured merchantman in tow. Prowse decided to close, with the intention of boarding what seemed a valuable prize, at which *Sirène's* captain fired his guns to alert Villeneuve that there were enemy ships behind him. The French admiral then ordered his fleet to wear in succession, thus reversing course and taking a southerly heading. Prowse was therefore suddenly faced with the leading ship of the enemy line of battle, the Spanish flagship *Argonauta* (90), as she appeared out of the haze. In accordance with the convention that ships of the line did not open fire on frigates, the Spanish admiral chivalrously ordered his guns to remain silent and this example was followed by the two ships next in line behind him, *Terrible* and *America.* By this time Calder's van had made contact with that of the enemy, and when the 3rd-rate *Hero* opened fire on *Argonauta,* the action became general and the Spanish *España* (64) fired on *Sirius,* killing two men and wounding three as Prowse escaped to the leeward. After the battle *Sirius* was dispatched to Plymouth with the captured Spanish *Firme* (74) in tow.

Villeneuve took his Combined Fleet into Cadiz on 21 August 1805 and *Sirius* was among the ships sent to build up the British blockade there. Vice-Admiral Viscount Nelson, on arriving to assume command from Vice-Admiral Cuthbert Collingwood, moved his main fleet out to sea, leaving a chain made up of his four frigates supplemented by four ships of the line to link him with Cadiz. Of these it was *Sirius* that first observed the indictors that Villeneuve had at last decided to put to sea and, at first light on 19 October, signalled her next in line, the frigate *Euryalus* under Captain the Honourable Henry Blackwood [3], with the message, 'Enemy have their topsails hoisted'. An hour later, at 7 a.m., *Sirius* hoisted the three flags for the numbers 370, code for 'Enemy ships are coming out of port or getting under sail', a message that, repeated from ship to ship in the chain, passed across forty-eight miles to reach Nelson's flagship, the 1st-rate *Victory* (104) at 9.30 a.m.

The next morning (20 October 1805), with part of the Combined Fleet still inside Cadiz harbour, *Sirius* and *Euryalus* were on station off the entrance when an unidentified vessel was sighted, approaching from the north-east. Prowse asked permission from Blackwood, commanding the frigates, to investigate but, by the time *Sirius* intercepted her, the French *Héros* (74) was within range. Under fire from *Héros*, Prowse nevertheless put a shot across the strange ship's bows and sent a boat with an examining officer, who found she was a neutral American merchantman. While *Héros* continued her cannonade, Prowse recovered his boat and sailed on, leaving the American to be stopped a second time and boarded by the French. Rainy squalls reached Cadiz about 10 a.m. just as the last of the Combined Fleet reached the open sea. The two British frigates lost contact with them in the bad visibility, but regained it about two hours later, after which Blackwood sailed to pass his information directly to Nelson. Prowse watched the enemy alone until Blackwood, after a round trip of some sixty miles, rejoined him at about 4 p.m.

At about 7.30 a.m. at **Trafalgar (21 October 1805)**, with the enemy fleet in full sight, Nelson signalled all four frigate captains to go on board *Victory*, where he gave them their battle orders. They were to take station to windward of the flagship, repeat his signals to the rest of the fleet, observe any enemy vessels escaping from the battle, capture any damaged enemy ships not otherwise being dealt with and take in tow any dismasted British ships or prizes. He then asked them all to go below into his cabin and witness his will, in which he left his mistress, Lady Hamilton, and their daughter, Horatia, 'as a legacy to my King and Country' if he were to fall in the coming engagement. They all duly signed, though they may well have thought that (as in the event proved to be the case) neither the King nor the Cabinet would be likely to provide for Nelson's extra-marital attachments. During the battle, *Sirius* kept station as Nelson had directed and, at the close, having suffered no damage nor casualties herself, took the dismasted *Victory* in tow. The following day, as the weather worsened, she handed over the tow to the 3rd-rate *Polyphemus* (64).

Prowse remained with *Sirius* in the Mediterranean, where Collingwood continued in the command to which he had succeeded on Nelson's death. On 17 April 1806, off Civitavecchia, on the east coast of the French-ruled Kingdom of Rome, *Sirius* engaged an enemy flotilla consisting of the corvette *Bergère* (18), three armed brigs, a bomb vessel, a cutter and three gunboats. *Bergère* put up a gallant fight while she covered the escape of the remainder of the flotilla into Civitavecchia, killing nine and wounding twenty of Prowse's crew before she was taken. Prowse was mentioned in dispatches and awarded a prize sword by the Patriotic Fund. After returning home to pay off in May 1808, Prowse was appointed to the 3rd-rate *Theseus* (74) in March 1810 and served in her in the North Sea until December 1813. He then went ashore and saw no further active service. Awarded the CB on 4 June 1815 at the end of the war, he was made a colonel of Royal Marines on 12 August 1819. He was promoted to rear-admiral on 19 July 1821 and died on 23 March 1826.

REDMILL, Captain ROBERT, CB (c.1762–1819) **[30]**
Robert Redmill joined the Navy at a young age and served during the American War of Independence prior to becoming a lieutenant on 24 December 1783, almost twelve months after the end of the war. The outbreak of the French Revolutionary War in February 1793 gave him the chance of further employment and he was promoted to commander in 1795, with appointment to the fireship *Comet* (14). He served in this ship with the Mediterranean fleet under Vice-Admiral William Hotham and was present off Toulon at the inconclusive battle of **Hyères (13 July 1795)**. Redmill was promoted to post captain on 16 December 1796 and commanded the 3rd-rate *Delft* (64), in the Mediterranean Fleet, between 1799 and 1801. There he served under Lord Keith in combined operations on the coast of Egypt leading to the defeat of the French army at the battle of Alexandria

(21 March 1801). Most of the French forces in Egypt surrendered on 27 June 1801 but those involved in the battle of Alexandria retreated behind the walls of that city, where they remained under siege until peace was signed in March 1802 and the Alexandria garrison was taken home in British ships. Redmill was among the senior officers awarded a gold medal by the Sultan of Turkey in recognition of the part played by the British in recovering his Egyptian domains.

War with France was renewed in May 1803 and with Spain in December 1804. In the summer of 1805, Redmill was appointed to the 3rd-rate *Polyphemus* (64), deployed to the Channel. On 30 August 1805, as part of a squadron under Vice-Admiral Sir Robert Calder, *Polyphemus* joined the British blockade of Vice-Admiral Pierre Villeneuve's Franco-Spanish Combined Fleet in Cadiz. She remained in the blockading fleet after the arrival of Vice-Admiral Viscount Nelson, who withdrew his ships to seaward in the hope this would encourage Villeneuve to sail. When the two fleets met at **Trafalgar (21 October 1805)** *Polyphemus* was in the rear group of the lee column led by Vice-Admiral Collingwood **[8]**. As they joined the mêlée, Captain Conn **[9]** next astern in the 2nd-rate *Dreadnought* (98), hailed Redmill for permission to pass, so as to get alongside the Spanish *Principe de Asturias* (112) on *Polyphemus*'s starboard bow. Redmill yawed *Polyphemus* to starboard to allow this and in the process came under heavy fire from *Principe de Asturias* and the two 74-gun ships next astern of her, the French *Berwick* and the Spanish *San Juan de Nepomuceno*. He altered course to head for *San Juan de Nepomuceno* but was unable to reach her as the 2nd-rate *Swiftsure* (98), originally behind *Dreadnought*, was too close to his starboard quarter. Redmill then went to the support of the hard-pressed 3rd-rate *Belleisle* (74) and drove away one of the two ships with which she was engaged, the French *Neptune* (84). After firing at the Spanish *Argonauta* (80), he joined in the attack on the last ship in the enemy line, the French *Achille* ((74). *Polyphemus*'s own damage in the fight was negligible, with casualties of two men killed and four wounded.

In the worsening weather that followed the battle, *Polyphemus* took over the tow of the disabled 1st-rate *Victory* from the frigate *Sirius* and, with Nelson's body aboard his former flagship, reached Gibraltar in safety. *Polyphemus* and *Sirius* both remained in the Mediterranean Fleet under Collingwood's command, and both were pursued by a French squadron in December 1805, when escorting a convoy from Gibraltar. In 1806 Redmill was relieved on medical grounds, after which he remained ashore for the rest of the war. He was awarded the CB on 4 June 1815 and died in March 1819.

ROTHERAM, Captain EDWARD, CB (1753–1830) **[31]**
Edward Rotheram, the son of a Northumberland medical practitioner, was born in Hexham in about 1753 and shortly afterwards moved with his family to Newcastle-upon-Tyne, where he grew up. After time at sea in a collier, he entered the Navy in April 1777, during the American War of Independence, and served in the Channel in the 3rd-rate *Centaur* (74), held briefly on the books as an able seaman before being appointed first a midshipman and then a master's mate. In April 1780 he moved from *Centaur* to the 2nd-rate *Barfleur* (98), flagship of Vice-Admiral the Honourable Samuel Barrington as second-in-command of the Channel fleet. On 13 October 1780 he was appointed acting lieutenant in the 3rd-rate *Monarch* (74) in which he was deployed to the West Indies under Rear-Admiral Sir Samuel Hood. There he took part in Hood's engagements against the French off Martinique (29 April 1781), the Chesapeake Capes (5 September 1781), **St Kitts (25 January–13 February 1782),** **Guadeloupe (9 April 1782)** and **The Battle of the Saintes (9–12 April 1782).** When the war ended, Rotheram returned home with *Monarch* in 1783, and was confirmed as lieutenant on 19 April 1783. He served in the Channel in the 3rd-rates *Bombay Castle* in 1787, *Culloden* in 1788 and *Vengeance* in 1790.

Rotheram returned to *Culloden* as her first lieutenant in 1790 and was still serving in her on the outbreak of the French Revolutionary War in February 1793. In **The Glorious First of June (1 June 1794),** he took a party from *Culloden* to board the battered French *Vengeur* (74) whose captain, though his ship was sinking under him, was still flying the tricolour and had set a small sail on the stump of his foremast. As the boats from *Culloden* and two other nearby British ships approached her, *Vengeur* sank and the British could do no more than save as many of her crew as possible from the water. About 400 souls, including her gallant commanding officer, Captain Renaudin, and his twelve year old son, were rescued out of a company of over 700. Rotheram was favourably noticed for his energy and coolness in directing operations and was promoted to commander on 6 July 1794. During 1795 and 1796 he commanded the store-ship *Camel* in the Mediterranean and from 1797 to 1800 the sloop *Hawk* (16), first in the North Sea and then in the West Indies. In the summer of 1800 he returned home as acting captain of the 6th-rate frigate *Lapwing* (28) and was promoted to post captain on 27 August 1800.

Peace was signed in March 1802, but hostilities were renewed with France in 1803 and Spain in December 1804. Rotheram was appointed in December 1804 to the four year old 2nd-rate *Dreadnought*, flagship of Vice-Admiral Cuthbert Collingwood [8] in the Channel. In March 1805, commanding an independent 'flying squadron', Collingwood sailed for the south-western coast of Spain, in the hunt for Vice-Admiral Pierre Villeneuve's Franco-Spanish Combined Fleet, which had sailed from Cadiz for an undisclosed destination. Discovering that Villeneuve, with Vice-Admiral Viscount Nelson and the Mediterranean fleet in pursuit, had reached the West Indies, Collingwood deployed his own ships in the blockades of Cadiz and Cartagena. When Villeneuve appeared off Cadiz on 20 August 1805, Rotheram's *Dreadnought* was one of the three ships of the line that Collingwood had there, and only skilful ship-handling in the British squadron enabled it to draw away and avoid a combat with overwhelming numbers.

Despite Rotheram's skilful management of his heavily-sailing ship on this occasion and indeed previously in the Channel, where the blockading fleet's great three-deckers found much difficulty in keeping off the land during the winter gales, Collingwood formed a low opinion of his flag captain. 'Such a captain, such a stick', he wrote to his sister at home in Northumberland at the end of August 1805, 'I wonder very much how such people get forward. I should (I firmly believe) with his nautical ability and knowledge and exertion have been a bad lieutenant at this day. Was he brought up in the Navy? For he has very much the stile of the Coal trade about him, except that they are good seamen.' The then Midshipman (later Rear-Admiral) Hercules Robinson, recalled in his memoirs that Collingwood once summoned across the deck 'his fat stupid captain, long since dead, when he had seen him commit some monstrous blunder, and after the usual bowing and formality ... said "Captain, I have been thinking, whilst I looked at you, how strange it is that a man should grow so big and know so little. That's all, sir, that's all." Hats off; low bows'. The story, however, may be something of an 'old salt's tale' as for one officer to criticize another in the hearing of a junior would have been a breach of the conventions that Robinson elsewhere stated that Collingwood was always punctilious in observing.

Dreadnought, her hull foul and weedy from being so long at sea, was ordered home by the Admiralty on 9 October, when her relief, the newly-refitted 1st-rate *Royal Sovereign* (100), arrived to join the fleet at Cadiz. The Admiralty also ordered Vice-Admiral Sir Robert Calder to return home in *Dreadnought* to face the court martial he had demanded in response to widespread criticism of his failure to destroy the Combined Fleet in **Calder's Action, Finisterre (22 July 1805)**. Nelson, who had arrived to take over command from Collingwood on 29 September 1805, granted Calder's plea to be allowed to go home in his own flagship, the 2nd-rate *Prince of Wales* (90) and retained *Dreadnought* in her place. Collingwood, who in any case would have had to shift his flag from *Dreadnought* into her replacement, was accordingly moved into *Royal Sovereign*, taking with him *Dreadnought*'s first lieutenant, James Clavell, on whom he had come greatly to rely. Rotheram also went with him as his flag captain, while Captain John Conn **[9]** and the first lieutenant under whom *Royal Sovereign* had come out from England exchanged into *Dreadnought*. It is possible that Nelson detected some tension between Collingwood and Rotheram as he declared about this time that 'in the presence of the enemy, all Englishmen should be as brothers'.

Royal Sovereign had previously been noted as a slow sailer and been dubbed 'the West Country Wagon', but her clean new copper bottom made her one of the fastest ships in the fleet. When Villeneuve put to sea and was met by Nelson at **Trafalgar (21 October 1805)**, *Royal Sovereign*, with Collingwood at the head of the lee column, was the first ship to come into action and was under fire for about ten minutes during the last mile of her approach to the enemy line. Rotheram aimed at the gap behind the Spanish flagship *Santa Ana* (112) through which Collingwood had directed him to steer, maintaining a steady course and speed, the latter diminishing as some of *Royal Sovereign*'s studding-sails, extensions set to catch as much as possible of the light wind, were shot away and began to trail in the water. He opened the battle on Collingwood's orders by firing an occasional gun to create smoke that, drifting alongside his ship, offered some cover, but not until breaking the line astern of *Santa Ana* and ahead of the French *Fougueux* (74) was he able to fire effectively on these two vessels. Aware that *Royal Sovereign* was the first to break the line, Collingwood unbent sufficiently to say to his flag captain, 'Oh Rotheram, what would Nelson give to be here.'

Rotheram then turned his ship to bring her so close to *Santa Ana*'s starboard (lee) side that the yard-arms of both vessels became locked together. *Royal Sovereign*'s first broadside, fired through *Santa Ana*'s vulnerable stern galleries, dismounted fourteen of her guns and killed 100 of her crew. After a quarter of an hour in which the two ships traded gunfire at close range, Rotheram went up to Collingwood and shook his hand, saying 'I congratulate you, Sir, she is slackening her fire and must soon strike'. In fact *Santa Ana*'s resistance was prolonged when *Fougueux*, together with the French *Indomptable* (80) and the Spanish *San Justo* (74) and *San Leandro* (64), came to her support, while *Royal Sovereign* was joined by her next in line, the 3rd-rate *Belleisle* (74), which engaged *Santa Ana* on one side and *Fougueux* on the other. After about an hour and a half's close combat, with his ship completely dismasted and 238 of his crew dead or wounded, *Santa Ana*'s captain finally struck his colours and sent his sword aboard *Royal Sovereign*.

During the battle, in which the closeness of the action left him with little to do as a flag officer, Collingwood had left Rotheram to handle his ship while he himself encouraged the gunners and marines on the quarterdeck. Rotheram appeared on deck at the beginning of the day wearing a large cocked hat decorated with gold braid, but even those who admired his courage thought it did not become him and urged him to take it off. He replied that he had always fought in a cocked hat and always would (in fact it had been eleven years since his last major fleet action). More fortunate than his C-in-C, whose own decorations attracted the fatal attention of enemy marksmen, Rotheram survived the battle unscathed, though almost everyone else on *Royal Sovereign*'s poop and quarterdeck became casualties. Losses among the ship's company amounted to three officers, two midshipmen and forty-two men killed, and four officers, a master's mate, four midshipmen, a boatswain and eighty-four men wounded.

Shortly after *Santa Ana* surrendered, *Royal Sovereign* lost her own badly damaged main and mizen masts and, with the fore-topsail-yard and most of the rigging of her foremast already shot away, become useless as a command platform. Collingwood then ordered Captain Blackwood [3] of the frigate *Euryalus* to take her in tow and, as the battle ended, transferred his flag to the frigate. Captain Gardoqui of *Santa Ana*, brought aboard as a prisoner, asked the name of the ship that had conquered him. When told that it was *Royal Sovereign*, he placed his hand on one of the quarterdeck guns and said that he thought it should be *Royal Devil*.

At dusk on the day after the battle, as the wind remained light and variable, and a heavy swell made towing conditions difficult, *Euryalus* suddenly lost way and *Royal Sovereign* ran into her. Collingwood then signalled the 2nd-rate *Neptune* (98) to take over the tow from *Euryalus*. At dawn, *Royal Sovereign*, rolling heavily in the strong gales and squalls then blowing, lost her foremast and its remaining sails and rigging. Soon afterwards the tow-rope parted and the two ships lost contact. Rotheram hoisted the signal 314 'ship is in distress and in want of immediate assistance', and fired several guns to draw attention to his plight, while his crew rigged a jury foremast and took soundings every half hour. Eventually they found a tow and reached Gibraltar, where on 4 November 1805 Rotheram was transferred to command of the 3rd-rate *Bellerophon* (74) whose previous commanding officer, Captain John Cooke [10] had fallen at Trafalgar. Together with *Belleisle*, she escorted *Victory* as she carried Nelson's body home to England.

Rotheram remained in *Bellerophon* and served in the Channel as flag captain to Rear-Admiral Sir Albemarle Bertie in 1807–08, after which the ship was paid off before being redeployed to the Baltic. He then went ashore and had no further service at sea. Rotherham was awarded the CB in 1815, the year in which the Napoleonic wars came to an end. In 1828 he was appointed captain of the Royal Naval Hospital, Greenwich, and died on 2 November 1830, while staying with friends at Bildeston, Suffolk. The cause of his death, apoplexy or stroke, was the same as that of his distinguished elder brother Professor John Rotheram, who had followed their father into the medical profession.

RUTHERFORD, Captain WILLIAM GORDON, CB
(1764–1818) **[32]**
William Rutherford was born in North Carolina in 1764, the son of John Rutherford of Bowland Stow near Edinburgh and his wife Frances, widow of Gabriel Johnson, late Governor of North Carolina. John Rutherford returned with his family to Scotland, where William Rutherford was educated in Edinburgh and at St Andrew's University before joining the Navy in 1778, during the American War of Independence. In 1793, after the outbreak of the French Revolutionary War, he was promoted to acting lieutenant in the 2nd-rate *Boyne* (98), flagship of Vice-Admiral Sir John Jervis as C-in-C, West Indies. With his promotion confirmed on 9 January 1794, Rutherford took part in the British capture of **Martinique (February–March 1794)**, where he served with distinction in

command of a naval landing party, **St Lucia (1–4 April 1794)** and **Guadeloupe (April–May 1794)**. He was mentioned in dispatches and promoted to commander on 4 July 1794, with appointment to the sloop *Nautilus* (16). He became a post captain on 15 November 1796 and was married in the same year. Much later, dining with other captains shortly before the battle of Trafalgar, he told them that it was foolish for a sailor to marry and that he himself had been married by that time for nine years, of which he had spent only one with his wife.

As a post captain he commanded successively the 5th-rate frigate *Adventure* (44), the 3rd-rates *Dictator* (64) and *Brunswick* (74) and the 5th-rate frigate *Decade* (36) and was present at the capture of the Dutch colony of Curacao, Venezuela, in September 1800. Peace with France and her satellites was signed in March 1802, but the war was renewed in May 1803. Rutherford and *Decade* returned home in 1804 to join the Channel fleet's blockade of Cherbourg, where they remained after Spain entered the war on the French side in December 1804.

From there, late in 1805, Rutherford was appointed to the 3rd-rate *Swiftsure* (74), after her return from Vice-Admiral Viscount Nelson's pursuit of Vice-Admiral Pierre Villeneuve and the Franco-Spanish Combined Fleet to the West Indies and back. On 30 August 1805 *Swiftsure*, in a squadron under Vice-Admiral Sir Robert Calder, joined the blockade of Cadiz, where Villeneuve had taken refuge. In the subsequent battle of **Trafalgar (21 October 1805)** she was among the five ships that brought up the rear of the British fleet's lee column led by Vice-Admiral Collingwood **[8]**. During the action she was engaged at various times with the Spanish *Argonauta* (80) and the French *Achille* (74), two of the rearmost ships in the enemy line, and went to the support of the hard-pressed 3rd-rate *Belleisle* (74) under Captain William Hargood **[18]**. When *Swiftsure* appeared through the smoke, those in *Belleisle* were unable to tell whether she was a friend or enemy until Rutherwood made an alteration in course that revealed her White Ensign. The ships' crews exchanged cheers and Hargood hailed Rutherford to ask him to engage the French

Aigle (74), to whose fire *Belleisle* had been unable to reply. *Swiftsure* crossed *Belleisle*'s stern and attacked another of her opponents, the French *Neptune* (84), while *Aigle* moved off as *Polyphemus* (64) also came to *Belleisle*'s aid.

Having entered the battle at a late stage, *Swiftsure* had suffered only her mizen-topmast shot away and her mizen-mast badly damaged and lost nine men killed and eight, including a midshipman, wounded. She was therefore ordered to take in tow the dismasted French *Redoutable* (74) which, under her heroic commanding officer, Captain Jean-Jacques Lucas, had engaged Nelson's flagship, the 1st-rate *Victory* (104), and tried to carry her by boarding. The attempt failed, but one of Lucas's marksmen had fired the shot that killed Nelson. Rutherford sent a prize crew on board and began the laborious work of towing a ship that *Victory*'s gunners had pounded almost to matchwood. Working together, the British and surviving French seamen tried to stop the holes in *Redoutable*'s hull and shore up her poop, while others pumped desperately to keep her afloat.

Captain Lucas noted that some of his men had concealed weapons in the orlop deck with the intention of retaking their ship, but the next morning Rutherford sent a boat to take him and his first lieutenant into *Swiftsure*. At noon, as the weather grew worse, *Redoutable* lost her sole remaining mast and at dusk, with a gale blowing, the prize crew made distress signals. Boats were sent to recover the prize crew and as many of the French as could be got into them. Lucas thought that none were left behind when the last boats returned almost empty. One hundred and sixty-nine French sailors, of whom 134 were wounded, reached *Swiftsure* but the sea state made it impossible for further boats to reach her and after five hours Rutherford cast off the tow as *Redoutable* sank by the stern, taking with her five of his own men and many of the French wounded. Some survived, however and, during the night, cries from the water were heard on board *Swiftsure*. Rutherford ordered out his boats and found a group of wounded clinging to a raft. The next day, two more rafts were spotted and, all told, about fifty men were rescued. *Swiftsure* then joined *Dreadnought* in taking men off the Spanish *San*

Agustin (74) and rescued another 116 men before the worsening sea state threatened to swamp the boats.

Rutherford subsequently went ashore where in 1814 he was appointed captain of the Royal Naval Hospital, Greenwich. In June 1815, the year in which the Napoleonic wars ended, he was awarded the CB. He died at Greenwich Hospital on 14 January 1818 and was buried in St Margaret's Church, Westminster, where a tablet was placed in his memory.

STOCKHAM, Captain JOHN (c.1764–1814) [33]

John Stockham was born in about 1764 and became a lieutenant on 29 April 1797. He thus reached this rank about ten years later in life than was the case with most of the Trafalgar captains and it is possible that, lacking an influential patron, he spent the early part of his seagoing career in the Merchant service before entering the Navy during the French Revolutionary War in February 1793. The war ended in March 1801 but hostilities with France were renewed in May 1803 and with Spain in December 1804. Stockham returned to sea and served in the Channel. As first lieutenant of the 3rd-rate *Thunderer* (74) he took part in **Calder's Action (22 July 1805)** in which Vice-Admiral Sir Robert Calder defeated, but failed to destroy, Vice-Admiral Pierre Villeneuve's Franco-Spanish Combined Fleet on its return from the West Indies. During a fight lasting some three hours *Thunderer*, stationed second from the rear of Calder's line, lost seven killed and eleven wounded and suffered damage to her masts, yards and rigging. Calder escorted his prizes and his most severely damaged ships, including *Thunderer*, towards Plymouth and eventually joined forces with the Channel Fleet off Ushant on 14 August 1805. Vice-Admiral Viscount Nelson, having pursued Villeneuve back to the Channel, reached them on 15 August and, after handing over his ships to the Channel fleet, went ashore. Calder was then sent south with orders to locate the Combined Fleet but, before he could make contact, it entered Cadiz on 21 August 1805. There, Vice-Admiral Cuthbert Collingwood [8] re-established his blockade after briefly being driven away by the arrival of Villeneuve's far superior numbers, and was reinforced by Calder's squadron on 30 August 1805. *Thunderer*, however, had not completed repairs and so did not reach Cadiz until 29 September 1805, when Nelson, in his flagship the 1st-rate *Victory*, arrived to take over command.

Nelson brought orders that Calder was to return to England, to face the court martial for which he had asked in response to public criticism of his having failed to destroy Villeneuve's fleet on 22 July. The orders stated that he should sail in the 2nd -rate *Dreadnought*, which was due home for a refit, but in response to Calder's pleas, Nelson allowed him to go home in his own flagship, the 2nd-rate *Prince of Wales*, and kept *Dreadnought* in her place. Any of the captains who had served under Calder in the engagement of 22 July and who wished to give evidence in his favour were allowed to go with him. Despite general sympathy with his plight, only two chose to do so, of whom one was the captain of the 3rd-rate *Ajax* (74) and the other was Captain Lechmere of *Thunderer*, so that when *Prince of Wales* left the fleet on 10 October 1805, both went with her. The two first lieutenants, Stockham of *Thunderer* and Pilfold [28] of *Ajax* then assumed command of their respective ships and were thus acting captains when Villeneuve put to sea and met Nelson at **Trafalgar (21 October 1805)**.

During the approach to battle *Thunderer* was among the rearmost group of ships in the lee column led by Collingwood in *Royal Sovereign*. This group thus came into action at a late stage and Stockham exchanged broadsides with the Spanish *San Ildefonso* (74), stationed towards the rear of the enemy line. Together with the 3rd-rate *Polyphemus* (64) he went to the support of the 3rd-rate *Revenge* (74), engaged by the Spanish three-decker *Principe de Asturias* (112) and the French *Neptune* (84). These two subsequently broke off the action and escaped back into Cadiz. *Thunderer*'s casualties amounted to four men killed and a master's mate, a midshipman and ten men wounded but, apart from a few shots that struck her main and mizen-masts and bowsprit, the ship was virtually undamaged. Accordingly, at the end of the battle, she was ordered by Collingwood (who had succeeded to the command on Nelson's death) to take in tow the captured Spanish three-decker *Santa Ana* (112).

Two days later, with a full gale blowing, the French Commodore Casmao-Kerjulien, in his pendant-ship *Pluton* (74) led five ships of the line out of Cadiz in an attempt to recover some of the prizes taken at Trafalgar. Stockham, with *Santa Ana* in tow, was unable to avoid them and so recovered his prize crew and cast her off. Collingwood ordered ten of his serviceable ships, including *Thunderer*, to form a line against the approaching enemy, and *Santa Ana*, together with the captured Spanish *Neptuno* (74), then escaped into Cadiz. Casmao-Kerjulien, faced by superior numbers, followed them, but in the continuing bad weather three of the ships he had brought out with him were driven ashore and wrecked. *Thunderer* subsequently took in tow the captured Spanish *San Juan de Nepomuceno* (74) and after anchoring with her, rode out the storm and brought her into Gibraltar on 28 October 1805, one of the only four prizes that were saved. In the distribution of awards that followed the battle, Stockham, like Pilfold, received the naval gold medal, the thanks of Parliament and the prize sword from the Patriotic Fund presented to all the captains who commanded at Trafalgar. He was promoted to post captain on 24 December 1805 without passing through the intermediate rank of commander and subsequently went ashore, where he died at Exeter on 6 February 1814.

TYLER, Admiral Sir CHARLES, GCB (1760–1835) **[34]**
Charles Tyler, the son of Captain Peter Tyler, 52nd Foot, and his wife, the Honourable Anna Maria Roper, daughter of Henry, eighth Lord Teynham, was born in 1760. He joined the Navy in 1771 as a captain's servant, carried on the books of the 2nd-rate *Barfleur* (98), guard-ship at Chatham. After a few months he was appointed to the 5th-rate frigate *Arethusa* (32) deployed to the North America station. In 1774 he joined the 4th-rate *Preston* (50), flagship of Vice-Admiral Samuel Graves, C-in-C, North America, and after the outbreak of the American War of Independence in 1776, pendant-ship of Commodore (later Admiral) William Hotham. Tyler was invalided home in 1777 with an injury to his left leg, which required the removal of a small bone and left him on crutches

for the next two years. Despite being left with a permanent limp, he returned to sea with promotion to lieutenant in the 3rd-rate *Culloden* (74) on 5 April 1779. He then served in the Channel in *Culloden* until September 1780, in Vice-Admiral George Darby's flagship the 1st-rate *Britannia* (100), until September 1782 and then, once more under Hotham, in the 3rd-rate *Edgar* (74).

Tyler was promoted to commander on 31 December 1782, twenty days before the war ended, and was appointed to the armed ship *Queen* (possibly in the Excise service, as the Navy's *Queen* at this time was a 2nd-rate three-decker of 98 guns). He was given command of another armed ship, *Chapman*, in July 1783. Between 1784 and 1789 he was stationed at Milford Haven, Dyfed, commanding the brig-sloop *Trimmer* (14) on anti-smuggling operations. Tyler was promoted to post captain on 21 September 1790, with appointment to the 6th-rate frigate *Tisiphone* (20) and remained on anti-smuggling operations, deployed in the Channel. In March 1793, a month after the outbreak of the French Revolutionary War, he was appointed to the 5th-rate frigate *Meleager* (32), in the Mediterranean fleet under Lord Hood. There he took part in the blockade, occupation and subsequent evacuation of **Toulon (August–December 1793)** and in the campaign in **Corsica (February–August 1794)**. In recognition of his services during the Corsican campaign he was appointed to the frigate *St Fiorenzo* (40), the former French *Minerve*, scuttled in Calvi harbour, Corsica, before the town surrendered to the British, and subsequently raised under Tyler's direction. In February 1795 he moved to the 3rd-rate *Diadem* (64) in the Mediterranean fleet under Vice-Admiral William Hotham, his former commodore. In *Diadem*, Tyler took part in the action off **Leghorn (13–14 March 1795)** where *Diadem* lost three killed and seven wounded out of her crew of 485.

In lieu of marines, *Diadem* carried a party of soldiers of the 11th Foot. Their senior officer, Lieutenant Gerald Fitzgerald, refused to accept that his men were subject to all orders of the ship's captain. Tyler, finding his authority defied, informed his C-in-C, who ordered Fitzgerald to be brought

before a naval court martial. Fitzgerald refused to recognize
the court's jurisdiction and declined to enter a plea. The court
overruled his objections, convicted him of insubordination
and sentenced him to be cashiered. This raised a number of
questions, not least the power of a naval court martial to
deprive an army officer of his commission, which unlike that
of a sea officer, was in most cases obtained by purchase and
thus represented a substantial capital investment. The case
reached the Duke of York, the King's second son, field
marshal and C-in-C of the British Army. He ruled that
soldiers, even when serving on board ship, were under
military, not naval, jurisdiction. The Admiralty protested that
this ruling was contrary to acts of Parliament and would
destroy discipline afloat. Fitzgerald left the Army, but the
incident hastened the end of the practice, unpopular on both
sides, of ships carrying soldiers to serve as marines.

Tyler served in *Diadem* off the coast of Italy and
commanded a small squadron in the Adriatic. He then
transferred to the 5th-rate frigate *Aigle* (38) in which he
captured a number of privateers in the Channel and the
Mediterranean. By the end of 1796, with Spain having joined
the war on the French side, and most of Italy under French
occupation, the British were forced to withdraw their fleet
from the Mediterranean for lack of bases. Early in 1798 a small
squadron under Commodore Horatio Nelson returned to
observe the French fleet at Toulon. More ships were sent to
reinforce him, *Aigle* among them, but en route she was
wrecked off Cape Farina, Spain, on 18 July 1798. Tyler and
his crew, including his young son Midshipman Charles Tyler,
were saved and he returned to sea in February 1799 on
appointment to the 3rd-rate *Warrior* (74) in the Channel.

Tyler took part in the naval expedition sent to the Baltic
under Sir Hyde Parker in 1801, and was at Nelson's victory
over the anchored Danish fleet at **Copenhagen (2 April 1801)**.
He was next deployed to the blockade of Cadiz, where he
was serving when a general armistice, signed on 1 October
1801 and followed by the formal peace treaty of Amiens in
March 1802, brought hostilities with France and her allies to
a temporary end.

As soon as the British lifted their blockade, Napoleon Bonaparte, First Consul of France, sent an expedition of twenty-two ships of the line and 25,000 troops to undertake the reconquest of the French colony of Santo Domingo (Haiti), where the former slaves had risen against their masters and established their own republic. The British ministers objected, but the strength of public opinion in favour of peace with France left them unable to do more than lodge a protest. Unable to reinforce their fleet in the West Indies until men pressed for war service had been replaced by volunteers, in January 1802 they sent a small squadron of four 3rd-rates from Gibraltar, led by Tyler in *Warrior*, to watch events in Haiti. He returned home with *Warrior* in July 1802.

After war with France was renewed in May 1803, Tyler was appointed to a district command in the Sea Fencibles, a force intended for the local defence of dockyards and landing places. Napoleon, now Emperor of the French, prepared an army of invasion, and his naval strength was increased when Spain declared war on the United Kingdom in December 1804. With the threat of a French invasion at its height, Tyler was appointed in February 1805 to the 3rd-rate *Tonnant* (80), in which he served first on blockade duties with the Channel fleet and then in a flying squadron under the command of Vice-Admiral Collingwood [8], deployed in the hunt for Vice-Admiral Pierre Villeneuve's Franco-Spanish Combined Fleet. On 8 May 1805, Collingwood detached two of his nine ships of the line to join Vice-Admiral Viscount Nelson, who had pursued Villeneuve to the West Indies. He then established a blockade of Cadiz with three ships of the line under his own command and sent Rear-Admiral Sir Richard Bickerton, with *Tonnant* and his three remaining ships of the line, into the Mediterranean to blockade Cartagena.

Villeneuve, having returned to European waters ahead of Nelson, appeared at Cadiz on 20 August 1805. Collingwood drew off towards Gibraltar, but resumed his blockade the next day, to be joined by *Tonnant* and the rest of Bickerton's squadron, hastily recalled from Cartagena, on 27 August. When Nelson arrived to take command of the steadily reinforced fleet on 29 September 1805, Tyler waited upon him with a compassionate problem. His son Charles, after their shipwreck in *Aigle* had served in a number of ships, including Tyler's own *Warrior* at **Copenhagen (2 April 1801)**, and was by this time a lieutenant. At Malta, he had left his ship and run away with an 'opera-dancer' (chorus girl) to Naples, where he was thought to have been imprisoned for debt. Knowing that Nelson was held in high regard by the King and Queen of the Two Sicilies (he had, indeed, been made a Neapolitan duke), Tyler asked his admiral to intercede for the errant son. Nelson, with his gift for leadership, not only found time to write to his royal friends but also, without telling Tyler, offered to pay the cost of the son's release.

When Villeneuve sailed and the two fleets met at **Trafalgar (21 October 1805)**, *Tonnant* was in the lee column led by Collingwood, at first stationed immediately behind his flagship, the 1st-rate *Royal Sovereign*. With the enemy in sight, Tyler called all hands and told them it would be a glorious day for them and the groundwork of a speedy return home, and then ordered bread, cheese, butter and beer to be served to every man at the guns. As the British fleet approached the enemy line, *Tonnant* began to lag behind the flagship so that the two ships astern of her, the 3rd-rates *Mars* and *Belleisle*, at that point respectively third and fourth in line, had to shorten sail. Observing that *Royal Sovereign* would become isolated at the head of her column, Nelson signalled Collingwood to order other ships to overtake *Tonnant* if she could not close the gap. Fifteen minutes later Collingwood signalled *Tonnant* and *Belleisle*, under Captain William Hargood [18], to change places. As *Belleisle* overtook her, *Tonnant*'s band played 'Britons, strike home' and the two captains hailed each other with cries of 'A glorious day for old England' and 'We shall have one apiece before night'. Two of the bandsman were subsequently killed in the opening shots of the battle, as the first four ships in Collingwood's line slowly neared the rear of the Combined Fleet and came under long-range fire.

Tonnant entered the battle fourth in her column, after *Mars* (74), with Tyler afterwards writing that he was so impressed by the performance of Collingwood's flagship that for a few moments he felt he had nothing to do but look on and admire. Then, going to the aid of the hard-pressed *Mars*, he engaged successively the French *Pluton* (74), the Spanish *Monarca* (74) and the French *Algesiras* (74), flagship of Rear-Admiral Medine. *Algesiras* fired a broadside into *Tonnant*'s stern, causing severe damage to the galleries and rudder and killing or wounding some forty men before attempting to board. The boarders were met with grapeshot from the forecastle guns and musketry from *Tonnant*'s marines, so that only one man succeeded in reaching her deck. He was pinned to the deck with a half-pike through his calf and about to be cut down when *Tonnant*'s third lieutenant intervened and sent him below to the surgeon. While this fight was going on, sharpshooters in *Algesiras*'s tops cleared *Tonnant*'s poop, and wounded Tyler himself in the left thigh, so that he had to be taken below and leave his ship to be commanded by the first lieutenant, Lieutenant John Bedford. Eventually *Algesiras* lost all her masts overboard and was boarded by *Tonnant* in her turn. At the end of the fight, the victorious British found fourteen of her guns dismounted, her flag-officer lying dead at the foot of the poop ladder and her captain mortally wounded, with 200 more of the ship's company dead or wounded.

On *Tonnant*'s forecastle, one of her officers, Lieutenant Benjamin Clements saw a nearby Spanish ship, *San Juan de Nepomuceno* (74) strike her flag. He hailed to ask if she had surrendered and when an officer shouted back that she had, ran to the quarterdeck to report this to Bedford. He was then told to pick two men and go across in the jolly-boat, *Tonnant*'s only remaining boat, but when launched, this too proved to be holed and began to sink. Clement could not swim, but his companions, helped by four men who jumped from *Tonnant*, managed to get him back to the ship where, half-drowned, he was hauled aboard through the damaged stern. *Tonnant*, having lost all three topmasts and the main-yard was, in the words of one of her seamen, drifting like a pig on a grating and had to let the Spaniard go. *Tonnant* lost one midshipman and twenty-five men killed, and her captain, his clerk, a master's mate, a boatswain and forty-six men wounded. At the close of the day, she was taken in tow by the 3rd-rate *Spartiate* (74). They survived the storm that followed and reached Gibraltar without further incident.

Tyler was granted a wound pension of £250 per annum and convalesced with his family at their home in Pembrokeshire. He remained on the active list, with promotion to rear-admiral on 28 April 1808 and appointment as second-in-command at Portsmouth in the following May. In June 1808, following the example of their Spanish neighbours, Portuguese patriots rose against French occupation and appealed to the British for aid. A British army landed and defeated the French at Vimiero (21 August 1808). Senior generals arrived to take over from the British commander, Sir Arthur Wellesley, and signed the subsequent Convention of Cintra (Sintra), providing for the French to be taken home in British ships and the Russian squadron in the Tagus to sail home to the Baltic under French protection. This squadron, first deployed to the Mediterranean at the end of 1805, was under the Anglophile Vice-Admiral D. N. Senyavin, who had himself served in the Royal Navy for six years. He had maintained cordial relations with Collingwood and had won a major victory over the Ottoman fleet on 1 July 1807. Shortly afterwards, following the meeting of the Emperors Napoleon and Alexander I at Tilsit and the establishment of friendly relations between Russia and France, Senyavin's squadron was recalled and in November 1807 was on its way home when driven by bad weather to take shelter in the Tagus. This had coincided with the arrival of a French army at Lisbon and the flight of the Portuguese Court to Brazil. Napoleon expected the Russian squadron to undertake operations in support of its new friends, but Senyavin resisted all pressure to do so and was still at anchor when the Portuguese rose against French rule. Vice-Admiral Sir Charles Cotton, commanding the British squadron off Lisbon, refused to accept the Convention of Cintra, arguing that neither British nor French generals had authority to negotiate in naval affairs. Accordingly, he made his own agreement with Senyavin (with whom he had been in contact for several months) whereby the Russian ships were to sail to England and be interned for the duration of hostilities. Tyler was sent from Portsmouth in September 1808 to escort the Russians back to Spithead. Four years later, after being invaded by Napoleon, Russia once more became a British ally.

Between 1812 and the end of the Napoleonic Wars in 1815, Tyler was C-in-C at the Cape of Good Hope, with his flag successively in the 3rd-rate *Lion* (64), the 5th-rate frigate *Semiramis* (32) and the 3rd-rate *Medway* (74). He was promoted to vice-admiral on 4 December 1813 and awarded the KCB on 2 January 1815. Sir Charles Tyler returned to England in March 1816 and thereafter remained ashore. He became an admiral on 27 May 1825 and a GCB on 29 January 1833. He died on 28 September 1835 at the Spa, Gloucester. Tyler was twice married, first to Miss Pike and later to Margaret, daughter of Alexander Leach, Esquire, of Corsan, Pembrokeshire, Dyfed. Charles Tyler, son of his first marriage, survived his war service and financial indiscretions to become a commander in 1812 and be placed on the retired list with promotion to captain in 1844. George, son of his second marriage, also served at sea during the Napoleonic Wars, being wrecked in the Mediterranean as a midshipman in August 1810 and losing an arm in a cutting-out expedition at Quiberon Bay in May 1811. He was promoted to lieutenant on 6 February 1813 and served as his father's flag lieutenant on the Cape of Good Hope station, rising eventually to become a vice-admiral and a knight of the Royal Guelphic Order of Hanover.

YOUNG, Commander ROBERT BENJAMIN (1773–1846) **[35]**
Robert Young, the son and grandson of lieutenants in the Royal Navy, was born in Douglas, Isle of Man, in 1773. He entered the Navy at the age of eight, in 1781 during the American War of Independence, but with hostilities effectively ending in the following year, and lacking an influential patron, he was still a midshipman on the outbreak of the French Revolutionary War twelve years later. He became acting lieutenant in the sloop *Thorn* (18) on the Windward Islands station, where on 25 May 1795 he was

mentioned in dispatches for his part in the capture of the French corvette *Courier National* (18) after a single-ship duel. Later in the year he was involved in counter-insurgency operations at St Vincent in the British Windward Islands where, encouraged by French revolutionary agents, the Carib population had risen against British rule. Young served with the seamen who landed to support the troops and was mentioned in dispatches a second time, with promotion to lieutenant on 26 January 1796.

Young was then appointed to the 6th-rate frigate *Bonne Citoyen* (20) and was in the small squadron under Commodore Horatio Nelson with which the British re-entered the Mediterranean on 9 May 1796. He served in this ship in Sir John Jervis' Mediterranean fleet at **Cape St Vincent (14 February 1797)** and was in the group of frigates that, after the battle, unsuccessfully pursued the disabled Spanish four-decker *Santisima Trinidad* (130). He subsequently transferred to the 3rd-rate *Colossus* (74) in which he served until she was wrecked in the Scillies on 10 December 1798. Young and all his shipmates were saved and he returned to sea in 1799, appointed to the sloop *Savage* (14). He was deployed to the North Sea, where at the end of August 1799 he was in the squadron that landed a British army on the Helder and captured the Dutch fleet at anchor in the Texel. The arrival of further reinforcements, including a large Russian contingent, held out prospects of a successful campaign, but inter-service disputes, lack of logistic support, and continued bad weather all combined to bring about its failure, so that the troops were re-embarked and carried back to England by November 1799.

The British government, responding to a national feeling of war-weariness, made a general armistice with France and her allies in October 1801, followed by a formal peace treaty at Amiens on 25 March 1802. It soon became clear that Napoleon Bonaparte, elected First Consul of France for life in a national plebiscite that followed the peace, saw this as little more than a truce. Pre-empting him, the British declared war on France in May 1802 and Young, serving as first lieutenant of the 3rd-rate *Goliath* (74), was deployed to the West Indies, where Bonaparte had sent an army to recover French Santo

Domingo (Haiti) from a slave insurrection. During 1803 *Goliath* captured the French *la Mignonne* off Haiti and the surviving French troops capitulated to the British at the end of the year.

Young's first command was the single-masted cutter *Entreprenante* (8), taken from the French in 1801 and put into commission as a dispatch vessel in 1803. In the late summer of 1805 she joined the blockade of Vice-Admiral Pierre Villeneuve's Franco-Spanish Combined Fleet in Cadiz . When the two fleets met at **Trafalgar (21 October 1805)** she was stationed on the weather side of the British fleet along with the four frigates and the schooner *Pickle*, all of them too slightly built to have any place in the line of battle. As the fighting died away, *Entreprenante* and *Pickle*, with boats from the frigate *Euryalus* and the 3rd-rate *Belleisle*, went to the aid of the burning French *Achille* and rescued 250 men from the sea (169 being packed aboard *Entreprenante*) before *Achille* blew up with a great explosion that marked the end of the battle. It was from one of *Entreprenante*'s boats that *Belleisle* some days later learned that the British C-in-C, Vice-Admiral Viscount Nelson, had been killed and command of the fleet had passed to Vice-Admiral Collingwood **[8]**.

The day after the battle, as the weather worsened, Collingwood sent *Entreprenante* and *Pickle* around his scattered fleet to tell them to close on *Neptune*, towing his dismasted former flagship *Royal Sovereign*. The weather grew worse still and *Entreprenante*, having split her mainsail and lost most of it, set her trysail and storm jib. Overloaded with survivors from *Achille* alongside her normal complement of forty officers and men, she shipped several heavy seas and, to prevent her being swamped, Young jettisoned his guns, the remains of the mainsail, hammocks and other expendable stores. Despite the foresail and storm jib being split by the gale force winds, this saved the ship and she survived to transfer her prisoners into the overcrowded 3rd-rate *Orion* and then to retrieve the British prize crew from the distressed Spanish *Bahama* (74). Collingwood wrote his dispatches and sent two copies, the first, on 26 October 1805, directly home in *Pickle*, and the second, on 28 October, to Faro, the nearest port on the south coast of neutral Portugal, in *Entreprenante*, to be taken overland to the British Ambassador in Lisbon for onward transmission to London.

Young received the 100 guinea prize sword given by the City of London's Patriotic Fund to all those who commanded at Trafalgar and remained in *Entreprenante* during 1806 and 1807, deployed in the blockade of Brest. In 1809, as first lieutenant of a troopship, the converted 5th-rate frigate *Ulysses* (44), he returned to the North Sea in the Walcheren expedition, involving 40,000 troops, 400 transports and 200 warships. The British landings aimed to destroy enemy shipping at Antwerp and Flushing (Vlissingen) and seize the mouth of the Scheldt, thus opening a second front in support of the Austrians then in the field against Napoleon. The Austrians, however, were defeated at Wagram on 5 July 1809 before the expedition had even sailed and, despairing of British aid, signed a truce two days later. The campaign proved a repeat of the ill-fated Helder expedition in which Young had taken part eleven years previously. The army landed under the guns of the fleet at the end of July and captured Flushing on 18 August, but delays in exploiting this success allowed the French to recover from their initial surprise. Logistic difficulties, bad weather and uncertain leadership literally bogged down the army in siege operations where the unfortunate redcoats dropped like flies from the effects of local fevers. The expedition failed and during September the fleet carried most of what was left of the army home again. On 14 October 1809 Austria accepted the Treaty of Schönbrunn, ceding a fifth of her territory to Napoleon and his satellites and losing, with her Adriatic provinces, her last outlet to the sea. Young was promoted to commander on 21 October 1810 but seems to have had no further sea service before the Napoleonic Wars came to an end in 1815. He became an out-pensioner of the Royal Naval Hospital, Greenwich, in 1839 and died at Exeter in 1846.

The Battles

Actions in which two or more of the Trafalgar captains took part
(the captains' names shown in italics)

Grenada (6 July 1779)

At the end of June 1779, the Comte d'Estaing, with a French
fleet of twenty-five ships of the line, evaded the British C-in-
C in the West Indies, Vice-Admiral the Honourable John
Byron, and captured the islands of Grenada and St Vincent.
Byron, with twenty-one ships of the line, arrived off Grenada
on 6 July 1779 and, sighting only a few of d'Estaing's ships,
ordered 'General Chase' with the intention of closing before
they could form a line of battle. The British ships, each sailing
at her best speed, entered the engagement as singletons, with
the leading vessels isolated from the main force. When a
freshening wind allowed the rest of d'Estaing's fleet to come
out of St George's Bay and join the battle, Byron appreciated
that he was outnumbered. He accordingly formed a
conventional line parallel to the French, though several of his
ships had suffered damage to their rigging from the fire of
French vanguard and shore batteries, and three were drifting
out of control. Rather than risk his possession of Grenada by
bringing on a fleet action, d'Estaing contented himself with
a distant bombardment of the three drifting British ships. The
French suffered heavier casualties than the British, but
retained possession of Grenada and the thirty laden
merchantmen captured in its harbour.

Morris; Prowse

The Moonlight Battle, Cape St Vincent (16 January 1780)

At the end of December 1779 Admiral Sir George Rodney
sailed from Plymouth with a fleet of twenty-two ships

escorting a convoy for the relief of Gibraltar. On 16 January, after rounding Cape St Vincent, Rodney met a Spanish blockading squadron of eleven ships of the line under Admiral Don Juan de Langara. The outnumbered Spanish attempted to escape, but a strong westerly wind allowed Rodney to come up with them after a four-hour chase. In the subsequent battle, continued by moonlight during a stormy night, *Santo Domingo* (70) blew up and six others, including Langara's flagship *Fenix* (80), were captured. Two of the prizes were subsequently retaken by their crews, but the relief convoy reached Gibraltar and returned home unopposed.

Carnegie (Northesk); Duff; Durham

Martinique (17 April 1780)

After his victory in **The Moonlight Battle (16 January 1780)**, Admiral Sir George Rodney was sent to the West Indies with four ships of the line to reinforce the British fleet there and to take over as C-in-C He arrived at Barbados on 17 March 1780, just ahead of the French admiral, the Comte de Guichen, who reached Fort Royal, Martinique, about thirty miles away, five days later, with a convoy of eighty-three merchantmen escorted by sixteen ships of the line. De Guichen collected the warships previously at Martinique and sailed on 13 April with twenty-two ships of the line and five frigates, carrying between them 3,000 invasion troops. Rodney, with twenty ships of the line and five frigates, sighted them at noon on 16 April but, not wishing for another 'moonlight battle', made no attempt to close until the next day. At dawn on 17 April the two fleets, heading in opposite directions, met in the channel between Martinique and Dominica. The French line extended over twelve miles and the British for six. Rodney's original plan was for his fleet to alter its formation from line ahead to line abreast so as to overwhelm the straggling enemy rear. De Guichen, however, ordered his ships to wear, so that each vessel reversed its heading by turning away from the wind and his well-organized van division became the rear.

At noon, with both fleets now heading in the same direction on a parallel course, Rodney, in his flagship, the 2nd-rate *Sandwich* (98), made the code signal No. 21, 'Every ship to bear down and steer for her opposite in the enemy line'. His intention was for each ship to attack the nearest enemy, but captains in the van division, conforming to the Admiralty's standard Fighting Instructions, made sail so as to get to the head of the enemy line and engage their opposite numbers there. Unable to recall them in time, Rodney attacked with only his centre and rear divisions, and *Sandwich* passed through the enemy line on her own, where she fought three French ships in a ninety-minute duel. At dusk the French broke off the action. Both sides claimed a victory, but neither side had lost a ship and, though the French had suffered greater casualties in terms of killed and wounded, the damage to his own ships prevented Rodney from giving chase.

The two fleets again made contact off Martinique on 10 May 1780, but Guichen avoided close action. Further indecisive actions took place on 15 May and again on 19 May, when both sides suffered damage and casualties. Rodney, after losing sight of the French, returned to his base at Barbados, while Guichen, abandoning his invasion plans, went back into Fort Royal.

Carnegie (Northesk); Duff; Prowse

Ushant (12 December 1781)

In this action, a large French convoy carrying troops and stores for the West Indies was intercepted some 150 miles south-west of Ushant by a British squadron of twelve ships of the line under Rear-Admiral Richard Kempenfelt. The French escort, nineteen ships of the line under Admiral the Comte de Guichen, was sailing so far from the convoy that Kempenfelt was able to reach the helpless merchantmen and capture fifteen of them while their escort was still well to their leeward. A few days later the French survivors were caught in a storm and only two ships of the line and five transports reached their destination.

Durham; Moorsom

St Kitts (25 January–13 February 1782)

Early in 1782, Rear-Admiral Sir Samuel Hood reached the West Indian island of St Kitts, where the British garrison was besieged by the Comte de Grasse. He lured de Grasse out to sea as if to a conventional naval battle and then crowded on sail and slipped behind him to enter the St Kitts roadstead. After beating off the larger French fleet when it made a series of attacks on his anchored line, Hood waited either for his C-in-C, Admiral Sir George Rodney to arrive with reinforcements, or for de Grasse to weary of the siege and sail away, but the British garrison, heavily outnumbered and cut off from the harbour, was starved into surrender on 12 February 1782. Appreciating that the enemy would turn their siege guns and heavy mortars onto his anchored fleet, Hood cut his cables and silently put to sea on the night of 13–14 February, leaving behind small boats with lanterns burning so that the French would suppose his ships were still there.

Duff; Rotheram

Guadeloupe (9 April 1782)

The British fleet in the West Indies, under Admiral Sir George Rodney with Rear-Admiral Sir Samuel Hood as his second-in-command, consisted at this time of thirty-six ships of the line against a French fleet of thirty-five under the Comte de Grasse, based at Fort Royal, Martinique. On 7 April 1782 de Grasse put to sea escorting a convoy of 100 merchantmen on the first leg of their journey home-bound for France. Delays in getting the convoy out of harbour allowed the British to catch up with de Grasse off Dominica on 9 April 1782. In the pursuit, eight ships of the van division, led by Hood, got ahead of the main British fleet and de Grasse, intending to defeat them in detail, ordered the convoy into the harbour of Basse-Terre, Guadeloupe, while he detached fifteen ships of the line to meet Hood. In the action that followed, four British ships suffered damage to their masts and rigging, but the French also suffered damage and no decisive result was achieved.

Hargood; Rotheram

The Battle of the Saintes (12 April 1782)

After the indecisive action at **Guadeloupe (9 April 1782)**, one French ship of the line had to be towed into Guadeloupe, but the convoy of French merchantmen, with two ships of the line as escort, resumed its course for France. De Grasse and his main fleet sailed westwards, intending to join forces with the Spanish in Santo Domingo and then attack Jamaica, but a collision between two of his ships during the night of 10 April 1782 left one, *Zèle* (74), damaged and the other, *Jason* (64), heading for repairs in Guadeloupe. With Rodney in chase, de Grasse was forced to lose time by protecting *Zèle*, though during the night of 11 April 1782 she was again in collision, this time with his flagship *Ville de Paris* (120) and had to be taken in tow.

At dawn on 12 April Rodney caught up with de Grasse (his fleet by this time reduced to thirty ships of the line) near the Îes des Saintes, a group of small islands between Guadeloupe and Dominica. Both fleets formed a conventional line and British gunfire inflicted heavy casualties but the French kept their distance until coming under the lee of Dominica, where they could not evade Rodney's determination to close. De Grasse ordered his ships to wear and reverse course, but they were already too near the British. When a sudden change of wind opened gaps in the French line, Rodney ordered his flagship, the 2nd-rate *Formidable* (90) through the enemy centre. With nothing in the Admiralty's Fighting Instructions about such a move, his next five ships followed him through the gap, raking the French ships either side of them as they went. Ahead of him in the British line, Captain Alan Gardner in another three-decker, the 2nd-rate *Duke* (90), also turned and broke through the enemy line. The British rear division under Hood broke through another gap and in the following mêlée British superiority in gunnery proved decisive.

The French, broken into three groups, were unable to reform. *Ville de Paris*, the largest warship then afloat, attempted to escape but was surrounded and, with heavy casualties, her sails gone and her ammunition exhausted, surrendered on the orders of de Grasse, one of only three men left standing on her upper deck. Four other ships of the line were captured, of which one caught fire and blew up with the loss of all on board. Total French casualties amounted to over 3,000 against about 1,000 British. Although Hood complained of Rodney's excessive caution in breaking off the battle at dusk and allowing the French to escape, Rodney's action in breaking the French line with captains who understood his intentions foreshadowed the tactics that Nelson would use with such success a generation later. His victory heartened the British public, facing the end of a disastrous war, and helped British diplomats negotiate from a position of greater strength. At the Treaty of Versailles (20 January 1783) the British were forced to recognize the independence of the United States, but regained possession of almost all their lost West Indian colonies.

Carnegie (Northesk); Cooke; Duff; Hargood; Morris; Rotheram

Toulon (Aug–Dec 1793)

Following the outbreak of war with Revolutionary France in February 1793, a British fleet of twelve ships of the line under Admiral Lord Hood was dispatched to the Mediterranean where it blockaded the major French naval base of Toulon. On 27 August 1793 pro-royalist citizens who had learned of Republican atrocities at Marseilles invited Hood to take possession of their city in the name of Louis XVII. The offer, including the great naval arsenal and dockyard containing thirty ships of the line, was at once accepted, though Hood could provide only 1,500 marines and seamen, hurriedly reinforced by a contingent of allied Spanish troops, to hold a perimeter of fifteen miles. British reinforcements were not immediately available, as the Cabinet had already committed its military assets variously to a continental campaign in Flanders, an expedition in support of royalist insurgents in Brittany, and to a colonial war in the West Indies. Nevertheless, two British regiments reached Toulon on 27 October 1793 and the Prime Minister, William Pitt, built up a multinational coalition, financed by British gold, that produced a total of 20,000 troops, including French royalists, Piedmontese, Neapolitans and Spaniards, for the defence of the city.

Against these the Jacobin government gathered an army of 35,000 men with siege guns under the young Napoleon Bonaparte. While the polyglot defenders of Toulon were weakened by disease and disputes between their commanders, the besiegers, inspired by revolutionary fervour and patriotic zeal, made steady progress. An assault made on the night of 17 December 1793 broke through the coalition lines, with only the Piedmontese, together with the British troops and seamen serving ashore, making any determined resistance. With Republican batteries able to reach the harbour, the allies decided to abandon the city to its fate. The following night some 15,000 refugees were packed into every available craft and taken out to the fleet. Of those who remained in the burning city, thousands of men, women and children were murdered by criminal gangs or executed wholesale by the vengeful Jacobins. In the confusion only thirteen of the thirty French ships of the line were destroyed, leaving the rest to sail again under the tricolour.

Fremantle; Hardy; Tyler

Corsica (February–August 1794)

Corsica had been sold to France by Genoa some twenty years earlier and its inhabitants only accepted French rule after years of Nationalist resistance. In the spring of 1793, under the Corsican patriot Pascal Paoli, they rose against the French Republic and drove its troops into their coastal fortresses. The British Cabinet at first ignored requests for aid but in February 1794 Admiral Lord Hood, having lost Toulon and needing a base for his Mediterranean fleet, arrived in San Fiorenzo (St Florent) and disembarked seamen, marines and 1,400 British troops who had arrived too late to defend Toulon. The insurgents, controlling the interior of the island, hailed the British as liberators, but the 3,500 French regulars secure behind the walls of Bastia and Calvi remained defiant. When the Army commander, Major-General David Dundas, reported that he could not take these positions with his available forces, Hood declared that the Navy would take them without him. Heavy guns were landed from the 3rd-rate *Agamemnon* (64) under Captain Horatio Nelson and, after standing a regular siege, Bastia was starved into surrender on 15 May 1794.

General Paoli and a national assembly then declared Corsica's independence, with George III as their new king. The arrival of large-scale troop reinforcements from Gibraltar allowed Hood to hand back the campaign to the Army. *Agamemnon's* guns went to Calvi where Nelson, serving in the siege batteries, was hit by flying debris that eventually cost him the sight of his right eye. Calvi surrendered on 10 August 1794. The island remained under a British viceroy for the next two years, but there were never enough troops either to suppress the brigands of the interior or to defend a coastline covering 400 miles. On 31 August 1796, with Spain about to enter the war on the French side and Bonaparte victorious in Italy, the Cabinet decided to withdraw from the Mediterranean and abandon Corsica, where French troops landed as the British sailed.

Nelson; Fremantle; Tyler

Martinique (14–21 April 1793)

The Revolution in France was followed by widespread disorders in the French West Indies. Taking their stand upon the Declaration of the Rights of Man, local freemen of mixed race or African descent demanded equality with the previously privileged white community, while African slaves rose in a series of savage insurrections. On the outbreak of war between the United Kingdom and the new French Republic in February 1793, French royalists in the West Indies asked for British help. The British, fighting revolution in Europe and fearing that their own West Indian slaves might follow the French example, agreed. On 14 April 1793 Vice-Admiral Sir John Laforey occupied Tobago with 500 British troops. On 16 June 1793, 1,100 British soldiers landed in Martinique, and with local French royalists, who had promised they would be welcomed as liberators, marched on St Pierre, the island's commercial capital. When the Republican governor showed fight, the royalists fled, leaving the British dangerously outnumbered. On 21 June, under the protection of the Navy's guns, the troops re-embarked for Barbados.

Bullen; Capel; Duff

Martinique (February–March 1794)

On 5 February 1794 the British returned to Martinique with 7,000 men under Lieutenant-General Sir Charles Grey, escorted by a fleet under Vice-Admiral Sir John Jervis. By 28 February 1794, despite determined resistance and the difficult terrain, they had captured the whole island except for the two forts defending the town of Fort Royal, the island's administrative capital (renamed Fort de France by the new Republican regime). With the aid of seamen from the fleet who were given their own battery, a formal siege was then begun, with gunfire support from ships in the harbour. On 20 March naval landing parties carried the seaward fort by storm while the town was taken by the Army's grenadiers and light infantry. The French commander held out in the landward fort for another three days before surrendering and Martinique remained in British hands until March 1802, when it was restored to France on the conclusion of the French Revolutionary War.

Bayntun; Hargood; Lapenotiere; Rutherford

St Lucia (1–4 April 1794)

After their success in capturing **Martinique (February–March 1794)**, the British attacked the nearby French island of St Lucia on 1 April 1794. As at Martinique, the troops made a series of landings under the protection of the fleet and then took the coastal defences from the landward side. The French garrison of 120 regulars surrendered on 4 April 1794 and were given passage home. The British were soon faced with a general rebellion of those to whom French Republican rule meant equal civil rights and the abolition of slavery. Counter-insurgency operations in the wooded mountains of the interior proved unsuccessful and, defeated by the combined onslaught of yellow fever and local resistance, the British garrison was evacuated by the fleet on 18 June 1795.

Lapenotiere; Rutherford

Guadeloupe (April–May 1794)

After an easy capture of **St Lucia (1–4 April 1794)**, Sir John Jervis and his fleet carried Sir Charles Grey's army to

Guadeloupe, where landings were made at Grand Bay on 11 April 1794, while the 5th-rate frigate *Winchelsea* (32) went close inshore to silence the shore batteries. Six battalions of grenadiers and light infantry, accompanied by a strong naval brigade, stormed Fort La Fleur, controlling Grande-Terre, the northern half of the island, on 12 April and the army then re-embarked and landed on the southern half of the island, Basse-Terre. Once again the coastal defences were taken from the landward side and the French commander surrendered on 21 April 1794. In June 1794, while Jervis and Grey were at St Kitts, commissioners from France reached Guadeloupe with 1,500 fresh troops. When they declared the end of slavery and the introduction of equal rights for all men, the Afro-Caribbeans rallied to their cause and provided recruits for a local army that vastly outnumbered the British. French royalists proved of little military value and many were massacred in what become a war between races as well as ideologies. The British, ravaged by yellow fever, were driven back into the coastal forts and after an eight-weeks' siege, the last garrison was evacuated by the Navy on 10 December 1795.

Bayntun; Lapenotiere; Harvey; Rutherford

The Glorious First of June (1 June 1794)

Early in 1794 Revolutionary France faced famine, resulting from the disruption of her economy by years of anarchy and a war with every kingdom on her borders. The harvest of 1793 had failed and the British naval blockade, in which foodstuffs were counted as contraband, cut imports from abroad. The French sent agents to the United States to charter cargo ships and buy grain, and the American grain fleet sailed on 11 April 1793.

Lord Howe, commanding the Channel fleet, sailed in search of the convoy, but failed to find it and returned to the blockade of Brest on 19 May 1794. In his absence the French Rear-Admiral Villaret-Joyeuse put to sea with twenty-six ships of the line to cover the grain fleet's arrival. After eight days searching, Howe, also with twenty-six ships of the line, made contact with Villaret-Joyeuse 400 miles west of Ushant and fought a running engagement with him during the next two days. By the evening of 29 March one British and four French ships were heading for home, but the next two days proved foggy, so that the two fleets only caught glimpses of each other, while the arrival of reinforcements brought the French fleet back to twenty-six ships against Howe's remaining twenty-five.

Dawn on 1 June 1794 revealed the French fleet four miles to windward of the British on a fine summer's day. Howe's plan was for each of his ships to steer for its opposite number in the enemy line, then pass astern of it and turn to engage it from the leeward. Most managed to do this, and the French line was pierced in some twenty places before Villaret Joyeuse was able to re-form it. Ten of his ships were left surrounded by the British, but he returned to rescue four of them. In all, six French ships were captured and one, *Vengeur*, sank after a duel with the 3rd-rate *Brunswick* (74), despite the latter losing her captain and a third of her crew. *Vengeur*'s captain, his twelve year old son and some 300 of her crew were rescued from the water and the rest went down singing the 'Marseillaise'.

After several hours fighting Villaret-Joyeuse broke off the battle and escaped to the north-west. The sixty-nine year old Howe, exhausted by four days and nights spent continually on deck before the battle, decided that his own fleet had suffered too much damage to follow him. Two weeks later the fleet returned to Portsmouth in triumph with its six battered prizes. The British government, badly in need of a naval victory after the disasters of the allied campaign in Flanders, was saved. George III went to Spithead and held a levee on board Howe's flagship *Queen Charlotte*. Honours, promotions and awards were distributed on a grand scale. Captains were awarded gold medals and first lieutenants were promoted to commander. The British population rejoiced, naming the battle 'The Glorious First of June'. The true victor of the campaign, however, was Villaret-Joyeuse, who had carefully drawn Howe away from the path of the grain convoy. The American merchantmen entered Brest on 14 June 1794, the day after Howe reached Portsmouth. At the cost of seven ships and perhaps 2,000 men, Villaret-Joyeuse had prevented the famine that would have brought down the Revolutionary regime. Howe had concentrated on defeating the enemy's battle fleet, the conventional aim of all British admirals. In the process, however, he lost the last chance of ending the war before France's increasing strength on land became too great for her enemies to counter.

Berry; Blackwood; Bullen; Codrington; Collingwood;
Conn; Cooke; Pilfold; Prowse; Rotheram

Leghorn (13–14 March 1795)

On 3 March 1795 a French squadron of fifteen ships of the line, six frigates and two brig-corvettes sailed from Toulon carrying troops intended for an invasion of British-held Corsica. The Mediterranean fleet, under Vice-Admiral William Hotham, at this time consisting of twelve ships of the line, four frigates and three minor combatants, supported by one ship of the line and two frigates from the Royal Neapolitan Navy, left its anchorage in Leghorn (Livorno) Roads on 9 March 1796 and sighted the French the next day. At first light on 13 March Hotham ordered a general chase, in squally weather during which the French *Ça Ira* (80) lost her fore and main topmasts in collision with her next ahead, *Victoire* (80). Captain Thomas Fremantle **[15]** in the 5th-rate frigate *Inconstant* (36) closed with *Ça Ira* and fired a broadside into her port quarter before exchanging fire with the French frigate *Vestale* when she arrived to take *Ça Ira* in tow. A broadside from *Ça Ira* damaged *Inconstant* and forced Fremantle to break off the engagement, leaving Captain Horatio Nelson in the 3rd-rate *Agamemnon* (64) to take his place.

This action continued until nightfall, after which the flagship *Sans-Culotte* (120), the only three-decker in the French squadron, lost contact with her consorts, so that at dawn these were faced with a force containing four British three-deckers. The badly damaged *Ça Ira*, towed by the frigate *Censeur*, was attacked by the British 3rd-rates *Captain* and *Bedford*, but put up so spirited a resistance that both British ships had to be towed out of the line. Fremantle and Nelson, however, had slowed *Ça Ira* so much that she was unable to escape and, with *Censeur*, was left behind to be captured while the rest of the French squadron made its way back to Toulon.

Nelson; Fremantle; Hope; Tyler

Hyères (13 July 1795)

On 4 July 1795 Admiral William Hotham, C-in-C Mediterranean Fleet, detached Commodore Horatio Nelson in the 3rd-rate *Agamemnon* (64) with the 5th-rate frigate *Meleager* (32) and three minor combatants to cruise off the coast of Genoa. On 7 July, off Cape Mele, western Liguria, they unexpectedly encountered the French fleet from Toulon, consisting of seventeen ships of the line, six frigates and two or three corvettes. Nelson immediately turned away and, with the French in pursuit, headed south-eastwards to San Fiorenzo (St Florent) Bay, the British fleet anchorage off northern Corsica. Alerted by *Agamemnon*'s signal guns, Hotham began to put to sea, but with most of his ships engaged in replenishment and revictualling, and hampered by contrary winds, did not succeed in doing so until dusk. The French, outnumbered by Hotham's twenty-three ships of the line (including two from the Royal Neapolitan Navy), of which six were three-deckers against only one in the French fleet, broke off the chase and headed for Toulon. Hotham pursued them and finally made contact on 13 July, off the Hyères Islands, some twenty-five miles east of Toulon. The three leading British ships came up with the three rearmost French, of which one, *Alcide* (74) caught fire and blew up. Three more British ships, including Nelson's *Agamemnon*, then joined the action but at this point Hotham decided they were too close inshore for safety and signalled them to break off. Both Nelson and Captain Rowley in the 3rd-rate *Cumberland* (80) at first disregarded the signal but when Hotham repeated it, prefixed by *Cumberland*'s distinguishing number, they were obliged to comply and allow the French to escape. Nelson and other British captains thought Hotham had been unduly cautious, and believed that, but for this, they could have taken or destroyed every ship in the French fleet.

Nelson; Redmill; Tyler

Bridport's Action, Île de Groix, Lorient (23 June 1795)

In May 1795 widespread discontent with the Republican regime inside France encouraged royalist exiles to attempt a restoration of the monarchy. The British gave them money and arms and allowed them to assemble an army in Hampshire. On 17 June 1795 the first contingent sailed for Brittany, escorted by a naval squadron under Commodore Sir John Borlase Warren, while the Channel Fleet under Admiral Lord Bridport (formerly Sir Alexander Hood), flying his flag in the 1st-rate *Royal George* (100), sailed with fourteen ships of the line to protect the expedition against the French fleet from Brest. The French, with twelve ships of the line under Vice-Admiral Villaret-Joyeuse, encountered five British ships of the line under Vice-Admiral Cornwallis on 17 June but did not press home its advantage and was discovered by Bridport off Belle Île on 22 June. Bridport signalled a general chase, but at dusk the wind failed and it was not until dawn on 23 June that the action began. Two British ships, the 1st-rate *Queen Charlotte* (100) and the 3rd-rate *Irresistible* (74), well ahead of Bridport's scattered fleet, caught up with the French 74-gun ships *Alexandre* and *Formidable* and were then joined by the 3rd-rates *Sans Pareil* (80) and *Orion* (74). The two French ships were crippled by gunfire and forced to surrender, while a third, *Tigre* (74) struck to *Sans Pareil* when the 2nd-rates *Queen* (98) and *London* (90) joined the engagement.

Shortly afterwards Bridport recalled his ships, judging that the chase had taken them too close to the land, so that Villaret Joyeuse escaped to the protection of the Île de Groix and thence into harbour at Lorient. British casualties totalled thirty-one killed and 113 wounded against estimated French losses of over 600 in the three prizes. Bridport was content with his victory, though others thought that he had been over-cautious in not following the French inshore. The French royalists disembarked in safety and were greeted as liberators by thousands of Breton peasants but, faced with a vigorous Republican counter-offensive and hampered by poor leadership, the expedition proved a disaster and most of its survivors were rescued by the boats of Warren's frigates on 21 June 1795.

Blackwood; Capel; Codrington; Durham; Grindall; Pilfold

Cape St Vincent (14 February 1797)

Early in February 1797, British fortunes were at a low ebb. A French descent on the coasts of Pembrokeshire, though easily defeated by the Yeomanry and Volunteers, had threatened a run on the banks and weakened the prestige of the British Cabinet. Austria, the United Kingdom's last major ally, had been defeated by Bonaparte at Rivoli and every port in Italy was closed to British shipping. The British fleet under Sir John Jervis had, for want of naval bases, been forced out of the Mediterranean. At the end of January 1797, with fifteen ships of the line, he took station off Cape St Vincent, the south-eastern tip of Portugal, to await a Spanish fleet that was expected to join the French in an attempt to invade Ireland. The Spanish, with twenty-seven ships of the line, left Cartagena on 31 January 1797 and reached Cape St Vincent on the night of 13–14 February 1797.

The next morning, Jervis, flying his flag in the 1st-rate *Victory*, made contact with the Spanish fleet. As the enemy ships emerged from the mist and his captain of the fleet, Captain (later Admiral Sir) Robert Calder reported their numbers from 'There are eighteen of the sail of line Sir John', up to 'There are twenty-seven sail of the line, Sir John, nearly double our own'. Jervis merely acknowledged each report with 'Very well, Sir' until finally declaring 'Enough, Sir! No more of that! The die is cast and if there are fifty sail of the line I will go through them.'

The Spanish commander, Don José de Cordoba, was not expecting the British to give battle, and had been proceeding towards Cadiz with his fleet in two divisions, the smaller, to his leeward side, consisting of seven ships of the line under Vice-Admiral Joaquin Moreno. On sighting the British fleet he attempted to form a line of battle with his larger division of seventeen ships. Jervis signalled his own fifteen, led by Captain Thomas Troubridge in the 3rd-rate *Culloden* (74), to pass through the gap between the two enemy divisions. As the British did so, both sides opened fire and Cordoba veered away so as to steer on a course roughly parallel with that of Jervis but on the opposite heading. Jervis then ordered his ships to tack in succession, each following the other so as to bring their line on the same heading as Cordoba's. As they did so, Moreno attempted to break through the British line and link up with Cordoba. One of Moreno's ships, steering well behind the British, succeeded, but his flagship, *Principe de Asturias* (112), was met by a series of broadsides from *Victory* and, with her steering assembly wrecked, drifted away with her consorts following her.

Commodore Horatio Nelson, with his pendant in the 3rd-rate *Captain* (74), third ship from Jervis's rear, appreciated that by waiting to tack in succession while still moving in the opposite direction, he would find himself well behind the enemy line, because it would have moved on in the meantime. With the rearmost British ships out of the way, Cordoba would then have been able to reverse his own course and link up with Moreno, so reuniting his numerically superior fleet. In fact Cordoba, with his flag in the four-decker *Santisima Trinidad* (130), had indeed changed direction to cut across the head of Jervis's line and possibly to turn once again while Jervis passed on an opposing course. Nelson therefore ordered *Captain* to wear rather than tack, turning away from the wind rather than going through it. After passing between the two ships behind him, the 3rd-rates *Diadem* and *Excellent*, he sailed directly to the head of the Spanish line and engaged the leading group of four ships, thus slowing Cordoba's progress. Jervis immediately signalled *Excellent*, under Captain Cuthbert Collingwood [8], to go to his aid, while *Culloden* and other ships of the British van came up in support.

Captain lost her fore-topmast in the mêlée and ran into *San Nicolas* (80) which, attempting to avoid *Excellent*'s broadsides, had already become entangled with *San Josef* (112). Nelson joined the boarders and after climbing through *San Nicolas*'s quarter-gallery windows, fought his way to the quarterdeck to find his friend Commander Edward Berry [2] hauling down the Spanish colours. They then boarded the three-decker *San Josef* and after a short fight captured her too. *Salvador del Mundo* (112) was taken by Captain James Saumarez's 3rd-rate *Orion* (74) while *Excellent* took *San Isidro* (74). *Santisima Trinidad*, struck her flag to Saumarez but rehoisted it again when, for lack of boats, he was unable formally to take possession of her. She sailed away to fight another day, notably when she and *Victory* met again at **Trafalgar (21 October 1805).**

This action, fought by a small British fleet against odds of almost two to one, demonstrated the high standard of gunnery, seamanship and ship-handling of which the Navy, especially when led by admirals of Jervis's quality, was capable at this time. The Spanish ships escaped into Cadiz, where they remained under blockade for the next two years. The invasion plan of which they were to form part was shelved. The British ministry, whose potential fall was averted by the news of this victory, was generous with its rewards, which including a peerage for Jervis as Earl St Vincent. Nelson's action in breaking away from the line was criticized by Calder as being contrary to the Admiralty's standard Fighting Instructions, but Jervis considered it fully justified as being in accordance with his known intentions, and gave Nelson his warmest thanks. *San Nicolas* was dubbed 'Nelson's patent bridge for boarding first-rates' and Nelson himself, promoted to rear-admiral at the age of thirty-eight (the youngest in the Navy), became a favourite with the fleet and the nation.

Nelson; Berry; Collingwood; Hardy; Prowse; Young

Santa Cruz, Tenerife (24–25 July 1797)
In April 1797 Commodore Horatio Nelson proposed an amphibious assault on the Spanish stronghold of Santa Cruz, Tenerife, in the Canary Islands, using the 3,500 British troops formerly in garrison at Elba. When these troops were ordered elsewhere, the scheme was shelved, only to be revived a few months later when intelligence reached Earl St Vincent, C-in-C of the Mediterranean fleet, that the annual Spanish treasure ship from the Far East was anchored there. Diverting its cargo from the Spanish to the British exchequer would be an important act of economic warfare as well as bringing a fortune in prize money to those involved, so St Vincent dispatched Nelson with three ships of the line, three frigates, and 200 extra marines under Captain Thomas Troubridge to make a surprise attack on Santa Cruz. Surprise was lost when

the initial attack, with 1,000 men being rowed ashore in boats, was disrupted by strong inshore currents and, after two attempts, had to be abandoned. A gale then kept the ships out to sea for two days and it was not until the night of 24–25 July that they tried again.

As they approached the harbour in misty rain, Spanish coast artillery opened a deadly fire on the boats and the town's church bells rang out the alarm. It soon became clear that reports of the garrison being weak, ill-trained and demoralized were completely inaccurate. Once more the strong current hindered the boats from reaching the mole and most were overturned by surf or smashed on rocks. Nelson, leading the attack, landed but was hit in the arm and caught by his stepson, Josiah Nisbet, who used his own stock as a tourniquet and put him back in his boat. Nelson insisted that as many others as could be pulled from the water should be got on board and was eventually taken to the frigate *Seahorse*, whose captain, Thomas Fremantle [15] had also been wounded and was still ashore.

About 300 marines and seamen led by Troubridge finally reached Santa Cruz's main square, where they came under musketry fire from the citadel and neighbouring houses. With their own powder wet, they could make no effective reply and took shelter inside a strongly-built convent. At dawn they found themselves out of ammunition and surrounded by 8,000 regulars and local militia. They prepared fireballs and torches with which, Troubridge declared, they would burn the town unless given safe conduct back to their ships. The Spanish governor called their bluff and Troubridge accepted a counter-offer of safe conduct in return for a British promise not to make any further attack on the Canary Islands. The governor, a generous and chivalrous foe, entertained the two surviving British captains to dinner and provided each of their men with a loaf of bread and a pint of wine before returning them to their ships in Spanish boats (no British boats having survived). Nelson, whose wound had cost him his arm, rallied and repaid this courtesy by ensuring that the governor's own official report of the action was delivered to Cadiz under flag of truce. This episode cost the British seven officers and 146 men killed in action, drowned or missing and five officers (including Nelson) and 100 men wounded. Like the attempted descent on **Boulogne (15 August 1801)**, another amphibious operation, it was one of Nelson's rare defeats.

Nelson; Fremantle.

The Nile (1–2 August 1798)

Early in 1798 General Napoleon Bonaparte proposed to the Directors of the French Republic that the best way of weakening their British enemy was to send an expedition, under his command, to the Levant and thence to attack their commercial empire in India. The Directors were happy for him to take his army out of France and a large expedition, including not only soldiers but engineers and scholars, was accordingly assembled. It sailed from Toulon on 19 May 1798 in a vast convoy of nearly 400 troopships and cargo vessels, escorted by thirteen ships of the line under Admiral Francois Brueys with his flag in *L'Orient* (120), the largest ship in the French Navy. Although the British knew that an expedition was planned, none supposed that its destination was Egypt. It was not, therefore, until after searching the Mediterranean for over two months, sometimes missing his quarry by the narrowest of margins, that Rear-Admiral Sir Horatio Nelson located the French in Aboukir (Abu Qir) Bay, Alexandria, off the western mouth of the Nile.

With the army safely disembarked at the beginning of July and Bonaparte having gained yet another brilliant victory at the battle of the Pyramids a fortnight later, Brueys had moored his fleet safely in a single line, two miles long, in Aboukir Bay. Its eastern side was protected by shoals and sandbanks, while strong shore batteries guarded the head of the line. Any attack, he seems to have appreciated, if made at all, would be on his centre and rear, where he placed his most powerful assets. Nelson, with fourteen ships of the line and his flag in the 3rd-rate *Vanguard* (74) reached the bay at sunset, but rather than wait until the next day, continued his approach. He had already told his captains that if he found the French fleet at anchor he would attack part of its line with the whole of his own and overwhelm it before the remaining enemy ships could join the battle.

Although the French were moored as closely as possible to the sandbanks on their port side, they were anchored only at the bow and therefore had to leave sufficient depth of water for them to swing if the wind shifted. Nelson and other experienced seamen in his fleet spotted that, where there was room for a ship to swing, there was room for a ship to sail. Captain Foley, leading the British line in *Goliath* (74) and the only officer in the fleet to have even a rudimentary chart of the shoals, accordingly went down the landward side of the French fleet, taking soundings as he went. He was followed by six others while Nelson led the remaining six (Captain Thomas Troubridge's *Culloden* (74) having gone aground in shoal water) along the seaward side, so that the seven leading French ships were engaged by thirteen British.

Close action continued until well after dark, when *L'Orient* caught fire and blew up. The same wind that carried the British into the bay prevented the rearmost French ships from going to the aid of their consorts at the head of the line and by dawn the survivors had drifted far downwind. When the British renewed the battle, two ships of the line and two frigates escaped to sea, two ran aground and surrendered, a third, dismasted, was taken the next day, and the last, also aground, was set on fire by her captain as the crew escaped ashore. This battle not only destroyed the French Mediterranean fleet but isolated the French army in the Levant. Eventually Bonaparte, leaving his veterans behind, returned to France alone, where his enemies said he should be tried as a deserter. His star, however, would carry him to higher things.

Nelson's own star shone out brilliantly in this action, his first great victory as an admiral. Before the battle, in consequence of his continued failure to find the French, there had been calls for him to be relieved of command. Afterwards, his reputation was made. The high standard of gunnery and seamanship in his fleet, his own tactical skill, and above all the mutual trust and understanding established between himself and his captains, his 'band of brothers', all combined to bring about not just the defeat but the annihilation of the enemy. Despite the courage of the French in battle, they had lost their admiral (dead of his wounds before his flagship blew up), 2,000 men killed and 3,500 captured, nearly half of them wounded. Out of thirteen ships of the line, nine had been taken and two destroyed. The British lost 200 men killed, including Captain Westcott of the 3rd-rate *Majestic* (74), and 700 wounded, including Nelson himself, who at one point had been temporarily blinded and had to leave the deck. After the battle, in a chivalrous gesture, he entertained six captured and wounded French captains to dinner in his cabin.

Nelson; Berry; Capel; Hardy

Malta (30 March 1800)

On his way to Egypt, Bonaparte had taken Malta from the Knights of St John and left a French garrison in their fortress capital of Valetta. Nelson's victory at **The Nile** left the Malta garrison isolated and the British began a siege and naval blockade. With his supplies failing, the French commander sent *Guillaume Tell* (80), the last French ship of the line surviving from **The Nile**, for help. She sailed after dark on 30 March 1800, hoping to take advantage of the gale then blowing, but was almost immediately intercepted by the frigate *Penelope* (36), under Captain Henry Blackwood [3]. Blackwood came up astern of her and engaged with *Penelope*'s port and starboard batteries alternately. *Guillaume Tell*, attempting to escape, could reply only with her stern-chasers, and Berry continued the action in this way until daylight, damaging *Guillaume Tell*'s topmasts and rigging and allowing the 3rd-rate *Lion* (64) to come up and join the fight at dawn.

An hour later the 2nd-rate *Foudroyant* (80), commanded by Captain Edward Berry [2], joined the battle, in which she fired eighty broadsides in two hours and ten minutes, with the loss of eight men killed and sixty-one wounded out of a crew of 718. *Penelope* lost her master killed, with a midshipman and two seamen wounded, and *Lion* lost eight killed and thirty-eight wounded out of her crew of 300. The outnumbered

Guillaume Tell put up a gallant fight, suffering some 200 casualties but, after being totally dismasted, was forced to surrender with a French rear-admiral and 1,200 men. *Foudroyant* herself was almost as badly damaged and had to be towed out of action by *Lion*. The siege and blockade of Valetta continued until 5 September 1800, when the French, down to their last rat, were starved into surrender.

Berry; Blackwood.

Copenhagen (2 April 1801)
In December 1800 Russia, Sweden, Denmark and Prussia formed the Armed Neutrality of the North to counter the British blockade of their seaborne trade with France. This alliance threatened British access to the Baltic's essential shipbuilding materials and also to ships carrying grain from eastern Europe to England, where the harvest had failed for a second year running. When the Danes placed an embargo on British shipping, the British Cabinet responded by assembling a powerful fleet at Great Yarmouth under Admiral Sir Hyde Parker, with Vice-Admiral Sir Horatio Nelson as his second-in-command. Parker, just returned from a lucrative command at Jamaica and having married an eighteen year old bride, made little effort to get his ships to sea. Alerted by Nelson, who appreciated the need to act before the Armed Neutrality could mobilize its full naval strength (amounting to 100 ships of the line), the Admiralty ordered Parker to sail without further delay. On 23 March 1801, after Parker had anchored his fleet at the entrance to the Baltic, the Danes rejected a British ultimatum to withdraw from the Armed Neutrality. Parker, reluctant to face the defences of Copenhagen, was in favour of waiting until the Baltic navies came out into the open sea to give battle. Nelson argued that the Danes must be attacked at once, before the Danish defences were improved still further while the ice at Kronstadt melted and allowed the Russians to join them. Parker agreed to let him attack with the shallowest-draught ships, while he himself stood off with the eight heaviest.

The Danes removed the various buoys and navigational aids marking their shoals but the British took soundings and replaced them. On 1 April 1801 Nelson moved his ships (twelve of the line, five frigates, seven bomb vessels and other minor combatants) to within two miles of Copenhagen, where the defences consisted of eighteen moored warships, hulks and floating batteries and coast artillery. The next morning he sailed in from the north, passing between the sand banks with the ships' leadsmen declaring their soundings as they went in a way that, in the surrounding silence, reminded one observer of the solemn responses in a church service. The Danes had placed their weakest units to the south, but in accordance with Nelson's plan, the 3rd-rate *Edgar* (74) led the fleet past them and anchored opposite the fifth ship from the head of the Danish line. The remaining British ships were then meant to pass *Edgar* so as to outnumber and engage those beyond. Their pilots however, used only to handling small Baltic traders, could not cope with major combatants, especially when they came under fire. Four British ships went aground or were swept out of position and Nelson's temporary flagship, the 3rd-rate *Elephant*, avoided the same fate only when, at the last moment, he ordered the helm put over. The remainder ranged alongside their selected opponents and the battle became a series of fire fights. The Danes resisted with great courage and boatloads of volunteers put out from shore to replace those killed or wounded. Despite nearly a quarter of his heavy ships being unable to play an effective part in the battle, Nelson's tactics proved successful and by noon the Danish flagship *Dannebrog* (24) was on fire, later to drift away and blow up with the loss of 270 out of her crew of 330. 'Hard pounding' said Nelson to Colonel Edward Stewart of the 49th Foot, on board *Elephant* with his regiment for an intended assault on the powerful Trekroner Battery at the head of the Danish line, 'but, mark you, I would not be anywhere else for a thousand pounds'.

An hour later, seeing only smoke and three stranded British ships flying distress signals, Parker hoisted signal No.39 (Discontinue Action). Nelson, appreciating that to break off the engagement at this critical time would be disastrous, made the famous remark that, with only one eye, he had the right to be blind sometimes and, putting his telescope to the blind eye, said that he really did not see the signal. He ordered his own No.16 (Engage the enemy more closely), always flown while a battle lasted, to be nailed to the mast. Only the frigates, engaging the Trekroner Battery and unable to see Nelson's signal, reluctantly obeyed Parker and stood out to sea, taking casualties as they went. Danish fire slackened as their vessels were driven ashore or forced to surrender. When British boats went to take possession, the Danes fired on them, and Nelson sent a message ashore under flag of truce, to say that the two nations were natural brothers rather than enemies, but if resistance continued, he would burn the prizes with their crews in them. This led to an armistice in which the Danish Crown Prince Frederick, to save his capital from bombardment, agreed to suspend membership of the Armed Neutrality and supply provisions for the British as they prepared to meet the Russians. Danish casualties amounted to 790 killed, 900 wounded and 2,500 prisoners of war, with twelve ships captured, though these had been so stoutly defended that eleven of them were fit only to be burned.

Despite Nelson's urging, Parker refused to advance into the Baltic without further orders from London. When they came on 5 May 1801, they told him to hand over command to Nelson and return home. A new Tsar, Alexander I, had come to the throne of Russia and, with the news of Copenhagen, decided (followed by the rest of the Armed Neutrality), to resume friendly relations with the British. Nelson visited Reval (Tallinn), the Estonian naval base of his new Russian friends, and was hailed as a young Suvarov. Returning home, where everyone knew that the victory was his, not Parker's, he was made a viscount, with his popularity and reputation higher than ever. Copenhagen, with British casualties of 350 killed and 850 wounded, was proportionately Nelson's costliest victory, but one in which his determination, courage and tactical skill were displayed to the full. It dissolved a powerful coalition that had threatened vital British interests and demonstrated that, with their survival at stake, the British would not shrink from attacking a neutral state.

Napoleon Bonaparte, First Consul of France, greeted the news by stamping and shouting with rage.

Nelson; Conn; Fremantle; Hardy; Tyler

Boulogne (15 August 1801)

On returning from the Baltic, Nelson was given a force of minor combatants for inshore operations in the Channel against the anticipated French invasion. Intending to sink or capture the invasion barges collected at Boulogne, he attacked the harbour with his ships' boats on the night of 15 August 1805 but the French defences, under Rear-Admiral Louis Latouché-Tréville, together with the fierce Channel current, proved too strong. The raid, one of Nelson's rare defeats, was repulsed with the loss of twelve boats and forty-four men to little purpose. He was, however, able to report on the barges and concluded that their flat-bottomed design meant they could neither row nor sail across the narrow seas and they therefore posed little threat.

Nelson; Conn

Calder's Action, Finisterre (22 July 1805)

On 9 July 1805 Lord Barham, First Lord of the Admiralty, read Nelson's report that the Franco-Spanish Combined Fleet under Vice-Admiral Pierre Villeneuve was heading home from the West Indies, with Nelson in pursuit. Barham accordingly sent Rear-Admiral Charles Stirling and the five ships of the line blockading Rochefort to join Vice-Admiral Sir Robert Calder's ten ships of the line at Ferrol, and ordered Calder to take station 100 miles off Finisterre so as to intercept the Combined Fleet as it returned to European waters. Villeneuve, who was sighted early on 22 August 1805, had twenty ships of the line against Calder's fifteen, but the British force included four three-deckers while the Combined Fleet had none. Both fleets formed a conventional line of battle but action was not joined until the early afternoon, by which time the morning haze had become a fog in which ships could scarcely see their opponents and fired mostly at enemy gun flashes. Two Spanish ships, *San Rafael* and *Firme*, fell out of their line and were captured and, with dusk approaching, Calder broke off the engagement. His casualties totalled forty-one killed and about 160 wounded against some 150 and 330 respectively of the enemy. Two of the British ships had lost a mast, but apart from the two prizes, Villeneuve's fleet suffered little damage. The two fleets remained within sight of each other during the next two days, after which, with neither admiral renewing the battle, they lost contact. Villeneuve made port in Vigo and Calder, after escorting his prizes and the two damaged ships safely towards Plymouth, resumed the blockade of Ferrol.

Calder was much criticized for failing to secure a decisive victory. Public opinion, accustomed to clear successes such as Nelson had achieved at **The Nile** and **Copenhagen**, was indignant that an enemy fleet had been allowed to escape, with ships that might cover the threatened invasion of England or prey upon vital British convoys. Sea officers on both sides, however, sympathized with him. Nelson commented that the outcome of a battle was never predictable. 'I should have fought the enemy, so did my friend Calder: but who can say that he will be more successful than another'. After Trafalgar, Captain Infernet, late of the French *Intrépide*, commented that the British had found fault with an admiral for fighting twenty capital ships with fifteen and only capturing two, and Villeneuve said 'I wish Sir Robert and I had fought it out that day, he would not be in his present situation nor I in mine'. Calder claimed that, already outnumbered, he could not risk a second battle in which Villeneuve might be joined by the sixteen Spanish ships of the line left in Ferrol. If his squadron had been destroyed or defeated, he argued, England or Ireland would have been open to the long-expected invasion. Nevertheless, public outcry and Barham's implied disapproval led him to demand a court martial, at which he was acquitted of cowardice but reprimanded for failing to renew the battle.

Durham; Conn; Pilfold; Prowse; Stockham

Trafalgar (21 October 1805)

On 19 October 1805 Vice-Admiral Pierre Villeneuve, commanding a Combined Fleet of eighteen French ships of the line and fifteen Spanish under Vice-Admiral Don Frederico Gravina, began putting to sea from Cadiz. His orders, dictated by Napoleon a month earlier, were to evade the British blockading fleet under Vice-Admiral Viscount Nelson, enter the Mediterranean, gather the Spanish ships in harbour at Cartagena and then land troops in Naples to counter the threat of an invasion from Malta by the British, supported by their new Russian allies. Villeneuve had learnt that, having failed to clear the way for an invasion of England, he was about to be superseded by Vice-Admiral François Rosily, whose arrival at Cadiz had been delayed by a broken coach (the British blockade making it imprudent to travel by sea). He had also learnt that four of Nelson's ships of the line had been detached to escort a troop convoy towards Malta, and another two, under Rear-Admiral Thomas Louis, were revictualling and replenishing at Gibraltar. Finally, there was an anticipated period of fine sailing weather in which his crews, after months cooped up in harbour, would find it easier to handle their ships.

Nelson had used the month since his arrival at Cadiz to prepare his battle plan and explain it to his captains. His appreciation was that it would take so long to form a fleet of nearly forty ships into a line of battle that it would be almost impossible to fight a decisive engagement in the remaining daylight. He therefore directed that the order of battle was to be the order of sailing, with the fleet in two parallel columns each of sixteen ships, led respectively by himself in the 1st-rate *Victory* (104) and his second-in-command, Vice-Admiral Cuthbert Collingwood [8] in the 1st-rate *Royal Sovereign* (100). His eight fastest 3rd-rates would form an advanced group able to reinforce either column if the need arose. When the enemy line (which Nelson expected to consist of forty-six ships) was encountered, Collingwood was to cut through it twelfth from the rear, thus allowing him to outnumber and defeat the last enemy twelve with his own sixteen. The weather column, led by Nelson, would cut the enemy line around its centre, where the enemy C-in-C was expected to take his station, and the advanced group would cut it three or four ships ahead of this, with the aim of isolating and capturing him and defeating the outnumbered enemy centre before the enemy van could turn back to its support. Before sailing, Villeneuve warned his own captains that Nelson would employ just these tactics.

On learning that Villeneuve had put to sea, Nelson (with his main force some fifty miles west of Cadiz) immediately sailed at his best speed south-eastwards, intending to intercept the Combined Fleet before it could enter the Straits of Gibraltar. In fact, Villeneuve did not succeed in getting all his ships out of harbour until the afternoon of 20 October, so that on the morning of that day, with no enemy in sight, Nelson supposed they had returned to Cadiz and began to head back to his previous position. In the afternoon, contact was re-established with the frigates that had kept Villeneuve under observation and Nelson, under the impression that the Combined Fleet was heading westwards, again changed course to intercept. At dusk the enemy was reported heading towards the Straits, and Nelson changed course twice more while his frigates shadowed Villeneuve through a squally night.

Dawn on 21 October revealed the two fleets in clear sight of each other, about ten miles apart. The Combined Fleet was steering almost due south, in an irregular curved line which in places was double-banked as ships struggled to take up their appointed places in the order of battle. Both sides were hampered by the lightness of the south-west wind that had replaced the previous squalls. An accompanying heavy swell, presaging a gale, placed the Combined Fleet's gunners at a disadvantage as their decks rose and fell while the British approached steadily from the windward. In the afternoon of 20 October Nelson absorbed his advance group into his main fleet. Having failed to make contact with Louis in the Straits of Gibraltar, he had only twenty-seven ships of the line with him instead of the nearly forty on which he had planned.

Nelson formed his fleet in an order of sailing of two columns, the van or weather column consisting of eleven ships led by himself and the rear or lee column of fifteen led by Collingwood. During the night, however, several of his ships had failed to keep their proper positions and he subsequently ordered the slowest, *Britannia*, *Dreadnought* and *Prince*, to 'take station as convenient without regard to the established order of sailing'. This meant that he risked these three-deckers, representing three of his seven most powerful assets, coming late into battle, but his main concern was to prevent Villeneuve turning back to Cadiz. Collingwood was equally anxious to close with the enemy and ordered his column to form a line of bearing, so that each ship would be in echelon behind him rather than directly astern, and so head straight for its opponent in the enemy line.

As a result, the British fleet approached the enemy in a series of groups, rather than in the carefully-spaced formation of two columns a mile and a half apart, with each unit 400 yards behind its next ahead that should, theoretically, have been the case. The light winds prevented ships from taking their proper stations and intervals and one officer in Collingwood's flagship thought that what was occurring was a general chase, in which ships had no set order at all. Afterwards, Captain Edward Codrington [7] of the 3rd-rate *Orion* (74) in the weather column recalled 'we all scrambled into battle as best we could' and Captain Robert Moorsom [25] of the 3rd-rate *Revenge* [74] in the lee column wrote 'the ships got down as fast as we could and into any space where they found the enemy, without attending to their place in the line'. Both flagships were at the head of their respective columns in a conventional order of sailing, instead of being near their centres, which was the usual station for flag officers in a conventional order of battle. Nelson's officers at one point persuaded him to order other ships to overtake *Victory* and Nelson himself twice ordered *Mars* to go to the head of Collingwood's column, but neither admiral would allow his flagship to reduce sail for this to happen, and when the 2nd-rate *Téméraire* succeeded in drawing alongside *Victory*, Nelson ordered her to resume her proper station.

The speed of all these movements was much affected by the light winds, so that the fastest ships could barely make three knots. Over six hours elapsed between the two fleets sighting each other and the first British ship reaching the enemy line.

In the interval, with their ships rapidly cleared for action, there was little for the British captains to do but ensure their men were fed and otherwise encourage them. Nelson had time to summon his frigate captains aboard for a final briefing and to act as witnesses to his will. To break the tension he told his signal officer he would 'amuse the fleet' and made his famous signal 'England expects ...'. Even the stoical Collingwood was feeling the tension of the slow approach to battle and said he wished Nelson would stop signalling. 'We all know well enough what to do', he said, in an unconscious tribute to the careful way that his old friend had long made his intentions clear.

The light wind equally affected the Combined Fleet, which had not completed the evolution of changing from order of sailing to order of battle when Villeneuve ordered it to reverse course by each ship wearing (turning away from the wind rather than through it) independently. Though this caused some further gaps in his line, he was still able to open a telling fire on the leading British ships. These, moving slowly towards an almost stationary opponent, suffered much heavier damage than they would have, had a stronger wind allowed them to reach the enemy more quickly.

Thus Collingwood's *Royal Sovereign*, the first British ship to come within range of the Combined Fleet, was under fire for about ten minutes before passing behind the Spanish flagship *Santa Ana* (112), fourteen ships from the rear of the enemy line, exactly at noon. She then fought alone for another ten or fifteen minutes before her next astern, the 3rd-rate *Belleisle* (74) joined her. Because of the gaps in the French line and the converging course of the two British columns, *Victory* broke the enemy line only five ships ahead of *Royal Sovereign* and about half an hour after her, having in the meanwhile endured a similar fire without being able to reply. She passed immediately behind Villeneuve's command ship *Bucentaure* (74) and then became involved in a mêlée that at one time had four ships of the line (*Victory*, *Téméraire*, *Fougueux* and the French *Redoutable*) entangled alongside each other.

Meanwhile the enemy van division, consisting of five French and three Spanish ships under Rear-Admiral Pierre Dumanoir, continued on its existing course, as Dumanoir had initially appreciated that the leading British ships might change course and come up with him to fight van to van in a conventional battle line. At about 1.30 p.m. he asked Villeneuve for orders and was told to tack and come back to support the centre division. In the light winds it took about two hours for him to comply but, before he could rejoin Villeneuve, the centre division was defeated as Nelson planned. At about 1.15 p.m. Nelson had been hit by a musket ball from *Redoutable* and carried below. Half an hour later, with *Bucentaure* dismasted and useless as a command platform, Villeneuve decided to move to another ship, but with no boats left to carry him, was forced to remain aboard and allow her captain to surrender to avoid further useless loss of life. When Dumanoir reached the battle area, his three Spanish ships broke company and he was eventually driven off by the rearmost British ships. Nelson lived long enough to be told of Dumanoir's defeat and of the surrender of fourteen or fifteen enemy ships. 'That is well' he said 'but I bargained for twenty'.

When the battle ended, about 5.30 p.m., seventeen enemy ships (eight French and nine Spanish) had surrendered and one, the French *Achille*, was on fire, finally blowing up when the flames reached her magazine. In the storm that began during the night of the battle and continued during the next five days, Collingwood, with the rocks of Trafalgar close on his lee, ordered the prizes, some dismasted and all badly damaged, to be abandoned and burnt so as to prevent their recapture. Only four, anchoring as Nelson had originally intended, survived to be taken to Gibraltar. Of the fifteen that escaped from the battle, Dumanoir's four headed home for France, but were intercepted and captured by a squadron under Sir Richard Strachan on 4 November 1805. The remaining eleven ships of the line re-entered Cadiz from where, on 23 October, Commodore Casmao-Kerjulien, the senior surviving French officer, led out five of them to try and recover some of the prizes. Two were recaptured, but of the rescue squadron two were wrecked trying to re-enter Cadiz and a third was captured, only to be driven ashore and wrecked on 25 October.

Thus the British lost no ships, though many were badly damaged, and 449 men (including their C-in-C and two of his captains) killed, with 1,241 wounded and about 200 drowned or taken prisoner serving as prize crews. The Combined Fleet lost eighteen ships in the battle, as well as its C-in-C and two flag officers captured, three other flag officers and seven captains killed or mortally wounded and over 5,000 men killed in action, wounded, taken prisoner or lost with their ships in the subsequent storm.

Turkish Straits (19 February–3 March 1807)

Late in 1806, with Napoleon's armies supreme on the Continent, the British Cabinet ordered Vice-Admiral Sir John Duckworth, second-in-command of the Mediterranean fleet, to Constantinople with a strong naval squadron. There, to keep Russia as a British ally by supporting her against the Turks, he was to enforce the surrender of the Turkish fleet and the dismissal of the French ambassador. If the Sultan refused, Constantinople was to be bombarded and a British army would be landed in the Ottoman province of Egypt. Duckworth, with his flag in the 1st-rate *Royal George* (100) arrived at the Turkish Straits (the Dardanelles) in February 1807, but waited a week before entering the Sea of Marmora and anchoring off Constantinople. On the way in, he lost six men killed and fifty-one wounded by fire from Turkish coastal forts. Against that, he could count a successful landing on the Asiatic shore by seamen and marines under Rear-Admiral Sir Sydney Smith and their destruction of one ship of the line, four frigates and various minor combatants. With seven ships of the line, two frigates and two bomb vessels (which had exchanged shots with the forts as they passed) Duckworth then waited while the British Ambassador bargained with the Sultan, who played for time while French military engineers helped his generals improve their defence works.

When negotiations failed, Duckworth, faced by strong currents and unreliable winds, feared that he would be trapped and decided to return to the Aegean. He reached Gallipoli on the morning of 3 March 1807 and initially responded to the fire of the shore batteries by firing a salute, hoping that the Turkish gunners would take this as a sign that an agreement had been made for a peaceful withdrawal. This ruse failed, and the squadron came under effective fire from both conventional ordnance and antique pieces hurling stone shot of up to 850 lbs. No ships were lost, but several suffered damage to their hulls or masts, with a total of twenty-nine men killed and 138 wounded. After reaching the open sea, Duckworth was joined by a Russian squadron of eight ships of the line and 2,000 soldiers. Their commander, Vice-Admiral D. N. Senyavin, an anglophile who had served in the Royal Navy, proposed a joint attack but Duckworth decided that, without a strong army to take the shore defences, this was impracticable. The British troops that could have supported him at Constantinople had been sent to Egypt, where they were defeated by the local Turkish commander, the Albanian-born Mehmet Ali, at the beginning of a career that later almost brought about a European war. Senyavin blockaded the Straits himself after Duckworth's departure and gained a naval victory over the Turks on 1 July 1807. Later that month the Emperors of France and Russia met at Tilsit and agreed to make peace. In sending a fleet to the Turkish Straits without an army and then giving the Turks time to strengthen their forts, the British in 1807 foreshadowed the same mistakes that they would make in 1915.

Blackwood; Capel

Copenhagen (16 August–7 September 1807)
Among the many provisions of the Treaty of Tilsit (9 July 1807), Napoleon and the Emperor Alexander I of Russia agreed to exclude British trade from their dominions and to coerce Denmark into joining them in forming a joint Northern fleet, to exclude the British from the Baltic. This threatened not only ordinary trade but the vital supply of timber, hemp, pitch and other shipbuilding materials essential to the Royal Navy. The British responded by sending Admiral Lord

Gambier to the Danish coast with seventeen ships of the line while a 30,000 strong expeditionary force was embarked at Great Yarmouth. At the same time, the Danes were sent an ultimatum, requiring them to hand over their fleet to the British, who would in return guarantee Denmark from attack by France and Russia and pay the Danes an annual rent of £100,000 for their ships. On 31 July 1807, just as Gambier reached the Skaw, at the northern tip of Denmark, Napoleon gave the Crown Prince of Denmark the choice of an alliance or war and began to assemble an army at Hamburg. Under this pressure, a week later the Crown Prince rejected the British terms, saying that he knew only too well what happened to allies of the United Kingdom against France.

By this time Gambier's warships were anchored in Roads and on 16 August 1807 the British troops arrived and marched rapidly towards Copenhagen. Taken by surprise, with their militia not yet mobilized and the French too far away to help, the Danes could offer little resistance. On 29 August their hastily-gathered troops were put to flight at Kioge by a division under Sir Arthur Wellesley, the future Duke of Wellington. On the evening of 2 September, outside the walls of Copenhagen, Lord Cathcart, commanding the military element of the expedition, having delayed his decision in the hope that the Crown Prince would yield to *force majeure*, reluctantly ordered his batteries to open fire on the city. Under a hail of explosive shells, red-hot shot and incendiary rockets which set the dry timbers of their city alight within minutes, the Danes held out for three nights before surrendering on the evening of 7 September. The Danish fleet of fifteen ships of the line and thirty smaller vessels passed into British hands and were prevented from falling into those of an enemy. The Danes subsequently rejected a British invitation to join an Anglo-Scandinavian League to keep the Baltic open to trade and, as soon as the British troops re-embarked, formally declared war. The episode was without doubt an infringement of neutrality by the British and Lord Gambier was among the many who were shocked at the burning of a major European city. Nevertheless the speed and secrecy with which the expedition was organized gave proof to Napoleon and the rest of Europe that the British government still had both the will and the means to act when a vital national interest was at stake.

Lapenotiere; Mansfield

Tarragona (June 1811)

In the summer of 1808, Tarragona, one of Catalonia's major seaports, joined the national revolt against French occupation, and was speedily reinforced by Spanish troops brought from the Balearic Islands under the protection of the Royal Navy. Aided by British cruisers and naval landing parties, it continued to defy the French for the next three years, until Napoleon decided that Catalan resistance must be ended. Marshal Louis-Gabriel Suchet, the best French general of the Peninsular War, defeated the Spanish regular troops and guerrillas and laid siege to Tarragona early in 1811. At the last moment British troops were sent to support the defenders but, under orders not to land unless they could be sure of being able to re-embark, remained in their ships until Suchet took Tarragona by storm on 28 June 1811. With Catalonia lost, the British frigates operating on this station dropped south to support the Spaniards still fighting in Valencia.

Bullen; Codrington

The Captains and their Ships at Trafalgar

(flagships underlined)

1. Bayntun, Captain Henry William *Leviathan* (74), 3rd-rate
2. Berry, Captain Sir Edward *Agamemnon* (64), 3rd-rate
3. Blackwood, Captain the Honourable Henry *Euryalus* frigate (36), 5th-rate
4. Bullen, Captain Charles *Britannia* (100), 1st-rate
5. Capel, Captain the Honourable Thomas Bladen *Phoebe* frigate (36), 5th-rate
6. Carnegie, Rear-Admiral William, Earl of Northesk <u>*Britannia* (100), 1st rate</u>
7. Codrington, Captain Edward *Orion* (74), 3rd-rate
8. Collingwood, Vice-Admiral Cuthbert <u>*Royal Sovereign* (100), 1st-rate</u>
9. Conn, Captain John *Dreadnought* (98), 2nd-rate
10. Cooke, Captain John *Bellerophon* (74), 3rd-rate
11. Digby, Captain Henry *Africa* (64), 3rd-rate
12. Duff, Captain George *Mars* (74), 3rd-rate
13. Dundas, Captain Thomas *Naiad* frigate (38), 5th-rate
14. Durham, Captain Philip Charles *Defiance* (74), 3rd-rate
15. Fremantle, Captain Thomas Francis *Neptune* (98), 2nd-rate
16. Grindall, Captain Richard *Prince* (98), 2nd-rate
17. Hardy, Captain Thomas Masterman <u>*Victory* (104), 1st-rate</u>
18. Hargood, Captain William *Belleisle* (74), 3rd-rate
19. Harvey, Captain Eliab *Téméraire* (98), 2nd-rate

20. Hope, Captain George Johnstone *Defence* (74), 3rd-rate
21. King, Captain Richard *Achille* (74), 3rd-rate
22. Laforey, Captain Sir Francis *Spartiate* (74), 3rd-rate
23. Lapenotiere, Captain John Richards *Pickle* schooner (10)
24. Mansfield, Captain Charles John Moore *Minotaur* (74), 3rd-rate
25. Moorsom, Captain Robert *Revenge* (74), 3rd-rate
26. Morris, Captain James Nicoll *Colossus* (74), 3rd-rate
27. Pellew, Captain Israel *Conqueror* (74), 3rd-rate
28. Pilfold, Lieutenant John *Ajax* (74), 3rd-rate
29. Prowse, Captain William *Sirius* frigate (36), 5th-rate
30. Redmill, Captain Robert *Polyphemus* (64), 3rd-rate
31. Rotheram, Captain Edward <u>*Royal Sovereign* (100), 1st-rate</u>
32. Rutherford, Captain William Gordon *Swiftsure* (74), 3rd-rate
33. Stockham, Lieutenant John *Thunderer* (74), 3rd-rate
34. Tyler, Captain Charles *Tonnant* (80), 3rd-rate
35. Young, Lieutenant Robert Benjamin *Entreprenante* cutter (4)

Bibliography

Adkins, Roy, *Trafalgar: The Biography of a Battle*, Little, Brown & Co., London, 2004

Allen, Joseph, *Battles of the British Navy; from AD 1000 to 1840*, 2 vols., A.H. Bailey & Co., London, 1842

Bennett, Geoffrey, *The Battle of Trafalgar*, Naval Institute Press, Annapolis, 1977

Boatner, Mark Mayo, *Cassell's Biographical Dictionary of the American War of Independence 1763–1783*, Cassell, London, 1966

Bouchier, Jane (ed.), *Memoir of the Life of Sir Edward Codrington, with selections from his public and private correspondence*, 2 vols., Longmans, Green & Co., London,1873

Bryant, Arthur, *The Years of Endurance 1793–1802*, Collins, London, 1942

— *The Years of Victory 1802–1812*, Collins, London, 1944

— *The Age of Elegance 1812–1822*, Collins, London, 1950

Clayton, Tim, and Craig, Phil, *Trafalgar: The Men, the Battle and the Storm*, Hodder & Stoughton, London, 2004

Colledge, J.J., (revised Warlow, B.), *Ships of the Royal Navy. The Complete Record of all Fighting Ships of the Royal Navy*, Greenhill Books, London, 2003

Collingwood, G.L. Newnham, *A Selection from the Public and Private Correspondence of Vice-Admiral Lord Collingwood interspersed with Memoirs of his Life*, James Ridgeway, London, 1828

Corbett, Julian S., *The Campaign of Trafalgar*, Longmans, Green & Co., London, 1910

Davies, David, *A Brief History of Fighting Ships. Ships of the Line and Napoleonic Sea Battles 1793–1815*, Robinson, London, 2002

Esdaile, Charles, *The Peninsular War. A New History*, Penguin Books, London, 2002

Feldbaek, Ole, (trans. Wedgewood, Tony), *The Battle of Copenhagen 1802. Nelson and the Danes*, Leo Cooper, Barnsley, 2002

Fremantle, Anne, (ed.), *The Wynne Diaries, 1789–1820*, Geoffrey Cumberlege, Oxford University Press, London, 1952

Goodwin, Peter, *Nelson's Ships. A History of the Vessels in which he served 1771–1805*, Conway Maritime Press, London, 2002

Hannay, David, *A Short History of the Royal Navy 1217–1815*, 2 vols., Methuen & Co., London, 1909.

Hibbert, Christopher, *Nelson. A Personal History*, Viking, London, 1994

Hill, Richard, *The Prizes of War. The Naval Prize System in the Napoleonic Wars 1793–1815*, Sutton Publishing, Stroud, 1998

Hore, Peter, *John Richards Lapenotiere and the HM Schooner Pickle*, creative multimedia communication, 2002

Howarth, David, *Trafalgar. The Nelson Touch*, Collins, London, 1969

Hughes, Edward (ed.), *The Private Correspondence of Admiral Lord Collingwood*, Naval Records Society, London, 1957

James, W.M., *The Naval History of Great Britain during the French Revolutionary and Napoleonic Wars*, 6 vols., Richard Bentley, London, 1847

Kennedy, Ludovic, *Nelson and his Captains*, Collins, London, 1951

King, Dean, *A Sea of Words, a Lexicon etc.*, 3rd edn., Henry Holt & Co., New York, 2000

Lambert, Andrew, *War at Sea in the Age of Sail 1650–1850*, Cassell, London, 2000

— *Nelson, Britannia's God of War*, Faber & Faber, London, 2004

Legg, Stuart (ed.), *Trafalgar. An Eyewitness account of a Great Battle*, Hart-Davis, London, 1966.

Mackenzie, Robert Holden, *The Trafalgar Roll containing the names and services of all officers of the Royal Navy and the Royal Marines who participated in the Glorious Victory of 21st October 1805*, George Allen & Co., London, 1913

Mackesy, Piers, *The War in the Mediterranean 1803–1810*, Longmans, Green & Co., London, 1957

Maine, Rene (trans. Eldon, Rita and Robinson, B.W.), *Trafalgar. Napoleon's Naval Waterloo*, Thames & Hudson, London 1957

Marcus, Geoffrey Jules, *A Naval History of England Vol. 2. The age of Nelson*, George Allen & Unwin, London, 1971

Miller, Nathan, *Broadsides. The Age of Fighting Sail*, John Wiley & Sons Inc., New York, 2000

— *Sea of Glory. A Naval History of the American Revolution*, Naval Institute Press, Annapolis, 1992

Murray, Geoffrey, *The Life of Admiral Collingwood*, Hutchinson, London, 1936

Oman, Carola, *Nelson*, Hodder & Stoughton, London, 1947

Parkinson, C. Northcote, *Britannia Rules. The Classic Age of Naval History 1793–1815*, Weidenfeld & Nicolson, London, 1977

Pocock, Tom, *Horatio Nelson*, Bodley Head, London, 1987

— *Stopping Napoleon. War and Intrigue in the Mediterranean*, John Murray, London, 2004

Pope, Dudley, *England Expects*, Weidenfeld & Nicolson, London, 1959

Purcell, I. Edward, *Who was Who in the American Revolution*, Facts on File, New York, 1993

Robinson, R.E.R., *The Bloody Eleventh. History of the Devonshire Regiment*, The Devonshire and Dorset Regiment, Exeter, 1988

Rodger, N.A.M., *The Command of the Ocean: A Naval History of Britain, 1649–1815*, Allen Lane, London, 2004

Sanderson, Michael, *Sea Battles. A Reference Guide*, Purnell Book Services, Abingdon, 1975

Sugden, John, *Nelson: A Dream of Glory*, Jonathan Cape, London, 2004

Tracy, Nicholas, *The Battle of Copenhagen 2 April 1801*, The 1805 Club, Shelton, 2003

Warner, Oliver, *Trafalgar*, Batsford, London, 1959

— *Nelson's Battles*, Batsford, London, 1965

— *The Life and Letters of Vice-Admiral Lord Collingwood*, Oxford University Press, London, 1968

White, Colin, *1797 Nelson's Year of Destiny*, Sutton Publishing, Stroud, 1998

— *The Nelson Encyclopaedia*, Chatham Publishing, London, 2002

— (ed.), *The Trafalgar Captains*, Chatham Publishing, London, 2005

Woodman, Richard, *The Sea Warriors. Fighting Captains and Frigate Warfare in the Age of Nelson*, Robinson, London, 2001

Index